D0813687

Letters of C. S. Lewis

Books by C. S. Lewis
available in paperbound editions
from Harcourt Brace Jovanovich, Publishers

The Dark Tower and Other Stories
The Four Loves
Letters to Malcolm
Narrative Poems
Of Other Worlds: Essays and Stories
On Stories
Poems
Reflections on the Psalms
Surprised by Joy
Till We Have Faces
The World's Last Night and Other Essays

Letters of C. S. Lewis

Edited, with a Memoir, by

W. H. LEWIS

A Harvest/HBJ Book
Harcourt Brace Jovanovich, Publishers
San Diego New York London

Printed in the United States of America

Library of Congress Cataloging in Publication Data
Lewis, Clive Staples, 1898–1963.
Letters of C.S. Lewis.

(A Harvest book, HB 300)
1. Lewis, Clive Staples, 1898–1963—Correspondence.
I. Lewis, Warren Hamilton.
PR6023.E926Z535 1975 828'.9'1209 [B] 74-13416
ISBN 0-15-650870-2

EFGHIJ

Letters of C. S. Lewis

MEMOIR OF C. S. LEWIS

by W. H. Lewis

My brother was born in one of the inner suburbs of Belfast on the 29th of November, 1898, when I was nearly three-and-a-half years old. I first remember him, dimly, as a vociferous disturber of my domestic peace and a rival claimant to my mother's attention: few detailed and particular memories remain of our first years together, though during these first years—up to our move to the new house in the spring of 1905—we laid the foundations of an intimate friendship that was the greatest happiness of my life and lasted unbroken until his death fifty-eight years later.

Looking back now upon the pattern of his life and work, I feel that one particular and even trivial circumstance in our early life together needs some emphasis. I refer to the wetness of Irish weather, and the nervousness of the parents of that time about damp and exposure. By the standards of present-day childhood in England, we spent an extraordinary amount of our time shut up indoors. We would gaze out of our nursery window at the slanting rain and the grey skies, and there, beyond a mile or so of sodden meadow, we would see the dim high line of the Castlereagh Hills—our world's limit, a distant land, strange and unattainable. But we always had pencils, paper, chalk, and paint-boxes, and this recurring imprisonment gave us occasion and stimulus to develop the habit of creative imagination. We learnt to draw: my brother made his first attempts at writing: together we devised the imaginary country of "Boxen", which proliferated hugely and became our solace and joy for many years to come. And so, in circumstances that might have been merely dull and depressing, my brother's gifts began to develop; and it may not be fanciful to see, in that childhood staring out to unattainable hills, some first beginnings of a vision and viewpoint that ran through the work of his maturity.

The highlight of our year was the annual seaside holiday. Children of today, accustomed as they are to be driven casually to the coast on any fine Sunday afternoon, can hardly imagine the excitement, the bustle and glory of preparation that these holidays entailed, the unique moment of arrival. Of many such holidays, two pictures remain in my memory. The first is of my father's gloomy detachment. He would sometimes come down for the week-end, but he never stayed with his wife and children throughout this summer holiday. Urgent business was his excuse —he was a solicitor—and he may also have felt that eleven months of our company every year was more than enough. It may have gone deeper than that. I never met a man more wedded to a dull routine, or less capable of extracting enjoyment from life. A night spent out of his own home was a penance to him: a holiday he loathed, having not the faintest conception of how to amuse himself. I can still see him on his occasional visits to the seaside, walking moodily up and down the beach, hands in trouser pockets, eyes on the ground, every now and then giving a heart-rending yawn and pulling out his watch.

Then, in the course of one holiday, my brother made the momentous decision to change his name. Disliking 'Clive', and feeling his various baby-names to be beneath his dignity, he marched up to my mother, put a forefinger on his chest, and announced "He is Jacksie". He stuck to this the next day and thereafter, refusing to answer to any other name: Jacksie it had to be, a name contracted to Jacks and then to Jack. So to his family and his intimate friends, he was Jack for life: and Jack he will be for the rest of this book.

Looking back in later years on our childhood, he once remarked to me that for one thing, and one thing only, he envied the modern child. In 1904 the rain kept us indoors, whether at home or in cramped seaside lodgings: the child of today splashes about outside, in gumboots and oilskins and sou'wester. Otherwise, not for a king's ransom did Jack wish to be a modern child, facing the stress and anxiety of today's world. This was no blind nostalgia, no mere regret for vanished class privilege and financial security: what he sighed for was the lost simplicity of country pleasures, the empty sky, the unspoilt hills, the white silent roads on which you could hear the rattle of a farm cart half a mile away.

These pleasures—all but unattainable to the modern child—were ours, and more especially after our move in 1905. Our new house, "Little Lea", was on the borderline—suburb one way, open hilly farmland the other. We both had bicycles, and in these golden years before school, Jack developed a passionate and life-long devotion to County Down. And the new house itself was a child's delight, by reason of its atrociously uneconomical design: on the top floor, cupboard-like doors opened into huge, dark, wasted spaces under the roof, tunnel-like passages through which children could crawl from one such space into another, with here and there a rectangular pit, floored with the ceiling of a bedroom—space which the architect had despaired of putting to use. Best of all, we had our own day-room in the attic, instead of a day-nursery and bedroom combined, as in the old house: in this glorious privacy, never invaded by officiously tidying maids, "Boxen" and the rest of our secret life flourished wonderfully. These were golden days, even after they became for Jack mere interludes in the horror of school: we remembered them with delight to the end.

But 1908 was a year of death, and the happy times ended. During that year my father lost his own father, then his wife, then his brother. If I gave any account of my mother's lingering illness and death, it would only be a poor paraphrase of what Jack wrote in *Surprised by Joy*. She died on my father's birthday, the 23rd of August: there was a Shakespearean calendar hanging on the wall of the room where she died, and my father preserved for the rest of his life the leaf for that day, with its quotation: "Men must endure their going hence".

In the Christmas term of that year, Jack followed me at the school referred to in *Surprised by Joy* as "Belsen". As he has made very clear, he hated the place, but he escaped its worse brutalities: he amused the headmaster, who even made something of a pet of him, so far as was possible for such a man.

Jack's letters and diaries of the time convey little of the full depressing story of this school and its headmaster. In 1901 a boy had been treated so brutally that his father brought a High Court action: this was settled out of court, but it confirmed local suspicions, and the school went downhill rapidly. In 1910 the headmaster wrote to my father that he was "giving up school work", which meant deliverance for Jack: in fact the school collapsed, the house was sold, and its proprietor retired to a country living. There, his behaviour towards his choir and churchwardens was such that he was put under restraint and certified insane: he died in 1912, soon afterwards. With his uncanny flair for making the wrong decision, my father had given us helpless children into the hands of a madman.

In the spring term of 1911, after a brief spell at Campbell College, Belfast, Jack came with me to Malvern—not to the College, of course, but to the preparatory school, which he calls "Chartres". Two years later, he entered for the scholarship examination to the College: when the day came, he was in bed with a high temperature, and I am inclined to rate his winning of a scholarship under these circumstances as the greatest academic triumph of his career. And so, in September 1913, he started his first term at Malvern.

There, as readers of *Surprised by Joy* will have gathered, he was something of a square peg in a round hole. By this time I had left the College and was reading for Sandhurst with W. T. Kirkpatrick, my father's old headmaster: that autumn, I visited Malvern to attend a House Supper, a noisy and cheerful function, of which I can remember only one thing—Jack's gloom and boredom, unaltered all through the evening, glaringly obvious to all, not calculated to increase his popularity with the House. He was no kind of failure academically—within a few weeks of arriving, still at the age of fourteen, he attracted the headmaster's attention with a brilliant translation from Horace—but Malvern was the wrong place for him: and in March 1914 he wrote home, imploring his father to take him away.

Much to my surprise, my father reacted to this letter by making an immediate and sensible decision: Jack was to leave Malvern at the end of the school year to become Kirkpatrick's pupil at Great Bookham in Surrey, reading for an Oxford scholarship. This meant one more term at the College, a burden that Jack carried bravely: then, at the end of July 1914, he left Malvern for ever with profound relief.

Here I feel it my duty to make some comment upon his criticisms of the school, as expressed in his letters of the time as well as in *Surprised by Joy*. "I would not", as Boswell says somewhere, "war offensively with the dead", and least of all with my brother: and yet I find it very difficult to believe in the Malvern that he portrays. In July 1913 I had been on more or less close terms with all the brutes of prefects whom he describes, and I found them (with one exception) very pleasant fellows. How did they come to change their characters entirely during the summer holidays of that year? As regards his lurid descriptions of the immorality of Malvern, I am far from denying that there was immorality; but when I got to Sandhurst and could compare notes with boys from every public school in the country, I found that there was little to choose between them in this respect. And it must be remembered that a boy in his first year at a public school knows very little of what goes on: he lives by scandal and rumour, and tends therefore to see immorality in every sentimental association between an older boy and a younger. Such associations—inevitable under a system which keeps a youth of eighteen isolated from feminine company for two-thirds of the year—are certainly silly and undesirable: but they are very often physically innocent, a fact that Jack seemed reluctant to see or admit.

When I first read *Surprised by Joy* I pointed this out to him, and drew his attention to his absurd statement that "there was only one topic of conversation" in the house. I could well remember many others—theatrical, sartorial, sporting, and so forth. I record the incident with pride, because on that occasion, and then only, I persuaded Jack to admit that he had been wrong.

The fact is that he should never have been sent to a public school at all. Already, at fourteen, his intelligence was such that he would have fitted in better among undergraduates than among schoolboys; and by his temperament he was bound to be a misfit, a heretic, an object of suspicion within the collective-minded and standardising Public School system. He was, indeed, lucky to leave Malvern before the power of this system had done him any lasting damage.

Of his days under Kirkpatrick's tutorship at Great Bookham, he has left a full and lyrical record in *Surprised by Joy*. The stimulation of a sharp and vigorous mind, the romantic beauty which the Surrey countryside then possessed, the ordered security of Jack's life, his freedom to read widely and gratuitously—these factors combined to develop his particular gifts and determine his future. 'He was born with the literary temperament', Kirkpatrick wrote to my father, 'and we have to face that fact with all that it implies'. And later: 'Outside a life of literary study, life has no meaning or attraction for him . . . he is adapted for nothing else. You may make up your mind to that'. There is a note here of warning and limitation, but for Jack these days were paradisal without qualification, his letters of the time being charged with the intoxication of literary discovery.

From time to time I would come home on leave from France, taking Jack with me to visit our father whenever I could; but already there were difficulties and reluctances in this respect, life at Little Lea having certain irksome and frustrating aspects. I mention this subject with reluctance: nevertheless, some awareness of my father's smothering tendency to dominate the life and especially the conversation of his household is necessary to an understanding of Jack's mind and life. This tendency had borne curious fruit in early days. Ever since the days of the old house, which we left in 1905, Jack had been trying to write: after his death, we found among his papers any number of childish but ambitious beginnings of histories, stories, poems, nearly all of them dealing with our private fantasy world of Animal-Land or Boxen. Then, in 1912, he had produced a complete novel, a creditable performance for a boy not yet thirteen; and the interesting thing to note is that this novel, like the sequel to it that followed soon after, revolved entirely around politics.

To anyone who recalls Jack's adult contempt for politics and politicians this will seem extraordinary: but this first predilection and his subsequent revulsion from the whole subject stemmed from the same root. In the upper-middle-class society of our Belfast childhood, politics and money were the chief, almost the only subjects of grown-up conversation: and since no visitors came to our house who did not hold precisely the same political views as my father, what we heard was not discussion and the lively clash of minds, but rather an endless and one-sided torrent of grumble and vituperation. Any ordinary parent would have sent us boys off to amuse ourselves, but not my father: we had to sit in silence and endure it. The immediate result, in Jack's case, was to convince him that grown-up conversation and politics were one and the same thing, and that everything he wrote must therefore be given a political framework: the long-term result was to fill him with a disgust and revulsion from the very idea of politics before he was out of his 'teens.

Now, during his happy days at Great Bookham, Jack's mind was developing and flowering on lines as unpolitical as can be imagined. His letters of the time are full of landscape and romance: they record his discovery of George Macdonald—a turning-point in his life—and his first and characteristic delight in Chaucer, Scott, Malory, the Brontës, William Morris, Coleridge, de Quincey, Spenser, Swinburne, Keats. In his friend Arthur Greeves he had found a kindred spirit, with whom he could share and celebrate these discoveries: they corresponded regularly, went on holiday together, and Jack enjoyed the hospitality of Arthur's home at Belfast. Here again, my father's temperament was a limiting and dampening influence. Jack would have liked to return Arthur's hospitality: had this been arranged, my father would certainly have welcomed his son's friend very cordially, but not for a moment would it have occurred to him that the two boys might want to talk together, alone. No: he would have joined them, inescapably, for a good talk about books, doing nine-tenths of the talking himself, eulogising his own favourites without regard to their interests. Two bored and frustrated youths would have been subjected to long readings from Macaulay's essays, Burke's speeches, and the like, and my father would have gone to bed satisfied that he had given them a literary evening far more interesting than they could have contrived for themselves.

That Arthur's visit would have this character was something all too obvious to Jack: he hinted delicately at the 'obstacle' of his father's temperament, and the visit never took place.

In December 1916 Jack went to Oxford to sit for a classical scholarship: passed over by New College, he was elected to an open scholarship by University. The full list of awards, published in *The Times* a few days later, included the names of Alfred C. Harwood and Arthur Owen Barfield: these two, elected to classical scholarships at Christ Church and Wadham respectively, were to be for the rest of Jack's life among his most intimate personal friends.

The prospects offered by war-time Oxford were, of course, limited and determined by the imminence of military service for most undergraduates: there were few men in residence, and arrangements were flexible. It was proposed that Jack should take Responsions in March and come up for the Trinity Term, joining the Oxford O.T.C.: this, it was suggested, offered him the best chance of a commission. And so, after further coaching at Bookham and a visit home, Jack matriculated, signed his name in the College book, and began his University career on the 28th of April, 1917.

It is noteworthy that in the circumstances of the time he was allowed to come into residence, having in the event failed the Responsions examination that Easter: one of his first concerns at Oxford was to find a coach and work harder at the elements of mathematics, with a view to another attempt. In fact, he never did pass this examination, being exempted from it later on by virtue of his military service. In this he was fortunate, for I do not believe that at any stage in his career he could have passed an examination of any kind in elementary mathematics: a view with which he himself agreed, when I put it to him many years later.

Before one full term was out, his papers came through, and Jack found himself a soldier, having crammed into those first few weeks at Oxford not only his unsuccessful work for Responsions and his O.T.C. training but also a good deal of miscellaneous reading, most of this (as recorded in his pocket-book) being characteristically a matter of poetry and romance. Joining the army was less of a break for him than for some others, since the cadet battalion to which he was drafted was billeted in Keble: he was able to keep in touch with his friends and even (for a time) to spend his week-ends in his own college.

Towards army life in war-time, his final attitude—as expressed in *Surprised by Joy*—was notably positive; and in these first days of initial training, his letters home conveyed more exhilaration than distress. It was during this period that a relationship first began that had a huge and determining effect upon the pattern of his subsequent life. Among the cadets at Keble, he found a few who were congenial company: one of them was E. F. C. ("Paddy") Moore, with whom he shared a room by alphabetic accident. In August, he had a couple of days' leave at home, and I had the misfortune to miss him by a few days: the next week-end he spent with Moore and his mother. On the 25th of September, Jack was commissioned in the 3rd Battalion of the Somerset Light Infantry and given a month's leave: he chose the same society for the first part of this leave, not coming home until the 12th of October. My father's pocket-book contains a wry note of this order of priorities: the situation did not reach full development until much later, but its character may have been apparent already.

I do not wish to dwell upon the barriers that existed between Jack and my father, nor to exaggerate their importance in connection with Jack's subsequent involvement with Mrs Moore and her affairs. These barriers were not only of a purely personal kind: between Ireland and England there stood in those days a kind of iron curtain of misunderstanding. There was no conscription in Ireland, no rationing, no shortages (as far as I could see) of any kind: the war was a very remote thing, merely a topic of conversation unless one had relatives fighting in France. I never went on leave without getting an eerie feeling that I had somehow or other been jolted back into 1913. Into this remote atmosphere, Jack despatched on the 15th of November a telegram—one that would have made it clear to anyone in England that he was on the eve of embarkation for overseas service. My father simply wired back that he could not understand the telegram, and asked for leisured explanations: he made no attempt to keep the rendezvous in Bristol—proposed clearly enough by Jack—for what might well have been a last meeting, and Jack had to sail for France and the war without seeing him again.

This must have been felt as a rebuff, though it was probably due to a genuine misunderstanding, a failure in 'communication'. But the same thing happened again much more seriously, seven months later. Jack reached the front line on his nineteenth birthday, the 29th of November, 1917: after an initial spell in the trenches and a short illness, he was among those who faced in March the final German attack on the Western Front, and in April he was wounded. I was able to visit him at once in hospital, and I still recall my overwhelming relief when I found him sitting up in bed and greeting me with a cheerful 'Hullo, I didn't know you A.S.C. people got as far up the line as this!'

His wounds were not serious, but he was sent home to recuperate in London, having heard a little earlier that Mrs Moore's son was missing and believed dead; and from the hospital in Endsleigh Gardens he wrote home, cheerfully but with his first frank expression of homesickness, begging his father to come and visit him.

One would have thought it impossible for any father to resist an appeal of this kind, coming at such a moment. But my father was a very peculiar man in some respects: in none more than in an almost pathological hatred of taking any step which involved a break in the dull routine of his daily existence. Jack remained unvisited, and was deeply hurt at a neglect which he considered inexcusable. Feeling himself to have been rebuffed by his father, he turned to Mrs Moore as to a mother, seeking there the affection which was apparently denied him at home.

There was no breach between Jack and his father: things remained, outwardly, as they had been. But after this, Little Lea lost its importance to Jack, and soon he was to write in his diary of 'coming home' in reference to the journey from his father's house to Oxford.

Before he was fit for any further service in France, the war was over; and after a certain amount of shifting around from one army camp to another, he was demobilised earlier than we had expected. I was at home on leave myself, not expecting to see him, when on the 27th of December 1918 he unexpectedly arrived, fit and free: in spite of all the stresses and tensions just mentioned it was a joyful reunion on all sides, a recovery of old days, the first occasion moreover on which I had champagne at home.

Within a month he was back at Oxford, and had embarked there upon a pattern of life that was to remain in many respects unaltered for the rest of his days. As such things are reckoned he had 'a successful career'; and in his progress from undergraduate brilliance through a double first to a fellowship and finally a professor's chair, in his world-wide celebrity as a writer on literary and religious subjects alike, there might appear to be an inevitable, even an effortless working-out of the destiny foreseen by Kirkpatrick.

My own contribution to the world's understanding of my brother must be limited: I do not propose in this memoir to give any full account of his work, and still less any evaluation of it. I offer only my own memories of Jack, as man, friend, and brother: and if these memories are to be useful to those who hope to understand his mind and his work, there must be no concealment of the difficulties under which he worked, the patterns of stress and tension that determined many aspects of his life.

There was, indeed, something natural and effortless about his strictly academic and literary work: Jack was one of those rare and fortunate people whose idea of recreation overlaps and even coincides with their necessary work. It was no matter of surprise that he should take a First in Honour Mods. (1920), a First in

Greats (1922), and a First in English (1923), or that he should win the Chancellor's Prize for an English Essay. But even for a scholar of his ability and achievement, it was then no swift and easy matter to embark successfully upon an academic career. Immediately after taking Greats, he sat for a Fellowship by Examination at Magdalen: before this, he had looked into the possibility of a classical lectureship at Reading: later on, he applied for Fellowships at Trinity and St John's. For all these posts, Jack saw other men chosen; and there were times during this period of uncertainty when he tended towards despair of any academic or literary success.

For the fact that he persevered, some credit must be given to the support—both moral and material—given by his own College and by his father. The authorities at Univ. had faith in him, and extended his original scholarship for a fourth year, spent very congenially in reading for the English School: his early reading gave him a flying start here, and academic affairs were then tending in a direction that made a double First of this particular pattern a very formidable qualification indeed. And in the end it was his own College that first offered him a post—a very minor post, certainly, but still a beginning: it was with considerable relief that Jack polished up his Greats reading and began his tutorial work in October, 1924.

This was strictly a temporary post, covering a single year's absence in America of one of the Fellows. Next Spring, it was announced that Magdalen proposed to make an election to a Fellowship in English. The competition seemed likely to be severe, and Jack applied listlessly, with little hope of success. The College elected him, nominally for five years: in fact, this appointment filled the bulk of his working life, from June 1925 until in 1954 he left Oxford to take up a professor's chair at Cambridge.

And so, after a long and discouraging struggle, Jack managed to fight his way into that apparently impregnable fortress which he had once described as 'the real Oxford'. Almost his first action was to write to his father in deep gratitude for six years of generous support. As I have hinted already, there was some degree of estrangement between them—though never any frank ill-feeling—and a certain amount of gloom and stress attended Jack's visits to Little Lea: nevertheless, my father had kept his promise made in 1923 of three years' further support for

Jack at Oxford, even though he knew that there was some risk of failure, and that it would then be no easy matter for Jack to launch himself in some totally new career at the age of 28 or so.

The stress occasioned by this limited family estrangement was only intermittent. But there was a further source of stress and difficulty in Jack's life, continuous, long-lasting, and to some degree self-inflicted. I have already indicated how during the war Jack started to display a marked preference for Mrs Moore's company, rather than his father's: afterwards at Oxford this relationship developed much more strongly. Mrs Moore had lost her son; Jack had many years earlier lost his mother and now his father too seemed to have failed him emotionally. He may have felt also some sense of responsibility, a duty perhaps of keeping some war-time promise made to Paddy Moore. Be that as it may, Jack now embarked upon a relationship with Mrs Moore which was almost that of son and mother; and as soon as his first year as an undergraduate was over, instead of moving from college into lodgings, he set up a joint ménage with her and her daughter Maureen. Having once embarked on this relationship with Mrs Moore, it was not in Jack's nature later to abandon her, and the ménage in fact continued in existence until her death in 1951; during this period Jack commonly referred to Mrs Moore as "my mother"—not always with any explicit indication that the relationship was conventional and adoptive.

The thing most puzzling to myself and to Jack's friends was Mrs Moore's extreme unsuitability as a companion for him. She was a woman of very limited mind, and notably domineering and possessive by temperament. She cut down to a minimum his visits to his father, interfered constantly with his work, and imposed upon him a heavy burden of minor domestic tasks. In twenty years I never saw a book in her hands; her conversation was chiefly about herself, and was otherwise a matter of ill-informed dogmatism: her mind was of a type that he found barely tolerable elsewhere. The whole business had to be concealed from my father of course, which widened the rift between him and Jack; and since an allowance calculated to suit a bachelor living in college was by no means enough for a householder, Jack found himself miserably poor. Nevertheless he continued in this restrictive and distracting servitude for many of his most fruitful years, suffering the worries and expense of repeated moves, until in 1930 we all settled at The Kilns, Headington Quarry.

I dwell on this rather unhappy business with some regret, but it was one of the central and determining circumstances in Jack's life. He hinted at it, darkly, in *Surprised by Joy*, and it is reflected with painful clarity in various passages in his books; the stress and gloom that it often caused him must not be played down.

On the other hand, it would be wildly misleading to suggest that my brother lived the life of a solitary and embittered recluse. The case was quite otherwise. As all his friends will bear witness, he was a man with an outstanding gift for pastime with good company, for laughter and the love of friends—a gift which found full scope in any number of holidays and walking tours, the joyous character of his response to these being well conveyed in his letters. He had, indeed, a remarkable talent for friendship, particularly for friendship of an uproarious kind, masculine and argumentative but never quarrelsome.

In this connection I must say something of the Inklings, a famous and heroic gathering, one that has already passed into literary legend. Properly speaking it was neither a club nor a literary society, though it partook of the nature of both. There were no rules, officers, agendas, or formal elections—unless one counts it as a rule that we met in Jack's rooms at Magdalen every Thursday evening after dinner. Proceedings neither began nor terminated at any fixed hour, though there was a tacit agreement that ten-thirty was as late as one could decently arrive. From time to time we added to our original number, but without formalities: someone would suggest that Jones be asked to come in of a Thursday, and there could be either general agreement, or else a perceptible lack of enthusiasm and a dropping of the matter. Usually there was agreement, since we all knew the type of man we wanted or did not want.

The ritual of an Inklings was unvarying. When half a dozen or so had arrived, tea would be produced, and then when pipes were well alight Jack would say, 'Well, has nobody got anything to read us?' Out would come a manuscript, and we would settle down to sit in judgement upon it—real unbiased judgement, too, since we were no mutual admiration society: praise for good work was unstinted, but censure for bad work—or even not-so-good work—was often brutally frank. To read to the Inklings was a formidable ordeal, and I can still remember the fear with which I offered the first chapter of my first book—and my delight, too, at its reception.

To indicate the content of those evenings, let me look forward to 1946, a vintage year. At most of the meetings during that year we had a chapter from Tolkien's 'new Hobbit', as we called it—the great work later published as *The Lord of the Rings*. My diary records in October of that year 'a long argument on the ethics of cannibalism'; in November, that 'Roy Campbell read us his translations of a couple of Spanish poems', and 'John Wain won an outstanding bet by reading a chapter of *Irene Iddesleigh* without a smile'; and of the next meeting, that 'David (Cecil) read a chapter of his forthcoming book on Gray'. In February 1949 we talked of red-brick universities; from where the talk drifted by channels which I have forgotten, to 'torture, Tertullian, bores, the contractual theory of mediaeval kingship, and odd place-names'.

Sometimes, though not often, it would happen that no one had anything to read to us. On these occasions the fun would be riotous, with Jack at the top of his form and enjoying every minute—'no sound delights me more', he once said, 'than male laughter'. At the Inklings his talk was an outpouring of wit, nonsense, whimsy, dialectical swordplay, and pungent judgement such as I have rarely heard equalled—no mere show put on for the occasion, either, since it was often quite as brilliant when he and I were alone together.

During the war years, and the even harder years after 1945, the routine would sometimes be varied slightly and Jack would give us all a cold supper in his rooms—a thing made possible by the great generosity of his many American admirers, whose tributes to him included many noble parcels of food. And there was also another ritual gathering, subsidiary to the Inklings proper: the same company used to meet for an hour or so before lunch every Tuesday at the Eagle and Child in St Giles', better known as the Bird and Baby. These gatherings must have attained a certain notoriety, for in a detective novel of the period a character is made to say 'It must be Tuesday—there's Lewis going into the Bird'.

In his Preface to *Essays Presented to Charles Williams*, Jack gave a lively and moving account of what this circle meant to him, with particular reference to one of the richest and most fruitful friendships of his life. For me to say anything further of Charles Williams in this context would be an unnecessary impertinence.

Through all these years, from 1925 onwards, Jack was bearing the exacting and sometimes tedious burdens of a college tutor and a University lecturer. He would take two or three pairs of pupils for tuition in his own rooms in College every morning, and then go to Headington for lunch; in the afternoon, if he was in luck, he would be allowed to take a walk, returning for tea, and then he would return to College for the rest of the day and for the night. He had, therefore, a precarious freedom from domestic drudgery: later on, however, he took to sleeping at home instead of in College, at some loss to this freedom.

His rooms at Magdalen were magnificent: a big sitting-room on the first floor of New Buildings, looking out on to the Grove, and another and smaller sitting-room and a bed-room, looking across to the Cloisters and the Tower. But he had to furnish these rooms himself at his own expense, and did so in perfunctory and notably economical style: the effect, described by Mr Betjeman as 'arid', continued long after Jack could have afforded new furniture, better chosen and more comfortable. My father suggested, plausibly, that Jack chose this furniture as he chose his clothes—by a hurried acceptance of the first thing offered to him by the shop-keeper. This was part of his general impatience with the mechanical business of living: to get his hair cut, to go to the bank, to go shopping—all such activities were a penance and a burden. His own clothes were a matter of complete indifference to him: he had an extraordinary knack of making a new suit look shabby the second time he wore it. One of his garments has passed into legend. It is said that Jack once took a guest for an early-morning walk round Addison's Walk, after a very wet night. Presently the guest brought his attention to a curious lump of cloth hanging on a bush. 'That looks like my hat!' said Jack; then, joyfully, 'It *is* my hat!' and clapping the sodden mass on to his head, he continued the walk.

This fine indifference was not extended to food: in that matter his requirements were simple but strongly-felt. Plain domestic cookery was what he wanted, with the proviso that if the food was hot the plates should be hot as well. What he really disliked was 'messed-up food', by which he meant any sort of elaborately dressed dish: he could never be persuaded to experiment with new foods. Normally, he drank nothing at table: on special occasions, he liked to share a bottle of Burgundy or Hock, and in College he usually drank a glass of port after dinner. One oddly feminine trait was the immense importance which he attached to afternoon tea. When we were off on a walking tour together, or out on my motor-cycle with Jack in the sidecar, the whole day had to be planned around the necessity of finding ourselves at four o'clock in some place where afternoon tea would be available. The only time I ever saw him really disgruntled in any matter of eating or drinking came in Ireland: we were motoring with a friend, and found no tea in a place where we had counted on it. The friend and I naturally dived into the nearest pub for whisky and soda: Jack refused even this consolation.

These various holidays and tours were a great feature of his life and mine: they were inspired by a joy in landscape that developed out of the Boxonian visions of our childhood and was—together with books—the most enduring element in cementing our friendship. Until 1939 our annual walking tour was a regular fixture: on these long days, and during the pleasant evening hours when we took our ease in an inn, Jack was always at his most exuberant, his most whimsical, his most perceptive—the over-worked cab-horse released from the shafts and kicking his heels.

Over-worked he certainly was: not only by the burden of his routine work as tutor and lecturer, not only by the domestic tasks laid on him by Mrs Moore ('He is as good as an extra maid in the house', she would say complacently to visitors), but also by the extent and depth of his own reading, the creative effort of original work both scholarly and religious, and (as the years passed) the increasing volume of his correspondence, much of it from total strangers. In view of all this, visitors to his rooms were often struck by the modest size of his personal library. In his younger days he was something of a bibliophile, but in middle and later life he very seldom bought a book if he could consult it in the Bodleian: long years of poverty, self-inflicted but grinding, had made this economical habit second nature to him—a factor that contributed, no doubt, to the extraordinarily retentive character of his memory.

For all their arid furnishings and their few books, those rooms in Magdalen came by habit and long association to seem cosy and home-like. When I left the army I made them my own headquarters, and was able to give Jack some help of secretarial and similar kinds: and it was in these rooms that many generations of students enjoyed and suffered the stimulation of his erudite and dialectical mind. Since his death, a number of tributes and reminiscences from former pupils have come into my hands: from these I would like to summarise one, provided by Mr H. M. Blamires, who began to read English with Jack in 1936, and who has managed to convey admirably the particular flavour of those tutorial hours.

'He was personally interested in his pupils and permanently concerned about those who became his friends. Though he was a most courteous and considerate person his frankness could, when he wanted, cut through the ordinary fabric of reticences with a shock of sudden warmth or sudden devastation, indeed of both at once. No one knew better how to nourish a pupil with encouragement and how to press just criticism when it was needed, without causing resentment. He did not think of himself as taking pupils through a course; rather he saw his pupils as having two years or so under his guidance, during which they could start on a process which would occupy the responsive ones for the rest of their lives. The literature stood waiting on the shelves; the pupil's appetite was to be whetted and fed. It would be wrong to give the impression that he encouraged indiscriminate reading. Once I went to a tutorial proudly nursing a substantial and, as I thought, admirably comprehensive essay on Abraham Cowley. Half-way through I undertook a critical survey of Cowley's historical epic, the *Davideis*. Well launched upon my reading of this survey, I was suddenly conscious of Lewis rocking in suppressed amusement. Eventually he interrupted me gently. "But you don't mean to say you've actually *read* the thing?" The tone was of mock horror. "Every word," I said. "I'm terribly sorry," he said gravely, as though nothing could atone for the suffering he had unwittingly brought upon me. Then he brightened, having found the crumb of consolation. "But think of it. You must be the only man in the country, perhaps the only man alive, to have read every word of Cowley's *Davideis*." He expected you to share his life-long companionship with his favourite authors. There was never a fit point in life for saying "Yes, I've *read*

Malory or Spenser or Milton". It would be like saying, "Yes, I've *eaten* bacon and eggs". There was a good deal of fun about tutorials. Lewis sat there on his vast Chesterfield, smoking a pipe and cigarettes alternately, periodically beaming and bouncing with good humour in a hugely expansive way. He looked big, sitting down opposite one, with his great fist bulging round a pipe bowl, eyes wide open and eyebrows raised behind a cloud of smoke. As a lecturer he was the biggest "draw" the English School had in the nineteen-thirties. He could fill the largest lecture rooms. He was popular because his lectures were meaty. He purveyed what was wanted in a palatable form. Proportion and direction were always preserved, but without forcing. Points were clearly enumerated; arguments beautifully articulated; illustrations richly chosen. The physical images of the Lewis of the 'thirties that stay with me are symbols rather than clearly defined pictures. One remembers his shapeless hat and ill-fitting overcoat seen to peculiar disadvantage from the top of a bus . . . the rich, chanting voice at one of his Thursday "Beer and Beowulf" evenings, the big red face bulging out of the graceless clothes, and alive with a zest and intensity which won and warmed you in defiance of aesthetic considerations. It is not easy to carry together in the mind the picture Lewis presented in a relaxed mood and the realization of the vast amount of work he did. His liking for beer and bawdy late-night talk might together have misled the unobservant with a completely false picture. His hospitality, like his help, generously but unforcingly offered, was easy to accept, easy to decline.

His "churchmanship" could not be labelled. It was never the meaningful things or the important things that displeased him from the "Catholic" side; it was excessive ritualistic concern over inessentials, or the exaggeration of trivialities.

It would be quite wrong to imagine that Lewis's deep and unfailing charity left him incapable of being decisive and frank about defect in others. He would not gossip. He would not sustain a malicious conversation. But he would not conspire to veil a person's deficiency if it might be harmful to veil it. He did his best to be scrupulously fair in his judgements. Praise and criticism were always absolutely honest. He had a near-fanatical devotion to Charles Williams, but when Williams wrote a bad book Lewis readily described it as "bloody awful".'

It was, of course, during these years at Magdalen that Jack underwent his re-conversion to Christianity, and also developed into a best-selling author of international reputation. A certain reticence in the one matter, and in the other a conviction that writers more scholarly than myself will be studying my brother's literary work for many years to come, lead me to pass over these subjects briefly.

I well remember that day in 1931 when we made a visit to Whipsnade Zoo, Jack riding in my sidecar: as recorded in *Surprised by Joy*, it was during that outing that he made his decision to rejoin the Church. This seemed to me no sudden plunge into a new life, but rather a slow steady convalescence from a deep-seated spiritual illness of long standing—an illness that had its origins in our childhood, in the dry husks of religion offered by the semi-political church-going of Ulster, in the similar dull emptiness of compulsory church during our schooldays. With this background, we both found the difficulty of the Christian life to lie in public worship, rather than in one's private devotions. In Jack's case, this difficulty was overcome slowly: he had been a practising Christian again for some time when he said to me, of Communion: 'I think that to communicate once a month strikes the right balance between enthusiasm and Laodiceanism.' In later years he saw that 'right balance' differently, and never failed to communicate weekly and on the major feast days as well.

I offer no gloss or comment upon his own experience and understanding of the Christian religion itself: to the profit of many thousands, he has himself told all that words can carry. So far as his outward life was concerned, his conversion had various consequences: it was the occasion of a notable literary development, of wide popularity coupled with hostility in some quarters, and of certain war-time lecturing engagements with the RAF and the BBC. It was in connection with his religious rather than his scholarly writing that his name became a household word in the 'forties and 'fifties, and the same emphasis may be behind the two honorary degrees conferred upon him—the Doctorate of Divinity (1946) by St Andrews, and the Doctorate of Literature (1952) by Laval University, Quebec. (A further honour, the

C.B.E., was offered by the Prime Minister in 1951, but Jack felt obliged to refuse this: his appearance in a Conservative Honours List might, he felt, strengthen the ill-founded case of those who identified religious writing with anti-leftist propaganda.)

The remarkable thing about his literary career is that it never occurred to him until a relatively late date that his great achievement would be in prose. *Spirits in Bondage* appeared in 1919, a collection of poems, some of them written in his Bookham days: *Dymer*, a narrative poem, was published in 1926, the fruit of much pain and effort during a peculiarly difficult period. During all these early years, he thought of himself (though with no great confidence) as essentially a poet. A certain feeling of alienation from the poetic currents of his time led him to publish pseudonymously: those first two books were by "Clive Hamilton" (his own first name, and his mother's maiden surname), and the many poems that he published in later years were signed "Nat Whilk" (Anglo-Saxon for "I know not who") or, more simply, "N.W."

In 1933 he published *The Pilgrim's Regress* and in 1936 *The Allegory of Love*. This latter book, on which he had been working since 1928, was immediately and permanently a success by every standard: and from that time on, my brother's life was one of continual writing and continual publication for an ever-increasing and ever more appreciative audience. It may be observed at this point that to become a best-selling author does not necessarily involve full success in the task of 'communication'. The two books into which Jack put most of himself—*The Pilgrim's Regress* and *Till We Have Faces*—were in his own estimation failures, misunderstood or ignored by the public.

It was with the publication of *The Screwtape Letters*, in the autumn of 1942, that Jack first achieved wide public success of the kind that brings money rolling in. He was not used to this—his early penury had not trained him for relative affluence—and he celebrated by a lavish and improvident scattering of cheques to various societies and individual lame dogs. Before the situation got completely out of hand, his solicitor intervened: a charitable trust was set up into which two-thirds of his royalties was thereafter paid automatically, and from which payments both large and numerous were made for all manner of charitable purposes. The financial side of his charity was by no means limited to this particular arrangement, and the total of his benefactions will never be known; but over and above this, he had in an extraordinary degree the deeper charity that can perhaps best be described as a universal and sympathetic neighbourliness to all and sundry, strangers as well as acquaintances.

Two examples of this quality come to my mind. One summer day he heard it mentioned casually that there was a sick man in a field some distance away. Jack said 'poor devil' and continued to write; then he suddenly jumped up in distress and said, 'I have sinned; I have shown myself lacking in all charity'. Out he went, found the man, brought him to the house, gave him a drink, heard his story, and then—being satisfied that the man was able to look after himself—saw him off, not (I am sure) forgetting the Samaritan's twopence. Then, on another occasion, he met a tramp while walking on Shotover—a tramp who turned the conversation to the subject of poetry, quoting Fitzgerald with gusto. Jack went home, armed himself with bottles of beer and a verse anthology, trudged up to the top of the hill again, gave book and beer to the tramp, and bade him a cordial farewell.

During all these Magdalen years until Mrs Moore's death in 1951, the domestic circumstances of Jack's life continued to impose a heavy strain upon this habit of charity. Relations with his father were peaceful but distant. Jack wrote home in regular and informative style, but visits to Little Lea had always a sad penitential character: in his later years my father became more and more of an inquisitor and tyrant, prying into every detail of his sons' lives, interfering blindly in even the most personal matters. We were always glad to get away. The three of us were at home together for the last time in 1927: it is pleasant to record that my father noted this in his journal as 'a very pleasant holiday—roses all the way'. In 1929 he died: I was in China at the time, and it fell to Jack to make the immediate arrangements for winding up the household at Little Lea.

And at Oxford, for more than three decades, Jack continued to live under the autocracy of Mrs Moore—an autocracy that developed into stifling tyranny, as I experienced myself during the years of my inclusion within this incomprehensible ménage. Mrs Moore was one of those who thrive on crisis and chaos; every day had to have some kind of domestic scene or upheaval, commonly involving the maids: the emotional burden so created had then to be placed squarely on the uncomplaining shoulders of Jack. In this atmosphere the physical inconveniences of the household seemed relatively unimportant: notable among them was the total unpredictability of any meal-time.

Jack's servitude was made more burdensome, as the years passed, by Mrs Moore's senility and invalidism: it was only broken by her admission to a nursing home in April 1950 and her death there nine months later.

Four years after this Jack's whole life changed, and for six years he was to experience first peace and then a delight and fulfilment which had never previously come to him.

In 1954 Jack accepted the offer of a new chair at Cambridge. He finished his last Oxford tutorial—with a certain sense of relief—on the third of December, and the New Year found him installed at Cambridge as Professor of Mediaeval and Renaissance English. His inaugural lecture, later printed under the title of *De Descriptione Temporum*, was a crowded and memorable occasion: it added a new phrase to the colloquial jargon of the time, and many people could be heard for a while thereafter proclaiming stoutly that they were, or were not, specimens of 'Old Western Man'. Dr G. M. Trevelyan, who was then Master of Trinity, presided on this occasion: he introduced Jack by revealing that this was the only university appointment in the whole of his experience for which the electing committee had voted unanimously.

Jack found the life at Cambridge and the company at Magdalene congenial, mentally stimulating yet relaxed. His years there were happy years. The break with his old life was not complete: he continued to live at The Kilns, passing there not only his vacations but also many week-ends in term. He necessarily resigned his Fellowship at Magdalen, but was immediately re-elected to an Honorary Fellowship: and with his Cambridge chair went a Fellowship there under the same patronage, at Magdalene.

Meanwhile he had met the woman who was to bring him so much happiness in love and marriage. Joy Davidman was American by birth and Jewish by race. She and her husband, William Lindsay Gresham, were avid admirers of Jack's work and became Christians partly under his influence. She met Jack for the first time in 1953, having already corresponded with him at some length. Later, and free now to marry again, she returned to England with her two sons, intending to live there permanently. By 1955 she was on close terms with Jack. For Jack the attraction was at first undoubtedly intellectual. Joy was the only woman whom he had met (although as his letters show, he had known with great affection many able women) who had a brain which matched his own in suppleness, in width of interest, in analytical grasp, and above all in humour and sense of fun. Further, she shared his delight in argument for argument's sake, whether frivolous or serious, always good-humoured yet always meeting him trick for trick as he changed ground. A woman of great charity, she had an unbounded contempt for the sentimental. Setting herself high standards, she could laugh at the seeming absurdities to which they sometimes carried her. With all this, she was intensely feminine.

Joy had cancer, and at the end of 1956 they were married, not in church but at the bride's bedside in the Wingfield Hospital, the civil ceremony having taken place some days earlier. Both knew she was a dying woman. Yet she did not then die: she made a temporary recovery and Jack brought her home to The Kilns. There were now for him three years of complete fulfilment. To his friends who saw them together it was clear that they not only loved but were in love with each other. It was a delight to watch them, and all the waste of Jack's years which had gone before was more than recompensed. Nevill Coghill has told how Jack at this time said to him, looking at his wife across a grassy quadrangle, "I never expected to have, in my sixties, the happiness that passed me by in my twenties."

Then on June 13th, 1960, after a return to hospital, she died.

A short episode, of glory and tragedy: for Jack, the total (though heartbreaking) fulfilment of a whole dimension to his nature that had previously been starved and thwarted. Joy's death was entirely expected. Even though her temporary recovery had made possible certain travels, including holidays in Ireland and Greece, none the less, the parting when it came was a shattering blow to him. His notes on the experience of those black days were later published, pseudonymously, as *A Grief Observed*: to this harrowing book, anyone can be referred who feels curiosity about the character and flavour of this love, this marriage.

It may not be amiss if I place on record here my own reaction to this side of Jack's life. For almost twenty years I had shared (to some degree) in his submission to matriarchal rule: the attitude that I have already expressed towards this rule, and towards Mrs Moore in person, may predispose some readers towards a suspicion that I may have been a possessive brother, jealous and resentful if any other person had importance in Jack's eyes. If this had been the case, I would have resented this marriage of his intensely: and in fact, my earlier experience did lead me to the preparation of plans for withdrawal and for the establishment of a home of my own in Eire.

But Jack and Joy would not hear of this; and so I decided to give the new régime a trial. All my fears were dispelled. For me, Jack's marriage meant that our home was enriched and enlivened by the presence of a witty, broad-minded, well-read and tolerant Christian, whom I had rarely heard equalled as a conversationalist and whose company was a never-ending source of enjoyment: indeed, at the peak of her apparent recovery she was at work on a life of Mme de Maintenon, which unfortunately never got further than several books of notes and an explanatory preface.

It would be an impertinence for me to compare my own sorrow at her death with his: nevertheless, I still continue to miss her sadly.

To speak temperately of the greater loss that overtook me three years later is difficult indeed. Jack was already in poor health by the time of his marriage: afterwards it became apparent that he needed an operation but was too weak to undergo it. In this situation, his health was bound to deteriorate steadily: no success attended the attempts to "fatten him up", as he put it, "for the sacrifice", and in July 1963 he very nearly died. He made some beginning of a recovery; but by early October it became apparent to both of us that he was facing death.

In their way, these last weeks were not unhappy. Joy had left us, and once again—as in the earliest days—we could turn for comfort only to each other. The wheel had come full circle: once again we were together in the little end room at home, shutting out from our talk the ever-present knowledge that the holidays were ending, that a new term fraught with unknown possibilities awaited us both.

Jack faced the prospect bravely and calmly. "I have done all I wanted to do, and I'm ready to go", he said to me one evening.

Only once did he show any regret or reluctance: this was when I told him that the morning's mail included an invitation to deliver the Romanes lecture. An expression of sadness passed over his face, and there was a moment's silence: then, "Send them a very polite refusal".

Our talk tended to be cheerfully reminiscent during these last days: long-forgotten incidents in our shared past would be remembered, and the old Jack would return for a moment, whimsical and witty. We were recapturing the old schoolboy technique of extracting the last drop of juice from our holidays.

Friday, the 22nd of November 1963, began much as other days: there was breakfast, then letters and the crossword puzzle. After lunch he fell asleep in his chair: I suggested that he would be more comfortable in bed, and he went there. At four I took in his tea and found him drowsy but comfortable. Our few words then were the last: at five-thirty I heard a crash and ran in, to find him lying unconscious at the foot of his bed. He ceased to breathe some three or four minutes later.

The following Friday would have been his sixty-fourth birthday. Even in that terrible moment, the thought flashed across my mind that whatever fate had in store for me, nothing worse than this could ever happen to me in the future.

"Men must endure their going hence."

In making this selection from my brother's correspondence, I have kept in mind not only those interested in the literary and religious aspects of his mind, but also—and perhaps more urgently—those who want to know what manner of man he was, and who may derive from these letters some idea of the liveliness, the colour and wit displayed throughout his life by this best of brothers and friends.

I should perhaps stress that this book is a selection. Not all the letters that Jack wrote were of permanent and public interest; he sometimes repeated himself; and a few letters, or parts of letters, must be held back on grounds of charity or discretion. In certain cases, the names of his correspondents have been altered or suppressed, for sufficient reason. In general, omissions have only been indicated where the reader might otherwise be misled or bewildered: I have considered the general reader's convenience, not aiming at any scholarly punctiliousness.

I am deeply grateful to those who passed Jack's letters to me, with permission to reprint; and also to Mr Walter Hooper and Mr Christopher Derrick for help in preparing the typescript for publication.

WARREN LEWIS

TO ARTHUR GREEVES. (*It seems appropriate to begin this selection from my brother's correspondence with his own first account of a major turning-point in his life, a major influence upon his thought and work.*)

(Undated: October 1915)

I have had a great literary experience this week . . . The book is Geo. Macdonald's 'Phantastes', which I picked up by hazard. . . . Have you read it? At any rate whatever you are reading now, you simply *must* get this at once. . . . Of course it is hopeless for me to try and describe it, but when you have followed the hero Anodos along the little stream of the faery wood, have heard about the terrible ash tree . . . and heard the episode of Cosmo, I know you will agree with me. You must not be disappointed at the first chapter, which is rather conventional faery tale style, and after it you won't be able to stop until you finish. There are one or two poems in the tale, which, with one or two exceptions, are shockingly bad, so don't *try* to appreciate them. . . .

I quite agree with what you say about buying books, and love the planning and scheming beforehand, and if they come by post, finding the neat little parcel waiting for you on the hall table and rushing upstairs to open it in the privacy of your own room. . . . I have at last come to the end of the 'Faerie Queen'; and though I say 'at last', I wish he had lived to write six books more as he hoped to do, so much have I enjoyed it. The two Cantos of 'Mutabilitie' with which he ends are perhaps the finest thing in it. . . . I well remember the glorious walk of which you speak, how we lay long drenched with sunshine on the moss, and were for a short time perfectly happy—which is a rare enough condition, God knows. . . .

TO ARTHUR GREEVES. (*The "Mrs. K" referred to here is Mrs Kirkpatrick. See Introduction, p. 4.*)

(Undated)

I am afraid you will be growing a very stodgy mind if you read nothing but Trollope and Goldsmith and Austen. Of course they are all very good, but I don't think that myself I could stand such a dose of stolidity. I suppose you will reply that I am too much the other way, and will grow an unbalanced mind if I read nothing but lyrics and faery tales. But I find it so hard to start a fresh novel; I have a lazy desire to dally with the old favourites again. . . . I have found my musical soul again . . . this time in the Preludes of Chopin. Aren't they wonderful? Although Mrs. K. doesn't play them well, they are so passionate, so hopeless, I could almost cry over them; they are unbearable. . . .

TO ARTHUR GREEVES.

(Undated)

I cannot urge you too strongly to go on and write something, anything, but at any rate *write*. Of course everyone knows his own strength best, but if I may give any advice, I would say as I did before, that humour is a dangerous thing to try; as well, there are so many funny books in the world that it seems a shame to make any more, while the army of weird and beautiful or homely and passionate works could well do with recruits. . . . And by the way, while I'm on this subject, there's one thing I want to say; I do hope that in things like this you'll always tell me the absolute truth about my work, just as if it were by someone we didn't know; I will promise to do the same for you. Because otherwise there is no point in sending them, and I have sometimes thought that you are not inclined to. (Not to be candid I mean). . . .

TO ARTHUR GREEVES.

(Undated)

I was rather surprised to see the notepaper of your last letter and certainly wish I could have been with you; I have some vague memories of the cliffs round there and of Dunluce Castle, and some memories which are not at all vague of the same coast a little further on at Castlerock where we used to go in the old days. Don't you love a windy day at a place like that? Waves make one kind of music on rocks and another on sand and I don't know which of the two I would rather have. . . . I don't like the way you say 'don't tell anyone' that you thought Frankenstein badly written, and at once draw in your critical horns with the 'of course I'm no judge' theory. Rot. You are a very good judge for me because our tastes run in the same direction. And you ought to rely more on yourself than on anyone else in matters of books—that is if you are out for enjoyment and not for improvement or any nonsense of that sort. . . .

TO ARTHUR GREEVES.

(Undated)

I have now read all the Tales of Chaucer which I ever expected to read and feel that I may consider the book as finished . . . some of them are quite impossible. On the whole, with one or two exceptions, like the Knight's Tale and the Franklin's, he is disappointing when you get to know him. He has most of the faults of the Middle Ages—garrulity and coarseness—without their romantic charm. . . .

I hope you are going on with 'Alice' or starting something else; you have plenty of imagination, and what you want is practice, practice, practice. It does not matter what we write at our age so long as we write continuously as well as we can write. . . . I feel that every time I write a page either of prose or of verse, with real effort, even if it is thrown into the fire next minute I am so much further on. . . .

TO ARTHUR GREEVES.

(Undated)

What is nicer than to get a book, doubtful both about the reading matter and the edition, and then to find that both are topping? By the way of balancing my disappointment in 'Tristan' I have just had this pleasure in Sydney's 'Arcadia'. Oh Arthur, you simply must get it. . . . I don't know how to explain its peculiar charm because it is not at all like anything I ever read before; and yet in places it is like all of them. Sometimes it is like Malory, often like Spenser, and yet different from either. . . . The story is much more connected than Malory; there is a great deal of love-making and just enough 'brasting and fighting' to give a sort of impression of all the old doings of chivalry without becoming tedious. . . .

TO ARTHUR GREEVES, *after a holiday spent together.*

27 September 1916

As you say, it seems years and years since I left. Portsalon is like a dream. . . . One part of my journey (to Bookham) I enjoyed very much was the first few miles out of Liverpool, because it was one of the most wonderful mornings I have ever seen—one of those lovely white misty ones when you can't see 10 yards. You could just see the nearest trees and houses, a little ghostly in appearance, and beyond that, everything was a clean, white blank. It felt as if the train was alone in space, if you know what I mean. . . .

Have you reached home yet? The country at home was beginning to look nice and autumn-y with dead leaves in the lanes and a nice nutty smell. . . . Here it is horrible bright summer, which I hate. . . . Love to all our friends such as the hedgepig etc.

TO ARTHUR GREEVES.

25 October 1916

I don't know when I shall buy some new books, as I am at present suffering from a flash of poverty. When I do, it will either be 'Our Village' or 'Cranford' or Chaucer's 'Troilus and Cressida'. . . . By all accounts it is much more in my line than the Canterbury Tales, and anyway I can take no more interest in them since I found out that my Everyman edition is abridged and mutilated. I wish they wouldn't do that (Lockhart you say is another case) without telling you. I can't bear to have anything but what a man really wrote.

I have been reading the quaintest book, 'The letters of Dorothy Osborne to Sir Wm. Temple'. . . . It is very interesting to read the ordinary everyday life of a girl in Cromwell's time, and tho' of course they are often dull there is a lot in them that you would like; especially the description of how she spends the day, and another of a summer evening in the garden. . . . I have read today some ten pages of 'Tristam Shandy'. . . . It is certainly the maddest book ever written, or 'ever wrote' as dear Dorothy Osborne would say. It gives you the impression of an escaped lunatic's conversation while chasing his hat on a windy day. Yet there are beautiful serious parts in it. . . . Tang-tang, there goes eleven o'clock. Don't you simply love going to bed? To curl up warmly in a nice warm bed in the lovely darkness, and then gradually drift away into sleep. . . . I'm turning out the gas. Bonsoir.

TO ARTHUR GREEVES.

30 October 1916

The beastly summer is at last over here, and good old autumn smells and colours and temperatures have come back. Thanks to this, we had a most glorious walk on Saturday. It was a fine, cool, windy day and we set out after lunch to go to a place called Friday Street, which is a very long walk from here, through beautiful woods and valleys that I don't know at all.

After several hours wandering over woods, fields etc., with the aid of a map, we began to get lost, and suddenly about four o.c. —we had expected to reach the place about that time—we found ourselves in a place where we had been an hour before. . . .

We had a bit of difficulty in at last reaching Friday Street, but it was glorious when we got there. You are walking in the middle of a wood when all of a sudden you go downwards and come to a little open hollow just big enough for a little lake and some old, old red-tiled houses; all round it the trees tower up on rising ground, and every road from it is at once swallowed up in them. You might walk within a few feet of it and suspect nothing, unless you saw the smoke rising up from some cottage chimney. . . . But best of all, when we came down to the little inn of the village and had tea there with—glory of glories—an old-time jackdaw hopping about our feet asking for crumbs. He is called Jack, and will answer to his name. The inn has three tiny, but spotlessly clean bedrooms and some day, if the gods will, you and I are going to stay there. . . .

TO ARTHUR GREEVES.

(Undated)

I can't let pass unchallenged that you should put 'Beowulf' and Malory together as if they belonged to the same class. One is a mediaeval English prose romance, and the other an Anglo-Saxon epic poem; one is Christian, the other Heathen; one we read just as it was actually written, the other is a translation. So you can like one without (liking) the other. . . .

TO HIS FATHER: *a scholarship candidate's first impressions of Oxford.*

(Undated: December 1916)

This is Thursday and our last papers are on Saturday morning. . . . This place has surpassed my wildest dreams; I never saw anything so beautiful, especially on these frosty nights; though in the Hall of Oriel where we do our papers it is fearfully cold at about four o'clock on these afternoons. We have most of us tried, with varying success, to write in our gloves.

TO HIS BROTHER.

(Undated: January 1917)

Many thanks indeed for the letter and the most acceptable enclosure which arrived, thank goodness, while P. was out, and so saved it from going the same road as my poor legacy. For you know I got £23 10. 0. the same as you, but of course I have never seen a penny of it; my humble suggestion that I might have a pound or two was greeted with the traditional "Ah such nonsense"! . . .

Is there any chance of your being made a permanent Captain before the war is over?—which I hope to God will be before my valuable person gets anywhere near it. . . .

Oxford is absolutely topping, and I am awfully bucked with it and longing to go up, tho' apparently I am not to do so until next October. . . .

TO HIS FATHER.

28 January 1917

At about half past eleven yesterday morning I went to Univ. and was led across two Quads, one behind the other, to a house in a beautiful old walled garden. This was the ogre's castle. He was a clean-shaven, white haired, jolly old man, and was very nice indeed. He treated me to about half an hour's 'Oxford manner', and then came gradually round to my own business. . . It seems that if I pass Responsions in March I can come up in the following term and join the O.T.C. This plan he thinks the best, because I have more chance of a commission from the Oxford

O.T.C. than from anything else of the sort. . . . After that he made me stay to lunch with his wife and his niece. . . . I am very pleased with my ogre after all. . . .

TO HIS FATHER, *on first taking up residence in wartime Oxford.*
(Undated: postmarked 28 April 1917)

The effect here of the war is much more startling than I could have expected, and everything is very homely and out of order. The College at present numbers 6 men, of whom four are freshmen! Others are coming all the time, but I do not think we shall be more than eleven all told. Last night we had dinner, not in Hall but in a small lecture room, and none of the Dons appeared. Hall is in possession of the blue-coated wounded, who occupy the whole of one Quad. . . . The first thing that strikes you is the enormous size of the rooms. I imagined a "sitter" something smaller than the little end room. The first one they showed me was rather larger than our drawing room, and full of the most beautiful oak. I wasn't left there however, and am now in a much humbler, and very nice set, on the other side of the Quad. It is a pity in a way that all the furniture and pictures really belong to a man who may be coming back after the war—it saves me expenses, but it prevents me from having what I want.

I have been to see the Dean, who turns out to be a beardless boy of about 25, and also my Tutor who is also the Bursar. They don't appear to suggest any real reading while I am in the Corps, but the Bursar has promised to find me a coach for elementary mathematics if possible. Corps does not begin until Monday evening, for which short respite I am very thankful. I think it will be quite cheap living in "this vast solitude"; the only serious expenses so far have been £2. 10. 0. for uniform (which seems very reasonable), and £1. 9. 0. for a cap and gown (which does not). . . .

TO HIS FATHER.

(Undated)

I am glad to say that my money 'pans out' quite sufficiently and is indeed just about the average. I mean the amount of pocket money is about the same as that of other people, though of course many have an allowance out of which they pay all their own bills—in which case the actual pocket money will vary with the ups and downs of their battles. To give you some idea of the latter I enclosed mine as supplied so far. . . . The first week was necessarily expensive, chiefly through ignorance, 'in which accomplishment', as de Quincy says, 'I excel'.

My scout is a very fatherly old man who has been here for forty-six years; he even once told me to change my socks when they were wet. His only failing is an impenetrable deafness which causes many conversations of the 'It's a fine day'—'No, not much to pay' type.

I'm afraid you must not build anything on the idea of my rowing, as I have almost given it up in favour of canoeing. You see a row boat can be used only on the big river where you run into all the real rowing men, as the Cherwell (much prettier and more interesting) soon gets too narrow for rowers to pass each other. Besides there is to me something very attractive about one of these little canoes—so very light and all-to-yourself. Perhaps when we all come back again from the war and there is no O.T.C. I will take up rowing again.

The O.T.C. gets more interesting as we go on. We spend a good deal of our time in the trenches—a complete model system with dugouts, shell holes etc. . . . I have nearly finished Renan, whom I find delightful. He seems to have written a good many books on different subjects. I am going to borrow Wells' new book from a man in college who is thinking of becoming a Catholic. He is an ardent Newmanite and we have some talk on literary subjects. Someone pointed out to me our present Poet-Laureate, Bridges, on the river last Wednesday.

TO HIS FATHER.

(Undated: postmarked 17 May 1917)

Our 'military duties' are as light as they well could be. We have a morning parade from 7 till 7.45, and another from 2 till 4, with occasional evening lectures on map reading and such-like subjects. . . . The early morning parade of course makes it impossible to go to Chapel, except to the Celebration on Sundays. . . . I am afraid that I usually find the place in possession of us freshers and the Dons. As to St Mary's, I have not been yet. The last two Sundays have been so fine that having been to early service, I felt justified in going off to bathe after 'brekker'. I have however found out enough about it to realize that it is rather different from what we imagine. There are only a few prayers, and a very long sermon, usually more of a philosophical and political than of a religious nature; in fact it is more a Sunday lecture room than a church in the true sense. The best place to go for a fine service is the Cathedral at 'The House' as Christ Church is called; it is typical of the House that it should have the Cathedral of the Diocese for its Chapel!

TO HIS FATHER, *recording the transition from an academic to a military life.*

(Undated)

Just a line in a hurry to let you know how things go. . . . The Cadet Battalion which I joined yesterday (of course it has nothing to do with the Varsity) is quartered in Keble. There are several gentlemen in it, and I am fortunate in sharing a room with one. It is a great comfort to be in Oxford, as I shall still be able to see something of my Univ. friends. . . . As to Responsions, I may or may not be able to persuade them to give me three days' leave to do it in; if they do, I should think that under the circumstances, my chance of passing would not be very bright. At any rate, six months service with the Colours will exempt me from it. . . .

TO HIS FATHER.

(Undated)

And now for some account of my new life. Well, at first when I left my own snug quarters and my own friends for a carpetless little cell at Keble with two beds (minus sheets and pillows), and got into a Tommy's uniform, I will not deny that I thought myself very ill-used.

I have quite recovered, and am now leading a very happy life, tho' not of course the life I would have chosen. In many ways it is a better life; I have never worked till now, and it is high time I began. As to my companions, they are really divided into three lots. The first and largest lot consists of rankers who have been out at the front for some time, and have come home to get commissions. They are mostly jolly good chaps; clean, honest, infinitely good-natured. . . . Most of our set get on very well with them. The next lot (about a third of the whole) consists of cads and fools pure and simple. They don't need much description; some of them are vicious, some merely doltish, all vulgar and uninteresting. They spit on the stairs and talk about what they are going to do when they get to the front—where of course none of them has been. Then comes the third, our own set, public school and varsity men, with all their faults and merits 'already ascertained'.

The daily round is of course pretty strenuous and leaves little time for dreaming or reading. However, I eat and sleep as I have never done before, and am getting rid of some adipose tissue. . . .

TO HIS FATHER.

(Undated: postmarked 18 July 1917)

Life here goes on pretty much as usual, except that the work gets more interesting and involves less actual "sweat of the brow". We do a good deal of night work, which I rather like, and which leads to getting up later in the morning. . . . You are allowed week end leave here every week, provided that you do not go out of Oxford. The last four weeks I have spent it over at Univ., enjoying all my old luxuries over again. Now however the Dean has vetoed the plan; on the ground that College is kept open in vacation for men who want to read, 'and not for use as an hotel'. I suppose he is quite right in a way, but it is rather a pity.

You can't imagine how I have grown to love Univ., especially since I left. Last Saturday evening when I was sleeping there alone, I spent a long time wandering over it, into all sorts of parts where I had never been before, where mullioned windows are dark with ivy that no one has bothered to cut since the war emptied the rooms they belong to. Some of the rooms were all dust-sheeted, others were much as their owners had left them—the pictures still on the walls, and the books dust-covered in their shelves. It was melancholy in a way, and yet very interesting. . . .

At present I am reading a countryman of ours, Bishop Berkeley, 'that silly old man' as Andrew Lang calls him; in fact, one of our few philosophers, and a very interesting fellow, whom I have always admired for the way he stood up to the ogre in Boswell. . . . Could you let me have some money to get boots for my officer pattern uniform? I find the Cadet School, so far, much more expensive than the Varsity. When does Warnie get his leave?

TO HIS FATHER.

(Undated: postmarked 22 July 1917)

I make every effort to cling to the old life of books, hoping that I may save my soul alive, and not become a great, empty-headed, conceited military prig. I am finding out that the military ideal in our army differs from the German one only in degree, not in kind. The Sergt. Major told us the other day that 'soldiering is more than 'arf swank. You've got to learn to walk out as if the bloody street belongs to you. See?' Well I hope that neither I nor any of my friends will ever attain to that degree of soldierhood.

The promised four days leave will come in about a fortnight's time. . . . On Saturday I drank tea with a dear old gentleman named Goddard, formerly an undergrad. of Balliol and now a Don of Trinity. What interested me most was his opinion of Jowett (here pronounced to rhyme with 'poet') who, he said, had spoiled the scholarly tone of Balliol by a vulgar running after lions. . . . Of Swinburne's prose, I have read the book on Charlotte Brontë, and the smaller one on William Blake. It is undoubtedly very bad prose (I did not find the coarseness), but it is so vigorous that you can forgive it. . . .

TO HIS FATHER.

(Undated: postmarked 10 October 1917)

The next amusement on our programme is a three day bivouac up in the Wytham hills. As it has rained all the time for the last two or three days, our model trenches up there will provide a very unnecessarily good imitation of Flanders mud. You know how I always disapproved of realism in art. . . . Tell Arthur I simply *can't* write.

TO HIS FATHER, *upon his being commissioned and posted to a Battalion then stationed in Devonshire.*

(Undated)

You will be anxious to hear what sort of thieves I have fallen among. . . . Of the officers . . . one or two of them I think I shall like, though of course it is hard to say at present. It must be admitted that most of them are hardly after my style; the subjects of conversation are shop (Oh, for the ancient taboo that ruled in officers' messes in the piping times of peace!), sport, and theatrical news recurring with a rather dull regularity—that is in the few moments of conversation which interrupt the serious business of bridge and snooker. However, they are for the most part well bred and quite nice to me. So that if this new life rouses no violent enthusiasm in me, it is on the other hand quite bearable and even pleasant.

The 'work' is a very simple matter. All the men, nearly, are recruits, and the training is carried out by N.C.Os. All you do is to lead your party onto parade, hand them over to their instructor, and then walk about doing nothing at all. This you do for several hours a day. It is a little tiring on the legs and I think will finally result in atrophy of the brain. However, it is much better than hard work, and I am satisfied. I was a bit too previous in wiring from Plymouth station that Crownhill was a barracks. It turns out to be a village of wooden huts, set up in the hills amid really very beautiful scenery. Besides the officer's mess—which is a sort of glorified golf club house—we each have our own room, with a stove in it. When it is lit up, it is really very snug. . . . So my verdict you see is quite favourable. . . .

TO HIS FATHER, *from France.*

13 December 1917

I am at present in billets in a certain rather battered town somewhere behind the line. It is quite comfy, but of course the work is hard and (what is worse) irregular. I have just finished 'Adam Bede' which I liked immensely—but don't send me any more of hers as I know a shop (or rather canteen) that has them in the Tauchnitz edition. . . .

TO HIS FATHER.

4 January 1918

I have been up in the trenches for a few days, attached to a company for instruction. . . . I am now back again on a course of bombing, where I live with the bombing officer, a very nice fellow of literary tastes, in a quite comfortable billet. The work, involving a good deal of chemical and mechanical questions, is not of the sort that my brain takes to readily, but so long as one is safe and has an unbroken night's sleep, there is nothing to grouse about I suppose.

You will be anxious to hear my first impressions of trench life. This is a very quiet part of the line and the dugouts are much more comfortable than one imagines at home. They are very deep, you go down to them by a shaft of about 20 steps; they have wire bunks where a man can sleep quite snugly, and braziers for warmth and cooking. Indeed the chief discomfort is that they tend to get *too* hot, while of course the bad air makes one rather headachy . . . I am now at 'The Mill on the Floss' . . . do you know of any life of George Eliot published in a cheap edition? If you can find one, I should like to read it. . . .

TO HIS FATHER, *from hospital in France.*

16 February 1918

Your letter has remained unanswered for some time, and if I had literally fulfilled my promise of 'writing when I got up', I fear the time would have been longer still. 'Trench fever' sounds a formidable name . . . which in plain English means merely a high temperature arising from the general irregularity of life at the front. In my case however, after they had got my temperature down to normal I had a relapse, and was pretty ill for a day or two. I am now on the highroad to recovery, though still in bed. I consider this little turn as an unmixed blessing; even if I get no leave by it, I shall have had a comfortable rest from the line. The place where I have dropped down is a little fishing village so far as I can make out. There are cliffs, and a grey sea beyond, which one is very glad to see again—and from my own window, pleasant wooded country. . . .

The next time you are in Mullans, I should be 'beholden' if you would ask them to look out some cheap edition of Burton's 'Anatomy of Melancholy'. . . . You see I make some desperate attempt to keep in touch with a life beyond the one which we lead here. . . .

TO HIS FATHER, *from another hospital to which Jack was sent after being slightly wounded. (For Mrs. Moore, see Introduction, p. 8.)*

14 May 1918

I am doing exceedingly well, and can now lie on my right side (not of course on my left) which is a great treat after you have been on your back for a few weeks. . . . The wound under my arm is worse than a flesh wound, as the bit of metal which went in there is now in my chest . . . this however is nothing to worry about, as it is doing no harm. . . . I am told that I can carry it about for the rest of my life without any evil results. . . .

My friend Mrs. Moore is in great trouble—Paddy has been missing for over a month, and is almost certainly dead. Of all my own particular set at Keble, he has been the first to go. . . .

TO HIS FATHER, *from hospital in London.*

20 June 1918

On Sunday I made my pilgrimage. Even to go to Waterloo was an adventure full of memories, and every station I passed on the way down seemed to clear away another layer of the time that had passed, and bring me back to the old life. Bookham was at its best; a mass of green, very pleasing to one 'that has been long in city pent'. . . . I opened the gate of Kirk's garden almost with stealth, and went on past the house to the vegetable garden and the little wild orchard with the pond where I had sat so often on hot Sunday afternoons, and there among the cabbages in his shirt and Sunday trousers, sure enough was the old man, still digging and smoking his horrible pipe. . . . I was led into the house with much triumph and displayed to Mrs. Kirk, whom we found fussing with the maid, just as old. I have seldom spent a more delightful afternoon; what talk we had, what reminiscences, how often my opinion was shown to be based ('bazed' as the Sage pronounces it) on 'An insufficient knowledge of the subject'.

I have bought an edition of Yeats which I ordered the bookseller to send home. . . . Of course I need not add that you are welcome to open the parcel if you would care to. Arthur at any rate would like to see it. . . . In the same shop I'm afraid I gave myself away badly. What first tempted me to go in was a battered copy of Burton's 'Anatomy'. . . . I went in and asked a courtly old gentleman to let me see it. 'H'm', said I, glancing over the dirty little volume, 'it seems rather worn; haven't you got a newer copy?' The gentleman looked at me in rather a pained way and said he had not. 'Well, how much is it?', I asked, rather expecting a considerable reduction. 'Twenty five guineas', said my friend with a bland smile. Ye Gods! Just think of it! There was I for the first time in my life, fingering a really valuable old edition and asking for a *newer* copy. I turned hot all over. However, the old gentleman was very forgiving, and turned his treasury inside out for me . . . and so, what could I do but bring away the Yeats? . . . Well, *ego in Arcadia vixi*, and it was something to have been in the shop of James Bain even for an hour.

It seems that now-a-days one is sent from hospital to be kept for some time in a convalescent home before going on leave. Of course I have asked to be sent to an Irish one, but there are only a few of these, and they are already crowded; we must not therefore expect too much, but wherever I am I know that you will come and see me. You know I have some difficulty in talking of the greatest things; it is the fault of our generation and of the English schools. But at least you will believe that I was never before so eager to cling to every bit of our old home life and to see you. I know I have often been far from what I should be in my relation to you, and have undervalued an affection and generosity which an experience of 'other people's parents' has shown me in a new light. But, please God, I shall do better in the future. Come and see me, I am homesick, that is the long and the short of it. . . .

TO HIS FATHER, *from a convalescent home near Bristol.*

(Undated)

Here all the 'gilded youth' among the patients, who have no interests in themselves, of course grow troublesome by being confined. The place echoes to the crack of their billiard balls and their loud, tuneless whistling. I was very miserable for the first few days until I discovered a little, almost disused writing room at one end of the house. Here I can sit in comparative safety and read Burton's 'Anatomy' . . . this cannot last for ever, and I hope to have a visit from you. . . .

The house here is the survival, tho' altered by continual rebuilding, of a thirteenth-century castle; the greater part is now stucco work of the worst Victorian period, but we have one or two fine old paintings and a ghost. I haven't met it yet, and have not much hope to. . . . Greatly to my chagrin the library is locked up. The park is several miles in extent, very pleasant, and stocked with deer; once or twice while wandering in the bracken I have suddenly come upon the solemn face and branching antlers of a stag within a few feet of me. He examines me for a moment, then snorts, kicks up his heels, and is gone; a second later head after head comes up—his panic has reached the rest of the herd, and they too scamper off after him like the wind. . . .

TO HIS FATHER, *who still failed to visit him.*

3 September 1918

Ever since my last letter to you I have been almost daily expecting to hear from you, and I am rather surprised that neither my answer to your proposal nor my suggestion that you should come over here, has met with any reply. Have you not yet decided on a date for coming over? It is four months now since I returned from France, and my friends laughingly suggest that 'my father in Ireland' is a mythical creation like Mrs. 'Arris. . . . I hope that there is nothing wrong and that I shall soon hear from you again. . . .

TO HIS FATHER. (*The poems mentioned were to be published as* Spirits in Bondage.)

9 September 1918

I write in haste to give you a piece of news which I hope will please you not much less than it did me. You are aware that for some years now I have amused myself by writing verses, and a pocket-book collection of these followed me through France. Since my return I have occupied myself by revising them, getting them typed with a few additions, and trying to publish them. After a refusal from Macmillans, they have, somewhat to my surprise, been accepted by W. Heinemann. . . . This little success gives me a pleasure which is perhaps childish, and yet akin to greater things. . . .

TO HIS FATHER.

27 October 1918

I succeeded in getting my day off to see Heinemann yesterday, after being stopped last week through a very ridiculous incident of a kind that is common in the army. In order to get leave for a day you have to write down your name, the time of leaving, and your destination, in a book which is then signed by the Medical Officer. Last week the book was lost; no objection was made to my going on either military or medical grounds, but—how could I go without the book? A suggestion that I might write the particulars on a slip of paper which could then afterwards be put in the book was treated as a sort of sacrilege. After a week, however, it occurred to the Adjutant (who must be a man of bold generosity and signal originality) that we might spend half a crown on a new book, and so I was able to go after all. . . .

Heinemann came in. . . . He is a fat little old man with a bald head, apparently well read, and a trifle fussy—inclined to get his papers mixed up and to repeat himself. . . . He told me that John Galsworthy (who publishes with them) had seen my MS and wanted to publish a certain poem in a new monthly called

'Reveillé' which he is bringing out in aid of disabled soldiers and sailors. I naturally consented because it is pleasant *laudari a laudato viro* and because it is an excellent advertisement. . . .

TO HIS FATHER.

(Undated)

Of course I shall be only too pleased if any influence of yours could succeed in getting me a discharge, though at the same time I am afraid it will be a very difficult business. As you have probably seen in the papers, we are to be drafted on demobilization to "Class Z Reserve", where I suppose we shall remain ready for the next scrape that some Labour government in the future may get the country into. I don't want to be pessimistic, but there does not seem to be much hope of ever being quite free of the army again. To get a discharge on the score of unfitness might be possible, but I do not think my degree of military unfitness will be sufficient to serve our turn. . . .

So far my readings, both in Latin and Greek, have been a pleasant surprise; I have forgotten less than I feared, and once I get the sound and savour of the language into my head by a spell of reading, composition should not come too hard either. In England I have started friend Trollope again—'The Small House at Allington'. . . .

TO HIS FATHER, *from Oxford.*

27 January 1919

After a quite comfortable journey (which showed me that 1st Class travelling is very little different to 3rd) I arrived somewhat late in the evening. The moon was just rising; the (College) Porter knew me at once and ushered me into the same old rooms. It was a great return, and something to be very thankful for. . . . There is of course a great difference between this Oxford and the ghost I knew before; true, we are only twenty-eight in College, but we *do* dine in Hall again, the Junior Common Room is not swathed in dust sheets, and the old round . . . is getting under weigh. The reawakening is a little pathetic; at our first meeting (of the J.C.R.) we read the minutes of the last—1914. I don't know any little thing that has made me realize the absolute suspension and waste of those years more thoroughly. . . . We have quite a number of old members who were up before the war and are a kind of dictionary of traditions.

Now as to work: I am 'deemed to have passed' Responsions and Divinity, and it was open to me to take Honour Mods. or go straight on to 'Greats'—as you know, the final fence. In consideration of my wish to get a Fellowship Poynton, my Tutor, strongly advised me not to avail myself of the opportunity of slurring over Mods. . . . Except for the disadvantage of starting 18 books of Homer to the bad, I find myself fairly all right; of course the great difference after Kirk is that you are left to work very much on your own. It is a little bit strange at first. . . .

The coal difficulty is not very serious. We have all our meals in Hall, which, if it abolishes the cozy breakfasts in one's own rooms and the inter-change of 'decencies and proprieties' is a little cheaper; we shall go back to the old arrangement as soon as we can. The library, one lecture room and the Junior Common Room are always warm, and the two former are quite quiet; then for the evening we can afford a modest blaze at one's 'ain fireside'. Our little body gets on well together, and most of us work. The place is looking more beautiful than ever in the wintry frost; one gets splendid cold colouring at the expense of tingling fingers and red noses. . . .

TO HIS FATHER.

7 February 1919

I find the work pretty stiff, but I think I am keeping my head above water. Poynton is, so far as I can judge, quite an exceptionally good Tutor, and my visits to him are enjoyable as well as useful—although he objects to my style of Greek prose—'I don't care very much for treacle *or* barley sugar myself'. So you have bequeathed to me some remnant of the old Macaulese taint after all. I drank tea with him last Sunday. Another man from Univ. went . . . and our host kept us very well amused . . . he is an excellent, if somewhat unjust raconteur. He came up to Balliol under Jowett and had a lot to say of the great man. . . .

Much to my surprise I have had greatness thrust upon me. There is a literary club in College called the Martlets, limited to 12 undergraduate members; it is over three hundred years old, and alone of all College Clubs has its minutes preserved in the Bodleian. I have been elected Secretary—the reason being of course that my proposer was afraid of getting the job himself. And so if I am forgotten as all else, at least a specimen of my handwriting will be preserved to posterity. . . .

TO HIS FATHER, *after publication of* Spirits in Bondage.

25 May 1919

I have not written to Heinemann as I found a circular from a press cutting agency to which I replied, enclosing 10/-. The results so far have been a very interesting review of 'The Principles of Symbolic Logic' by C. S. Lewis of the University of California. I am writing back to tell them that they have got rather muddled. Symbolic Logic forsooth! I started reading it without noticing the title and was surprised to find myself—as I thought—being commended for a 'scholarly elucidation of a difficult subject'.

As nearly everyone here is a poet himself, they have naturally no time left for lionizing others. Indeed the current literary set is one I could not afford to live in anyway, and tho' many of them have kindly bought copies of the book, their tastes run rather to modernism, 'vers libre' and that sort of thing. I have a holy terror of coteries; I have already been asked to join a Theosophist, a Socialist and a Celtic Society. By the way the distinction which one finds in such books as Tom Brown by which the poor, the industrious, and the intellectual, are all in one class, and the rich, the brainless, and the vicious, all in another, does not obtain. Some 'poor scholars' are bad lots, and some of the 'gilded youth' are fond of literature. . . .

TO HIS BROTHER, *with some indication of difficulties at home: see Introduction, p. 11.*

22 June 1919

I have just got your letter, to which I am replying immediately. Of course I quite see your point, and am greatly relieved to hear from you as I had—of course—lost your address and wanted to get in touch with you. Now will you please wire me at Univ. and let me know the day and approximate time of your arrival at Oxford; I will then report at the station at a suitable hour. If by any chance I am absent from parade you must drive to Univ. and wait for me, even if I do not turn up at once. The Porter will have means of getting on to me if I am out. The programme you sketch is very attractive, and it would be grand to have ignorance exposed by the Knock again. You understand why I behave so queerly—the effort to avoid being left alone at Little Lea. With you to back me up however, I have no doubt that we shall depart up to scheduled time. . . .

TO HIS FATHER.

(Undated: postmarked 4 February 1920)

I am preparing to wait upon my great aunt Warren this afternoon, with transports as moderate as Warnie's. I think this particular form of introducing strangers by letter, on the theory that blood is thicker than water ('and a good deal nastier' as someone added) is one of the most irritating of social amenities. It always reminds me of two hostile children being shoved into a room and told to 'have a nice game' together. . . .

I am inclined to agree with you and Mrs. Ward about the lack of charm in Wells; but there are other qualities as important, if less delightful.

I am reading 'Lavengro' at breakfast every morning, and should like it very much if one could cut out the anti-Catholic propaganda. . . .

TO HIS FATHER, *from a village in Somerset.*

4 April 1920

I am glad to be able to begin with a bit of good news. I did get a First (in Honour Mods.) after all. Unfortunately that is almost all I can tell you, as the names in each class are given only in alphabetical order. . . . Now as to our movements; as this is the shortest Vac., and also as I felt in need of some 'refresher' I thought it a good opportunity of paying off an engagement with a man who has been asking me for some time to go and 'Walk' with him. We are at present at this tiny little village in a perfectly ideal cottage . . . from which as a base we shall set out when the weather clears. We are quite alone, and live an idyllic life on eggs, bully beef, and—divine treasure—an excellent ham . . . The country is delightful, consisting of high moors with charming valleys full of orchards between them and everything is a mass of white blossom. It is on the borders of Somerset and Devon. Our address will of course be moveable, but letters sent here will reach me after some delay. I am sorry to desert you for the present, but it had to be polished off sooner or later.

I am just getting over a rather tiresome cold and cough, and am beginning to feel much better than I have done for a long time. I have brought Waverley to clean out my mind—there is great comfort in these solid old books. . . .

TO HIS FATHER, *from the same village.*

11 April 1920

I had quite forgotten about aunt Warren. She must be pretty old, and dresses (with cap and white collar) in a style that makes her rather more so. At the same time there is nothing senile in her conversation or manner. We talked chiefly about Mountbracken and Irish politics. The only one of 'the girls' present was Daisy, who is I suppose, over forty. She struck me as being ecclesiastical in a high degree; for instance, from her point of view, the chief argument in favour of expelling the Turks from Europe was 'that it would re-establish the Patriarch at Constantinople and thus create a balance to the Papacy'. After the Armenian massacres, not to mention the war, that would hardly have appeared to me—nor you I presume—the most important reason. . . .

As you see, we have not yet moved; indeed the weather has not encouraged us to set out, though it has not prevented us from a great deal of walking. It is more beautiful here almost than any place I have ever seen—whether in the valleys full of orchards or up on the big, heathery hills from which one looks down on the sea and the Welsh coast far away on the horizon.

You need not have any fear about our cuisine here. Remember we are almost in Devonshire and the clotted cream of this country is a host in itself; also—shades of Oldie—the real 'Deevonshire' cider in every thatched and sanded pub.

A few miles away is a little fishing town called Watchet, which saw at least one interesting scene in its obscure history; it was here that Coleridge and the Wordsworths slept (or 'lay' as they would have said) on the first night of their walking tour. During the afternoon the germ of the Ancient Mariner occurred in conversation and in the inn at Watchet the first lines were jotted down. . . .

TO HIS FATHER, *from Oxford.*

6 June 1920

I thought I had said something about the anthology. It is being got up as a kind of counterblast to the ruling literary fashion here, which consists in the tendencies called 'Vorticist'. Vorticist poems are usually in 'vers libre' (which means that they are printed like verse, but neither rhyme nor scan, a line ending wherever you like). Some of them are clever, the majority merely affected, and a good few—especially among the French ones—indecent; not a sensuous indecency but one meant to nauseate, the whole genus arising from the 'sick of everything' mood. So some of us others who are not yet sick of everything, have decided to bring out a yearly collection of our own things in the hope of persuading the gilded youth that the possibilities of metrical poetry on sane subjects are not yet quite exhausted because the Vorticists are suffering from satiety. Of course we may end by proving just the opposite, but we must risk that. . . .

TO HIS FATHER, *after a visit to the other university.*

(Undated: postmarked 8 December 1920)

It was very interesting . . . to see Cambridge. In many ways it is a contrast; there is something, I can hardly say whether of colour or atmosphere, which at once strikes a more northern, a bleaker and harder note. Perhaps the flatness of the country, suggesting places seen from the railway beyond Crewe, has something to do with it. The streets are very narrow and crowded; the non-university parts are depressing enough. Some things, such as King's College Chapel, in which I was prepared to be disappointed, are indeed beautiful beyond hope or belief; several little quadrangles I remember, with tiled gables, sun dials, and tall chimneys like Tudor houses, were charming. One felt everywhere the touch of Puritanism, of something Whiggish, a little defiant perhaps. It has not so much Church and State in its veins as we. The stained windows in the Halls show figures like Erasmus and Cranmer. Oxford is more magnificent, Cambridge perhaps more intriguing. Our characteristic colour is the pale grey almost yellow of old stone; theirs the warm brown of old brick. A great many Cambridge buildings remind one of the Tower of London. Most of the undergrads I met I liked very much. Their Dons, as judged by those who were at the 'do', are certainly inferior to ours in charm of manner and geniality. . . .

TO HIS FATHER. (*"The work on 'Optimism'" is the essay that won the Chancellor's Prize.)*

21 January 1921

My history tutor has handed me over to a gentleman at Magdalen whom he recommended to me by telling me that he was a grandson of Mendelssohn's; a trifle irrelevant I thought.... The new man deserves to be known to fame. I had not been many minutes in his room until I had a sense of strange yet familiar neighbours. When he went out for a moment I discovered what it was—pigs! Do not mistake me; not live pigs; but pigs of bronze, of clay, of stuff and stone; pigs jovial and pigs quizzical, kindly pigs and severe pigs, Falstaffian pigs and pigs philosophical. I counted 28 in a few seconds, and still had not got beyond the mantelpiece. This porcine seraglio of a lonely old batchelor is one of the little comedies I would not have missed for a good deal. And yet how wise. Here are companions for every mood, who need practically no upkeep and are never untrue or unkind.... I am still smoothing and varnishing the work on 'Optimism'.

Here is a story which will please Warnie. The other night at the Martlets old Carlyle read a paper. He is a foxy looking old gentleman with a clean-shaven face as red as a berry and straight hair the colour of snuff—a very comical face and a high croaking voice. He began by saying that he ought to apologise for his paper 'because h'm—to tell the truth—I had meant to publish it—but h'm—h'm, it was so unsatisfactory that I—I just sent it to an American magazine'. That's the proper spirit....

TO HIS FATHER, *in reply to the news of W. T. Kirkpatrick's death.*

28 March 1921

I am glad you sent me the wire. I am a poor reader of papers and should have been sorry through ignorance, to let such a thing pass in silence. Poor old Kirk. What shall one say of him? It would be a poor compliment to that memory to be sentimental; indeed if it were possible, he himself would return to chide the absurdity. It is however no sentiment but plainest fact to say that I owe him in the intellectual sphere as much as one human being can owe another. That he enabled me to win a Scholarship is the least that he did for me. It was an atmosphere of unrelenting clearness and rigid honesty of thought that one breathed from living with him—and this I shall be the better for as long as I live. And if this is the greatest thing, there are others which none of us will forget; his dry humour, his imperturbable good temper, and his amazing energy—these it is good to have seen. . . . The more one sees of weakness, affectation, and general vagueness in the majority of men, the more one admires that rigid, lonely old figure—more like some ancient Stoic standing fast in the Roman decadence than a modern scholar living in the home counties. Indeed we may almost call him a great man. . . .

TO HIS BROTHER: *a serial letter, written on various dates, the first part undated.*

I am waiting to hear your address, and in the meantime have begun—tho' with what promise of continuance I don't know—my journal letter. . . . As we talk a good deal of fragments out of odd books when we are together, there's no reason why we should not reproduce the same sort of tittle-tattle. Perhaps one of the reasons why letters are so hard to write and so much harder to read is that people confine themselves to news—or, in other words think nothing worth writing except what would not be worth saying. . . .

Going into College today, I met —— in the porch, who carried me to his rooms in Merton St. . . . He was too young for the war, and I always look on him as rather a child, though some people think I am wrong in this. I mention him for the amusing passages he showed me in two books. One was a tour of the County of Cornwall, written in the 17th century. . . . Under the heading of Beastes we find (after those of Venery and Draught), Rats . . . described as 'not only mischievious by day for their devouring of clothes, writings, and meats, but cumbersome by night for their rattling and jaunting as they gallop their gaillards in the roof'. This sentence I at once learnt by heart.... —— is an enthusiastic Cornishman and some are bored by his persistency in talking of his native scenery, habits, language, and superstitions. I rather like it.... Cornwall is of course all mines; they are full of beings called Nackers whom one hears knocking at the ends of the lonelier galleries. The workmen leave little bits of their food for them, for they are terrible bringers of good and bad luck....

12 March 1921

Everyone is going down today. Such days have all the atmosphere of a school end of term with its joy taken out of it... and lest empty rooms and stacks of suitcases should not be sufficiently offensive, we have the intolerable institution of 'Collections'.... From 9 till noon the Master and his 'auxiliary fiends' sit at the high table in Hall and one by one sheepish or truculent undergraduates are called up, walk up the long emptiness, mount the dais, and stand foolishly gaping while he delivers a little homily.... It is extraordinary that any ceremony which is designed to make you feel like an inky schoolboy will succeed in making you feel like an inky schoolboy. I doubt if even our father could have invented anything more subtly undermining of one's self-respect.... Try to imagine it, and then add the idea of 9 in the morning; and that your collar has broken loose from its stud at the back; and that there is a smell of last night's dinner about; a fly on your nose; a shaving cut beginning to bleed—but no, it is too painful....

13 March 1921

I waited after breakfast on P., in his rooms at Unity House; this is a cottage in a lane by Headington Church where the buildings are so ruinous that it looks like a bit of France as the cant goes—well *fairly* like it. P. is my oldest ally; he used to write poetry but is now too engrossed in history, and he has also become engaged—that fatal tomb of all lively and interesting men. Unity House is ruled by a strangely ugly woman.... I had an excellent walk with P. We sat in a wood full of primroses. Dammit, how gushing generations have teased the language till the very name of a primrose sounds sentimental; when you come to look at them they are really rather attractive. . . .

14 March 1921

I received this morning a letter from my obliging friend X. . . . He writes poetry. The annoying thing is that it is exactly like mine, only like the bad parts of mine; this was my original opinion and it has been confirmed by others. Perhaps you can imagine the sensations I feel in reading it. X's letter was to say that he had mentioned to Yeats 'my double claim to distinction as an Irishman and a poet', and would I come along this evening and see him? I accordingly repaired to X's lodging. . . . He is a married man; his wife is an American; she is the sister of a woman who is married to a brother of Mrs. Moore's. She was a woman of implacable sullenness who refused even to say good evening to me. . . . X was finishing a very nasty meal of cold fish and cocoa; but he soon put on his coat, and after asking his lady why there were no stamps in the house, and receiving no answer, swung out with me into the usual Oxford theatrical night. . . . I reflected that I was now to meet at last William Butler Yeats and felt a veritable Bozzy. But enough of that.

We were shown up a long stairway lined with rather wicked pictures by Blake—all devils and monsters—and finally into the presence chamber, lit by tall candles, with orange coloured curtains and full of things I can't describe because I don't know their names. The poet was very big, about sixty years of age; 'aweful' as Bozzy says. When he first began to speak I would have thought him French, but the Irish sounds through after a time. Before the fire was a circle of hard antique chairs. Present were the poet's wife, a little man with a grey beard who never spoke all evening, and Father ——. Fr. —— is a Catholic priest, a little twinkling man like a bird, or like Puck. . . . I used to go to his lectures in the old days. . . . I was preparing to sink into the outlying chair . . . but the poet sternly and silently motioned us into the other ones. . . .

Then the talk began. It was all about magic and cabbalism and 'the Hermetic knowledge'. The great man talked while the priest and Mrs. Yeats fed him with judicious questions. . . . I lost my morale. I understood how it is possible for a man to terrify a room into silence. . . . Some good angel guided me, for presently I really had something to say—a case mentioned by Coleridge which was most apposite and indeed crying for a quotation on something just said. But thank God I didn't, for a minute later the priest did.

YEATS (*thumping his chair*): 'Yes, yes, the old woman in Coleridge. That story was published by Coleridge without the slightest evidence. Andrew Lang exposed it. I've never had a conversation on this subject that *someone* didn't bring in Coleridge's old woman. It is anonymous in the first place and everyone has taken it over without question. It just shows that there is no limit to the unscrupulousness that a sceptical man will go to——'

PRIEST: 'Oh surely Mr. Yeats——'

YEATS: 'Yes. There is a professor living in Oxford at this moment who is the greatest sceptic in print. The same man has told me that he entered a laboratory where Mme Blavatsky was doing experiments; saw the table floating near the ceiling with Mme B. sitting on it; vomited; gave orders that no further experiments were to be done in his laboratory—and refused to let the story be known.'

But it would be ridiculous to record it all; I could give you the insanity of the man without his eloquence and presence, which are very great. I could never have believed that he was so like his own poetry. . . . Finally we were given sherry or vermouth in long curiously shaped glasses, except the priest who had whiskey out of an even longer and more curiously shaped glass, and the orgy was at an end. . . .

21 March 1921

This night (at Yeats's house) we were shown to a study up in the ceiling and entertained by him alone. And would you believe it, he was almost quite sane, and talked about books and things, still eloquently but quite intelligently? Of course we got on magic in the end. It was really my fault for I mentioned Bergson. 'Ah yes', said he, 'Bergson. It was his sister who taught me magic'. . . . We spoke of Andrew Lang.

YEATS: 'I met him once at a dinner somewhere. He never said a word. When we began to talk afterwards he just got up and took his chair into a corner of the room and sat down facing the wall. He stayed there all the evening.' Of the 'great Victorians' he said, 'The most interesting thing about the Victorian period was their penchant for selecting one typical Great man in each department—Tennyson, *the* poet, Roberts, *the* soldier; and then these types were made into myths. . . .'

(Undated)

About the coal strike you have, I suppose, heard *ad nauseam* from the papers; what it means to me personally is that I have done a good deal of wood sawing. Have you ever sawed wood? If not, you probably have an idea that one sets the saw lightly on the log, gets to work, and continues steadily deepening until the two halves fall apart. Not a bit of it; you set the saw lightly on the log and then try to move it. It darts aside with a sound like a swallow, and you wrap a handkerchief round your hand; when the blood has soaked through this, you go into the house and get some court plaster. Next time you go more cautiously, and after the saw has chirped a whole song a bit of bark comes off; by this time you are fairly warm. Then you really get to it; back and forward you go, changing uneasily from your right to your left hand and feeling the blisters arise, while the shadows lengthen and the sweat pours down. When you go to bed at night . . . you get visions of getting through that log on your thirtieth birthday. . . . I am very glad you have become a convert to Milton; what put you on to him, and what parts are you reading? I wonder will you ever get to the end of the Bible; the undesirable 'primitives' around you will enable you to appreciate the Hebrews who were class A primitives after all. . . .

TO HIS FATHER.

23 April 1921

I can of course appreciate your feelings about poor Kirk's funeral. Stripped of all wherewith belief and tradition have clothed it, death appears a little grimmer—a shade more chilly and loathsome—in the eyes of the most matter of fact. At the same time, while this is sad, it would have been not only sad but shocking to have pronounced over Kirk words that he did not believe, and performed ceremonies which he himself would have denounced as meaningless. Yet, as you say, he is so stamped on one's mind, so often present in thought, that he makes his own acceptance of annihilation the more unthinkable. I have seen death fairly often and never yet been able to find it anything but extraordinary and rather incredible. The real person is so very real, so obviously living and different from what is left, that one cannot believe something has turned into nothing. It is not faith, it is not reason—just a 'feeling'....

TO HIS BROTHER.

10 May 1921

Here term is still new enough to be interesting. It is still pleasant to see fewer foreign visitors pacing the High with guide books and taking photos of spires—where I know they'll get them crooked—and to see one's friends again instead.... The only strictly social function I have attended so far this term was tea with the ——s in their most charming house. It is a place which I greatly envy; long, uneven rooms with beams in the ceiling and wide stone grates where a little kind of brazier sits in a deep cave of Dutch tiles. I need hardly say that in Oxford houses all such things were unearthed only fairly recently; the XVIII century had very decently covered them over with plaster, 'substituting' as they would doubtless have said, 'elegance and civility for Gothic rudeness'....

People talk about the Oxford manner and the Oxford life and the Oxford God knows what else; as if the undergraduates had anything to do with it. . . . The real Oxford is a close corporation of jolly, untidy, lazy, good-for-nothing, humorous old men, who have been electing their own successors ever since the world began and who intend to go on with it. They'll squeeze under the Revolution or leap over it when the time comes, don't you worry. When I think how little chance I have of ever fighting my way into that unassuming but impregnable fortress, that modest unremoveability, that provokingly intangible stone wall, I think of Keats's poison

> Brewed in monkish cell
> to thin the scarlet conclave of old men.

Today the 11th, little —— appeared after lunch and bade me go for a bike ride. As I had decided to work, I thought this would be an excellent opportunity for breaking my resolution. . . . After stopping for a drink at Garsington, we rode along the top of a long hill, where you look down into a good, woody English valley with the Chilterns, rather sleek and chalky . . . on the horizon. It was a grey day, with clouds in muddled perspective all round. Just as the first drops of rain began to fall, we found a young man looking as if he was going to be hanged, crossing a field. He turned out to be one Smith of Univ., who is now gone down and is incarcerated at a High Church Theological Seminary in the neighbouring village of Cuddesdon. 'He would have liked to ask us into tea, but couldn't—indeed oughtn't to be talking to us—because they were having a *quiet day*!' Ye gods; a lot of young men shut up together, all thinking about their souls! Isn't it awful? After this it was quite fresh and lively to investigate an old windmill near Wheatley; it had the sort of atmosphere we felt at Doagh. . . . We rode over Shotover Hill through sandy lanes with gorse on each side and passing occasional warm, comfortable English barns and haystacks. Most attractive signposts, 'Bridle path to Horsley'—a bridle path always sounds mysterious. Dozens of rabbits and whole bunches of bluebells; and view far off . . . of where the first Mrs. Milton used to live. About the time he wrote 'L'Allegro' and 'Il Penseroso' he would be often riding over here from his home to court her—God help her. . . .

TO HIS FATHER: *referring initially to the Chancellor's Prize.*

29 May 1921

Everyone has been very nice about it ('Optimism'), particularly the Mugger who is delighted, and this ought to be of use to me later on. Some of my congratulations indeed have made me feel rather ashamed, coming from people I have been used to class generically as 'louts'. By louts I denote great beefy people unknown to me by name, men with too much money and athletic honour, who stand blocking up passages. . . . I suppose the explanation is that in their view we have done so badly on the river that any success—even in so unimportant a field as letters—should be encouraged. . . .

I have been reading the oddest book lately—Newman's 'Loss and Gain'. I never knew that he had written a novel. As fiction or drama it is of course beneath contempt, but it has some real satirical humour. . . . The picture of the then Oxford with its ecclesiastical controversies etc., is something more remote from my experience than ancient Britain or modern Cathay. . . .

We are old, disillusioned creatures now, and look back on the days of 'buns and coffee' through a long perspective, and only seldom come out of our holes; the young men up from school in immaculate clothes think we have come to clean the windows when they see us. It happens to everyone here. In your first year you drink sherry and see people; after that your set narrows, you haunt the country lanes more than the High, and cease to play at being the undergraduate of fiction—there will be no revelry by night.

TO HIS FATHER.

27 June 1921

The event of last week was one of the unforeseen consequences of my winning 'Optimism'. I had almost forgotten, if I had ever known, that 'prizemen' have to read portions of their compositions at our ceremony of Encaenia. Being of the troglodytic nature I have never before exerted myself so far as to assist at this show; but having now been compelled, I am glad.

It is a most curious business. We unhappy performers attend (tho' it is at noon) in caps, gowns, and *full evening dress*. It was held in the Sheldonian Theatre. . . . During the long wait while people trickled in, an organ (much too large for the building) gave a recital. The undergraduates and their guests sit round in the galleries; the 'floor' is occupied by the graduates en masse, standing at barriers in all their war-paint. At noon the Vice-Chancellor enters with his procession of 'Heads of Colleges, Doctors, Proctors, and Noblemen'—a very strange show they make, half splendid and half grotesque, for few Don's faces are fit to bear up against the scarlet and blue and silver of their robes. Then some backchat from the Vice-Chancellor's throne and the Public Orator led in the persons who were to receive honorary degrees; with the exception of Clemenceau and Keyes (the Zeebruggeman) they were not well known to the world at large. Keyes was a very honest-looking fellow and Clemenceau the tough, burly, 'people's man' whom one expected; but what was beyond all was the Canon of Nôtre Dame; a great theologian apparently, with some name like Raffitol.[1] Such a picture of a great priest with all the pale dignity that one has imagined, I never saw. . . . He would have appealed to you immensely. After the honorary degrees the Professor of Poetry made an oration in Latin. . . .

The performance of us prizemen was of course very small beer after all this. We had been instructed to read for about two minutes each; I had some difficulty in finding a short passage which would be intelligible by itself. . . . I have had a good lesson in modesty from seeing my fellow-prizemen. I was hardly prepared for such a collection of scrubby, beetle-like, bespectacled oddities. . . . It brings home to one how little I know of Oxford; I am apt to regard my own set, which consists mainly of literary gents, with a smattering of political, musical and philosophical—as being central, normal, representative. But step out of it, into the athletes on one side or the pale pot-hunters on the other, and it is a strange planet. . . .

[1] Batiffol.

TO HIS BROTHER.

1 July 1921

Here another term has blossomed and faded. . . . I have lived my usual life; a few lectures until—as happens about half way through every term—I got tired of it all; work, meetings with friends, walks and rides, solitary or otherwise, and meetings of the Martlets. These, by the way, were all invited to dinner by the Don Martlets a few weeks ago, and I again had the opportunity of peeping into the real Oxford; this time through the medium of a very excellent meal ('with wine' as Milton says with the air of a footnote) in cool, brown oaky rooms. . . .

The great event of *my* term was of course 'Optimism'. . . . I managed to make myself audible I'm told, and beyond nearly falling as I entered the rostrum, I escaped with success. (They *do* actually call it a rostrum, so that I was delighted; for the whole gallery of the Dammerfesk seemed to gaze at me, and the jarring ghosts of Big, Polonius Green and Arrabudda to lend me consequence). . . .

I had not meant in my other letters to bring any serious charge against the Oxfordshire country. Tried by European standards it takes a lowish rank; but I am not such a fool as to depreciate any decent country now, and rather wrote in depreciation for fear you'd fancy I was 'writing up' a place in which you would remember no particular beauties. Of landscapes, as of people, one becomes more tolerant after one's twentieth year. (The rate at which we both advance towards a responsible age is indecent.) We learn to look at them, not *in the flat* but *in depth*, as things to be burrowed into. It is not merely a question of lines and colours but of smells, sounds and tastes as well; I often wonder if professional artists don't lose something of the real love of earth by seeing it in eye-sensations only?

From the house where we are now living there are few good walks, but several decent rides. Last Saturday we rode to Standlake. In the heat of the day it was an heroic undertaking. . . . We had to begin by climbing the 'warm, green-muffled Cumnor hills' a long, long pull, all on foot. . . . We really enjoyed nothing until beyond Cumnor we sunk into the long grass by the side of the road under one of the deplorably rare trees, and tackled our luncheon basket. A local pub supplied beer for me and lemonade for the children, and we had a basket of cherries. After this it became better, and when after a long and pleasant decline through corkscrew lanes full of meadowsweet (that's the white dusty stuff with a nice smell, you know) we reached Bablocke Hythe, it was quite delightful. Beyond this the country is very flat, very tree-y—full of villages rather too 'warm and muffled'; they make you feel like a bumble bee that has got into damp cotton wool. . . .

This country is much favoured of the Muse. A few miles beyond us was Kelmscott where Morris lived and built that 'red house' whose brick nudity first defied the stucco tradition. . . . A little to our right, at Stanton Harcourt, is an old Manor with a tower room where Pope wrote his famous parody—which he called a translation—of the Iliad. And of course as you know, every mile smells of Arnold. . . . By the way I have found the ideally bad edition of *Thyrsis* and the *Scholar Gipsy* . . . illustrated with photographs, one to almost every two stanzas . . . best of all—there is a line somewhere I can't remember, about a 'battered merchantman coming into port'—illustrated with a photo of two racing yachts! How are such things possible? . . .

The steps by which you became a Miltonian are very interesting. Can one quite have done by labelling him a republican and a puritan? Puritanism was after all (in some of its exponents) a very different thing from modern 'dissent'. One cannot imagine Milton going about and asking people if they were saved; that intolerable pride is the direct opposite to sentimentalism. He really had the virtues and vices of the aristocracy writing for 'fit audience tho' few'. He always seems to look down on the vulgar from an almost archducal height. 'How charming is divine philosophy, Not harsh and crabbed as dull fools suppose'. The dull fools are the ordinary mass of humanity, and though it has its ridiculous side, that deliberate decision of his, taken at my age, 'to leave something so written that posterity would not willingly let it die' takes a little doing. *Paradise Regained* I only read once; it is a bit too much for me. In it the Hebrew element finally gets the better of the classical and romantic ingredients. How can people be attracted to things Hebrew? However, old Kirk really summed up Milton when he said, 'I would venture to assert that no human being ever called him Johnnie.'

TO HIS BROTHER, *describing an English holiday taken with various relations from Ireland.*

7 August 1921

It so happened that the Irish party only stopt at Oxford for lunch, and then took me on with them for a week. . . . The first piece of scenery I saw was our father himself, outside the Clarendon in Cornmarket. You've no idea how odd he looked, almost a bit shrunk; pacing alone with that expression peculiar to him on a holiday—the eyebrows half way up the forehead. I was very warmly greeted by all; and with the exception of Aunt Annie, we all took a short stroll before lunch. I heard from our father that he found the heat intolerable, and that he had not slept a wink since he left home. He seemed dazed by his surroundings and showed no disposition to go and see my rooms, though he observed that 'the College had treated me very shabbily as they distinctly mentioned free rooms as one of the privileges of scholars'—a statute by the way completely unknown at Oxford, however familiar at Little Lea. We lunched heavily at the Clarendon; I succeeded in getting some cold meat (suitable to a shade temperature of near 90), in spite of the frequently advanced proposition that it would be 'better' (how or why?) if we all had the table d'hôte.

We addressed ourselves to the road as soon as the meal was over. . . . Our direction was South and West, so we ran out over Folly Bridge and towards Berkshire. . . . The weather was oppressively hot . . . when you dropped to 20 at a turn or a village, a stifling heat lept up round you at once . . . this first run was almost the only one where our father sat behind with me, and it was about half an hour south of Oxford that he made his first *mot* and one of the best of his life by asking, 'Are we in Cornwall yet, Gussie?'

[*The party were unable to get rooms at Malmesbury.*] Our father was in favour of going on to Bath and stopping at the largest hotel there—being reduced to a painful uneasiness when we told him that he could get supper, not dinner, of a Sunday evening in these small towns. . . . It ended in our pushing on to a place called Chippenham . . . where we took rooms for the night. . . . Chippenham is one of (I suppose) a thousand English towns that one has never heard of, but once having seen, remembers kindly. . . . The streets widen occasionally into what are called squares, being, after the manner of English country towns, any other shape in Euclid rather than a square. . . . After dinner of course we 'strolled'. . . . When we got back to our hotel . . . our father offered us drinks. Uncle H. would have some beer, and so would I. Our father (in his 'desperate' voice): 'I'll have a bottle of soda water. Here. Waitress. Two half pints of bitter beer and a bottle of soda water—(pause)—and if you'd just put a little Scotch whiskey in it'. (The waitress goes and returns) 'Here you are, Gussie. Is this my soda water?' Waitress. 'Yes sir. With the whiskey in it'. (Roars of laughter from Uncle H.). Our father: 'Hm'h'. This was truly in our best manner, wasn't it? . . .

On this second day . . . we drove through a hilly country, the weather a little cooler, by Farringdon Gurney and Chewton Mendip to Wells. This landscape has everything, though on a small scale: rocks, hills, woods and water. Chiefly you run along the sides of winding valleys. . . . I steered our course very satisfactorily. Our father only advanced so far as to get hold of the Michelin every day and look up hotels; usually he looked up some place *he* thought suitable to lie at; once or twice it was a place we had stopped at the night before.

We lunched at Wells after seeing the Cathedral. . . . I am no architect and not much more of an antiquarian. Strange to say it was Uncle H. with his engineering more than our father with his churchmanship that helped me to appreciate it; he taught me to look at the single endless line of the aisle, with every pillar showing at once the strain and the meeting of the strain (like a ship's framework inverted); it is certainly wonderfully *satisfying* to look at. The pleasure one gets is like that from rhyme—a need, and the answer of it following so quickly that they make a single sensation. So now I understand the old law in architecture, 'no weight without a support, and no support without an adequate weight'. For the rest, Wells is particularly rich in a wilderness of cloisters all round the Cathedral where one can cut the cold and quiet with a knife. There is a fine castle with the only *real* drawbridge I ever saw. . . .

We were on the road again by two. . . . We ran through Westbury, Cheddar ('Are we in Cheshire, Gussie?' asked our father), Axbridge, Highbridge, Bridgewater etc. . . . I had been able to name Dunster to Uncle H. as a likely stopping place. I had at first been rather troubled lest my apparent knowledge of the place should lead to long and tedious questioning from our father; but I found him advancing from his own resources that I had got to know it whilst stationed at Plymouth—and did not pursue the subject. . . . Through the village of Nether Stowey we climbed up through the Quantocks; they are a tremendous barrier of moor, with the most wonderful valleys, called 'combes', running down them. From the high ground we looked down into the last valley in Somerset—a little piece of ground that I love as well as any I have ever walked in. On your right is the Bristol Channel with the faint line of the Welsh coast beyond it. Ahead are the enormous hills of the Devonshire border. . . . I pointed the Welsh coast out to our father. He replied 'Ah the thing has got twisted. It ought to be round to our left'. I should like to draw his map of England. . . .

We made Dunster about 4 o.c. and had our first engine trouble just as we drew up at the Luttrel Arms. . . . Uncle H. treated the business with admirable sang froid. . . . Our father insisted on standing by, making irritating suggestions. I made one or two efforts to remove him, out of sympathy for our uncle, but of course they were unsuccessful. Later on he discussed the situation with me in private. I remarked that Uncle G. took it very well. Our father: 'Ah, you don't know the fellow as I do. Making a mess of things like this just hits him on his sore point; he's as vain as a peacock. He's just fuming under the surface. That's why I waited—just to smooth things over'. Why by the way is any misfortune that happens to anyone but himself always described by our father as the sufferer's 'having made a mess of things'? I am afraid that from my description this (Dunster) may sound a typical guide-book village: as a matter of fact there is nothing really curious enough in it to attract the tourist, and it is more completely tucked away than anywhere . . . the hills so close up and the rare paths in the heather . . . give one a great sense of snugness. . . . Nobody talks loud, nobody walks fast, rooms are deep and shady. . . . It has a personality as definite as, though antithetical to, Doagh. . . . It is off the main road, nobody goes there. . . . I have a notion that nobody ever leaves it either. . . . Our father was now quite in love with Dunster (which he called 'Dernster', 'Deemster' and other weird names), and was still talking of a day of rest. I noticed that he was usually in love with some place we had left; after anything good he could hardly be brought to admit merits anywhere else, and when he was, the whole process began over again. Thus for the first few days, if one ventured to praise anything, you were told that it was not to be compared with the Welsh mountains. After that it was Dunster which blotted out every other halt; then Land's End; and when I left them he had settled down to the view that 'none of these places came up to Salisbury'. . . .

But to proceed; we ran very comfortably through Minehead, and immediately began to climb. . . . At Porlock Uncle G. was just changing gear for the next appalling hill when something stuck again. Telephoned back to Minehead for the same mechanic. More buttoning up of coats and stiffening of upper lips as per previous night. Aunt Annie and I went and looked at the Church —we found it cooler both psychologically and physically—for the sun was terrific. . . . We were held up here for some three quarters of an hour, greatly to the annoyance of the other traffic; and the heat as we stood still made us very glad to be in motion again. . . .

Our objective was now Lynmouth. . . . Let me solemnly warn you against ever attempting this ride. . . . The toll road is detestable . . . and the humourist who owns it has also left it without any kind of barrier at the outside, and everywhere the banking is all wrong. I must confess that mountain scenery is often seen most impressively when I for one would be least ready to enjoy it. To look back as you attack an almost perpendicular corner, down an enormous cliff; to see other hills piled up on the far side of the gorge and in their unusual perspective from such a position, giving the whole scene a nightmare appearance . . . to remember that the cheery man from the garage told us that a car backed over into the sea further along the road a few days ago; to wonder what exactly you'd do if one of those charabancs came down—on my life I had the wind up. . . . The descent from this into the next hole was even worse than the ascent. You just wind down the cliff edge on a road about 7 ft. wide, which touches, at times, the pleasant gradient of $1/4\frac{1}{2}$. . . .

We were exceedingly glad to drop into Lynmouth . . . the heights all round are perhaps too beetling, and to live there permanently would be like living at the bottom of a well. Our hotel had a verandah above the river, where we sat very pleasantly after tea and watched a water rat manoeuvring from stone to stone.... We all walked out after dinner up the road which we were to follow next day. Uncle H. and I outstripped the others. It was a fine evening, delightfully cool and dewy. The road was good ... big gorges ... mysterious and chaotic landscape—'forest on forest piled'.... Whenever you were still, the sound of a stream many feet below and the 'EEE-ee' of bats worked a kind of counterpoint on the general theme of silence. We walked faster; we talked most entertainingly. Finally we reached the top where these valleys, getting shallower and shallower, at last come out on the surface of the moor. We sat under a haystack enjoying the smell and the air of a good, starless, moonless English country night.... I find that I have few distinct images left of the next day's run.... We lunched at Clovelly. It carries the West Country tradition of living in holes to its logical conclusion, consisting simply of a stairway some 250 yards long with whitewashed houses on each side, ending in a cove and a jetty. The local tramway consists of a dozen well-cared-for donkeys on which lazy people travel up and down; goods are carried or trailed in a kind of wooden sledge. The bump-bump from step to step is one of the most characteristic sounds of the place.... Arrived at the beach, our father sternly refused the unanimous advice of his companions to facilitate his ascent by mounting one of the donkeys....

This day we passed into Cornwall. I had always imagined Cornwall a place of rocky heights and gulfs. At first I was very disappointed; for, to be candid, it is so like Co. Down or parts of Antrim that it felt uncanny. The same absence of bright colours, the same cottages, the same sloping, somewhat bare hills, grey rather than green. The only thing that disturbs the illusion are the continual engine-houses of the tin and copper mines ... they rather increase the general Celtic dreariness and 'oddness' (you know what I mean) which brings it at times so close to our own country—a thing by the by far more insidious than the sensuous idleness of richer scenery....

The show parts of Cornwall—the parts one has read about—are all on the coast. We lay this night at Tintagel, storied name. There is a generally-diffused belief that this place is connected with King Arthur; so far as I know from Malory, Layamon, and Geoffrey of Monmouth, it is not; it is really the seat of King

Mark and the Tristram story. This has not however deterred some wretch . . . from erecting an enormous hotel on the edge of the cliff, built in toy Gothic, and calling itself the King Arthur Hotel. The interior walls are made of cement with lines stamped on them to represent stone. They are profusely illustrated with toy armour from Birmingham; a Highland target, suitable for Macbeth, jostles a reproduction of late Tudor steel plate and is lucky to escape a Cromwellian helmet for its next door neighbour. In the centre of the lounge, with the Sketch and Tatler lying on it is—of course—*the* Round Table. Ye gods!! Even the names of the knights are written on it. Then there are antique chairs—on which very naturally we find the monogram K.A. stamped.

I have not yet exhausted the horrors of the place; I was glad to see a bookcase in the lounge. All the books were uniformly bound, and I was surprised to see such titbits as the Ethics of Aristotle and the works of the Persian epic poet Firdausi. I solved the mystery by finding out that they were a uniform series of *The Hundred Best Books*. . . . How I abominate such culture for the many, such tastes, ready-made, such standardization of the brain. To substitute for the infinite wanderings of the true reader through the bye-ways of the country he discovers, a charabanc tour. This whole place infuriates me. But the coast was wonderful; very like the Antrim coast, only better; foreland after foreland stretching away on both sides. In the evening I extracted honey even from the 100 best books by reading an excellent play of Molière's. . . . We left Tintagel after breakfast. By the way it is of course pronounced Tintagj-le; which was a sufficient reason for our father's insisting on calling it TINtagEL, with a hard G. . . . At Penzance we put up our side-screens and excluded the view. But nothing would deter Uncle H. from going on to Land's End; I indeed thoroughly agreed, but I was his only supporter.

Of the last bit of England I saw nothing . . . outside there was only a genuinely Celtic greyness. . . . We began to pass several hotels, every one of which announced that it was 'the last hotel in England'. Some of them looked as if this was perfectly true. Our uncle scorned them all and drove on until we reached the real end of the world where the road stops on a cliff outside the really last hotel. It was pouring with rain and blowing a terrific gale. It is a place well worth seeing . . . the same driving mist continued all the time we were there, clearing up for ten minute intervals with extraordinary suddenness every now and then. When this happens, the blue suddenly leaps out of the grey and you see the clouds packing all along the cliffs for miles, while a lighthouse on some rocks about three and a half miles out, turns up from nowhere. Indeed the appearance and disappearance of this place is what I most remembered . . . first the blank mist—then the outlines, rather ghostly in it—then golden—then quite clear with hard outlines and waves breaking on it—then blurred again and so back to the fog. . . .

A big lacuna occurs here; some pages of the journal have been lost and I do not propose to re-write them. Dartmoor and the New Forest must remain unsung. . . . At Warwick Uncle Hamilton could get no cover for the car which had to spend the night—a threatening night—in an open yard. When I lamented this fact our father said, 'Ah well, the holiday is nearly over now'. This remark contains so many distinct trains of thought that you may spend a wet afternoon in disentangling them. . . . At a certain cathedral city in the Midlands I found the masterpiece of comic or satiric statuary. It represents a little eighteenth century gentleman with a toy sword. It cannot explain how cunningly a kind of simpering modesty is combined with a certain profound vanity in this figure . . . need I add that the town was Lichfield and that the statue bore the name—BOSWELL.

From Lichfield I returned to Oxford by train. . . . I was delighted with your letter and have much to say in answer which must at present wait. I liked particularly your description of the rains—I can see that. Just one word about *Paradise Regained*—surely the shrinkage of Satan is the very proper one that since the great days of *P. Lost* he has spent sixty centuries in the Miltonic hell? . . .

TO HIS FATHER, *after the holiday described above.*

31 August 1921

I still feel that the real value of such a holiday is still to come, in the images and ideas which we have put down to mature in the cellarage of our brains, thence to come up with a continually improving bouquet. Already the hills are getting higher, the grass greener, and the sea bluer than they really were; and thanks to the deceptive working of happy memory our poorest stopping places will become haunts of impossible pleasure and Epicurean repast.

As to myself, I do not propose, as you may be sure, to spend the whole Vac. here. I will do what I can; but I must 'sit to my book' for a little while yet. The fault of our course here is that we get so little guidance and can never be sure that our efforts are directed exactly to the right points and in the right proportions. I suppose that is part of the education—part at any rate of the game. . . .

TO HIS FATHER.

(Undated: postmarked 30 November 1921)

A dread portent has arisen above our horizon here—an immoralist, nihilist, determinist, fatalist. What are you to do with a man who denies absolutely everything? The joke is that he's an army officer on a course. He talks you blind and deaf. The more I see of him the clearer becomes my mental picture of his brother officers en masse imploring him to take advantage of a two-year course at Oxford—or Cathay or on the Moon. . . .

From his journal.

1 April 1922

I walked to Iffley in the morning and called on ——. . . . He talked about Atlantis, on which there is apparently a plentiful philosophic literature; nobody seems to realize that a Platonic myth is fiction, not legend, and therefore no base for speculation. . . .

2 April 1922

I sat in my own bedroom by an open window in bright sunshine and started a poem on Dymer in rhyme royal.

5 April 1922

Saw —— in order to get the address of the 'London Mercury'. He told me with a solemn face and admirable naivety how he got his poems accepted. Two or three were sent back by return post. Whereupon he went up to London and called on the Editor, saying, 'Look here Mr. Squire, you haven't taken these poems of mine and I want to know what's wrong with them'. If the story ended there it would merely be a sidelight on ——, but the joke is that Squire said, 'I'm glad you've come to talk it over; that's just what I want people to do', and actually accepted what he had formerly refused. Truly the ways of editors are past finding out. . . .

7 April 1922

I wish life and death were not the only alternatives, for I don't like either; one could imagine a via media.

15 April 1922

Tried to work at Dymer and covered some paper; but I am very dispirited about my work at present specially as I find it impossible to invent a new opening for the Wild Hunt. The old one is full of clichés and will never do. I have leaned too much on the idea of being able to write poetry and if this is a frost I shall be rather stranded. . . . A dissatisfying day but, praise God, no more headaches. . . .

18 April 1922

In the afternoon I walked into Oxford and looked up Civil Service exam papers in the Union. 'Greats' is child's play compared with them. . . . I called on A.S., hoping to hear something of the Civil Service. He tells me that there is no vacancy this year, and that probably there will be none next. . . . Thus ends the dream of a Civil Service career as suddenly as it began; I feel at once that I have been in alien territory—not mine, and deep down, impossible. . . .

21 April 1922

Got up shortly before seven, cleaned the grate, lit the fire, made tea, 'did' the drawing room, made toast, bathed, shaved, breakfasted, washed up, put the new piece of ham on to boil, and was out by half past ten. . . . Washed up after lunch. Worked on Greek History notes until tea when Miss Baker came. Had got settled to work when Mrs. Moore called me down 'for five minutes' to talk about Maureen's programme for next term. This would not have mattered, but before I could make my escape Miss Baker began to be 'just going' and continued so. When she finally got away it was time to get supper and to clear the tea things which Maureen had kindly left in statu quo. A good hour wasted altogether. . . .

3 May 1922

Met —— in the High. It had now cleared and we walked down to St. Aldate's and over the waterworks to Hinksey. I talked of staying up for another year and lamented that all my friends would be down; he said he had not got to know any new people of interest since his first year. We both agreed that to find people who had any interest in literature and who were not at the same time dam'd affected dilletanti talking 'l'art pour l'art' etc., etc., was almost impossible—in fact he put Baker, Barfield and me as the only exceptions in his own circle; and even the 'hearty' men were preferable to the usual literary sort. . . .

TO HIS FATHER.

18 May 1922

And now I want to talk about my plans. You will remember a talk we had when I was last at home. On that occasion I repeated to you a conversation which had taken place some time before between one of my tutors and myself. I had asked him for a testimonial, preparatory to giving my name to the employment agency. Instead of giving me one he advised me very earnestly not to take any job in a hurry; he said that if there was nothing for me in Oxford immediately after Greats, he was sure there would be something later; that College would almost certainly continue my scholarship for another year if I chose to stay up and take another school, and that 'if I could possibly afford it' this was the course which he would like me to take. . . . I was not particularly keen at the time about doing so; partly on your account, partly because I did not care to survive most of my contemporaries.

At that time there seemed to be one or two things in view—a vacant fellowship at Lincoln, another at Magdalen. Soon however it 'transpired' that one of these was to lapse and the other be filled from its own college without open election. I thought of the Civil Service. . . . The advice of my first tutor was repeated by the other one; and with new points. The actual subjects of my own Greats school are a doubtful quality at the moment; for no one quite knows what place Classics and Philosophy will hold in the educational world in a year's time. On the other hand the prestige of the Greats School is still enormous; so what is wanted everywhere is a man who combines the general qualifications which Greats is supposed to give, with the special qualifications of any other subject. And English Literature is a 'rising' subject. Thus if I could take a First or even a Second in Greats, *and* a First next year in English Literature, I should be in a very strong position indeed. . . . In such a course I should start knowing more of the subject than some do at the end; it ought to be a very easy proposition as compared with Greats.

All these considerations have tended to confirm what my tutor said in the first place . . . the pros and cons. I ought in fairness to say that I am pretty certain to get a job of some sort as I am; but if it comes to schoolmastering, my inability to play games will count against me. Above all, I hope it is clear that in no case will Greats be wasted. The point on which I naturally like to lean is that the pundits at Univ. don't want me to leave Oxford. . . . Now if, on all this, you feel that the scheme is rather a tall order and that my education has already taken long enough, you must frankly tell me so, and I shall quite appreciate your position. If you think that the chance thus offered can, and ought to be taken, I shall be grateful if you will let me know as soon as may be. . . .

From his journal.

19 May 1922

After tea I bussed back into College and called on the Mugger. . . . We talked of my plans. He said the days were past when one could walk out of Schools into a Fellowship; even in minor universities there was a demand for men who had done something. . . . He advised me however to take the extra year. He said that College was very hard up, but that he thought they could manage to continue my scholarship. I asked him whether if I 'came a cropper in Greats' he would still advise the extra year, and he said he would. . . . A dear old man, but the inexhaustible loquacity of educated age drove me to the City and University to recoup on a Guinness. . . .

24 May 1922

Bussed into Oxford, meeting Barfield outside the Old Oak. After finding a table, we decided to go to the Good Luck instead. An excellent lunch. . . . From there we walked to Wadham gardens and sat under the trees. We began with "Christina dreams"; I condemned them—the love dream made a man incapable of real love, the hero dream made him a coward. He took the opposite view and a stubborn argument followed. We then turned to *Dymer* which he had brought back; to my surprise his verdict was even more favourable than Baker's. He said it was 'by streets' the best thing I had done, and 'Could I keep it up?' He did not feel the weakness of the lighter stanzas. He said Harwood had 'danced with joy' over it, and had advised me to drop everything else and go on with it. From such a severe critic as Barfield the result was very encouraging. We then drifted into a long talk about ultimates. Like me, he has no belief in immortality etc., and always feels materialistic pessimism at his elbow. . . .

27 May 1922

I called on Stevenson and asked him to let me know of any tutorial work for the Vac. which he might hear of. I then called on Carritt and made the same request to him. He also promised to give my name to the Manchester Guardian for some reviewing. In the course of the morning I met Blount who said he was sure he could get me a schoolboy from Lynam's. . . . I also visited Williams, who is the local agent for Trueman & Knightley; he gave me a form, and said that by narrowing the field to Oxford I reduced my chances, but that if there was anything my qualifications would get it. He advised me also to put an advertisement in the *Oxford Times*. . . .

24 June 1922

Breakfasted before eight and cycled to the station to catch the 9.10 to Reading. . . . I found my way to University College and left my bike at the lodge. I saw a great many undergraduates of both sexes walking about; a nice looking lot. I then strolled about until 11 o'clock when I was taken to the Principal's room. . . . All were very pleasant to me, but Childs very firmly ruled out my idea of living anywhere else than in Reading. . . . Dodds showed me round the College which is pleasant and unpretentious, and left me in the Senior Common Room to wait for lunch. . . . I left the College at two and cycled to Bradfield. . . . The theatre is perfectly Greek—simple stone steps to sit on, and incense burning on the altar of Dionysus in the orchestra. Unfortunately the weather was perfectly English . . . most of the actors were inaudible and as the rain increased . . . it completely drowned them. . . . The audience were spectacle enough; rows of unhappy people listening to inaudible words in an unknown tongue and sitting bunched up on stone seats under a steady downpour. . . . I then noticed that J. was standing on the last tier where the amphitheatre merged into the hillside. . . . I crept up to join him—'Oh think of a cup of steaming hot tea' said he. We exchanged a pregnant glance; then I led the way and in a trice we had plunged into the bushes, plugged our way on all fours up the ivy bank, and dropped into a lane beyond. Never shall I forget J. shaking streams of water off his hat and repeating over and over again, 'Oh it *was* a tragedy'. We then repaired to a marquee and had tea. . . .

30 June 1922

After lunch I packed up my things for the night and biked into Oxford . . . and on to Beckley through wind and rain. I was warmly welcomed by Barfield and Harwood. . . . We got into conversation on fancy and imagination; Barfield could not be made to allow any essential difference between "Christina dreams" and the material of art. In the end we had to come to the conclusion that there is nothing in common between different people's ways of working, and as Kipling says, 'every single one of them is right'. At supper I drank cowslip wine for the first time in my life. It is a real wine, green in colour, bittersweet, as warming as good sherry, but heavy in its results and a trifle rough on the throat—not a bad drink however. After supper we went out for a walk into the woods on the edge of Otmoor. Their black and white cat Pierrot accompanied us like a dog all the way. Barfield danced round it in a field—with sublime lack of self-consciousness and wonderful vigour—for our amusement and that of three horses. There was a chilling wind, but it was quite warm in the wood. To wander here as it got dark . . . and to hear the wind in the trees . . . had a strong de la Mare-ish effect. On the way back we started a burlesque poem in Terza Rima, composing a line each in turn; we continued it later, with paper, by candlelight. It was very good nonsense. We entitled it 'The Button Moulder's Story'.

2 July 1922

In the evening Mrs. Moore and I discussed our plans. It was hard to decide yes or no about the Reading job, and she was so anxious not to influence me that I could not be quite sure what her wishes were—I am equally in the dark as to what my own real wishes are. . . .

TO HIS FATHER.

(Undated: July 1922)

I am now close to my viva and of course on that subject I have nothing new to tell you. The details for the Magdalen Fellowship have however been published at last. The subjects are, as we expected, identical with those of Greats; but it is also notified that candidates may send in a dissertation on any relevant subject in addition to competing on the papers. I felt at once that this gave me a great pull. . . . I am all agog to begin . . . but naturally I shall not sit seriously to the work until my viva is over. Under these circumstances you will understand that I cannot promise an early return home. I must see how I get on. No doubt this is disappointing for us all. . . . I feel it would be folly to throw away any chances for the sake of an immediate holiday. Also—odious factor—in my present position it is advisable to be on the spot, to be seen, to let people remember that there is a young genius on the lookout for a job. . . .

I thought I had got hold of a temporary job for next year the other day . . . a classical lectureship at University College, Reading. For geographical reasons I had hoped this would combine—by means of a season ticket—the diplomatic or 'advertisement' advantages of keeping in touch with Oxford with the advantages of a salary. This however turned out to be impossible. As well pure classics is not my line. I told them quite frankly, and they gave the job to some one else. Perhaps also I was too young. My pupils would nearly all have been girls. . . .

From his journal.

24 July 1922

Baker had been at Tetsworth yesterday to see Vaughan Williams.... He is the largest man Baker has ever seen—Chestertonian both in figure and habits. He eats biscuits all the time while composing. He said that after he had written the first bar on the page of a full score, the rest was all mechanical drudgery and that in every art there was 10% of real 'making' to 90% of spadework. He has a beautiful wife who keeps a pet badger—Baker saw it playing both with the dog and the kittens, and it licked his hand....

30 September 1922

Started to work again on the VIth Canto of *Dymer*. I got on splendidly—the first good work I have done for a long time. ... An absurd episode during lunch. Maureen had started saying that she didn't mind which of two alternative sweets she had; and Mrs. Moore, who is always worried by these indecisions, had begun to beg her to make up her mind in a rather weary voice. Thus developed one of those little mild wrangles about nothing, which a wise man accepts as in the nature of things. I however, being in a sublime mood, allowed a silent irritation to rise, and sought relief in jabbing violently at a piece of pastry. As a result I covered myself in a fine shower of custard and juice; my melodramatic gesture was thus deservedly exposed and everyone roared with laughter.

13 October 1922

Shortly before one I saw Farquharson. He told me to go to Wilson of Exeter for tuition in English. He then gave me a lecture on an academic career which was not (he said) one of leisure as popularly supposed.... He advised me, as he has done before, to go to Germany for a time and learn the language. He prophesied that there would soon be a school of modern European literature and that linguistically qualified Greatsmen would be the first to get the new billets thus created. This was attractive, but of course circumstances make migration impossible for me. . . .

15 October 1922

Worked all morning on my piece in Sweet's Reader and made some progress. It is very curious that to read the words of King Alfred gives more sense of antiquity than to read those of Sophocles. Also to be thus realizing a dream of learning Anglo-Saxon which dates from Bookham days. . . . After tea went on with Troilus. . . . It is amazingly fine stuff. How absolutely anti-Chaucerian Wm. Morris was in all save the externals. . . .

16 October 1922

Bicycled to the Schools after breakfast to a 10 o.c. lecture, stopping first to buy a Batchelor's gown at the extortionate price of 32/6. According to a usual practice of the Schools we were allowed to congregate in the room where the lecture was announced, and then suddenly told that it wd. be in the North School; our exodus of course fulfilled the scriptural condition of making the last first and the first last. I had thus plenty of time to feel the atmosphere of the English School which is very different from that of Greats. Women, Indians, and Americans predominate and—I can't say how—one feels a certain amateurishness in the talk and the look of the people. The lecture was by —— on the history of language. He spoke for an hour and told us nothing that I haven't known these five years. . . . After lunch I bicycled again to Schools to seek out the library of the English School. I found it at the top of many stories, inhabited by a strange old gentleman who seems to regard it as his private property. . . .

18 October 1922

Bicycled to Schools for a 12 o.c. lecture on Chaucer by Simpson, who turns out to be the old man I found in the English School library. Quite a good lecture . . . Jenkin arrived and I went to him in the drawing room. We talked of Troilus and this led us to the question of Chivalry. I thought the mere ideal, however unrealized, had been a great advance. He thought the whole thing had been pretty worthless. The various points which I advanced as good results of the Knightly standard he attributed to Christianity. After this, Christianity became the main subject. I tried to point out that the mediaeval knight ran his class code and his church code side by side in watertight compartments. Jenkin said that the typical example of the Xtian ideal at work was Paul, while admitting one would probably have disliked him in real life. I said that one got very little definite teaching in the gospels; the writers had apparently seen something overwhelming, but been unable to reproduce it. He agreed. . . .

TO HIS FATHER.

28 October 1922

I think I know my own limitations and am quite sure that an academic or literary career is the only one in which I can hope ever to go beyond the meanest mediocrity. The Bar is a gamble . . . and in business of course I should be bankrupt or in jail very soon. . . .

Anglo-Saxon is great fun. One begins it in a Reader constructed on the admirable system of having nearly all the text in one dialect and nearly all the glossary in another. You can imagine what happy hours this gives the young student—for example, you will read a word like 'Wado' in the text; in the glossary this may appear as Wedo, Waedo, Weodo, Waedu, or Wiedu. Clever bloke, aint 'e? The language in general gives the impression of parodied English, badly spelt. Thus the word 'Cwic' may baffle you, until you remember 'the quick and the dead'. Or again 'Tingul' for a star, until you remember 'Twinkle, Twinkle little star'. . . . I spend most of my hours with her [his tutor] trying to reproduce the various clucking, growling, and grunted noises which are apparently an essential to the pure accent of Alfred. . . .

From his journal.

29 October 1922

Aunt Lily has been here for about three days and has snubbed a bookseller in Oxford, written to the local paper, crossed swords with the Vicar's wife, and started a quarrel with her landlord. . . . She is still engaged on her essay which started three years ago as a tract on the then state of woman's suffrage, is still unfinished and now embraces a complete philosophy on the significance of heroism and maternal instinct, the nature of matter, the primal one, the value of Christianity, and the purpose of existence. . . . She thus combines a good deal of Schopenhauer with a good deal of theosophy; besides being indebted to Bergson and Plotinus. . . . She told me . . . that women had no balance and were cruel as doctors, that what I needed for my poetry was a steeping in scientific ideas and terminology, that many prostitutes were extraordinarily purified and Christ-like, that Plato was a Bolshevist, that the importance of Christianity could not have lain in what He said, that Pekinese were not dogs at all but dwarfed lions bred from smaller and ever smaller specimens by the Chinese, that matter was just the stop of all motion and that the cardinal error of all religions made by men was the assumption that God existed for, or cared for us. . . . I got away, with some difficulty, at one o.c. . . .

2 November 1922

Went to the Schools library. Here I puzzled for the best part of two hours over phonetics, back voice stops, glides, glottal catches, and open Lord-knows-whats. Very good stuff in its way, but why physiology should form a part of the English School I really don't know. . . .

25 December 1922

We were awakened early by my father to go to the communion service. It was a dark morning with a gale blowing and some very cold rain. . . . As we walked down to Church we started discussing the time of sunrise; my father saying rather absurdly that it must have risen already or it wouldn't be light.

In Church it was intensely cold. Warnie offered to keep his coat on. My father expostulated and said, 'Well at least you won't keep it on when you go up to the Table'. Warnie asked why not, and was told it was 'most disrespectful'. I couldn't help wondering why. But Warnie took it off to save trouble.... Another day exactly similar to yesterday. My father amused us by saying in a tone, almost of alarm, 'Hullo, it's stopped raining. We ought to go out' and then adding with undisguised relief, 'Ah no, it's still raining, we needn't'. Christmas dinner, a rather deplorable ceremony, at quarter to four. Afterwards it had definitely cleared up; my father said he was too tired to go out, but encouraged Warnie and me to do so—which we did with great eagerness and set out to reach Holywood by the high road and there have a drink. It was delightful to be in the open air after so many hours confinement in one room. Fate however denied our drink; for we were met just outside Holywood by the Hamiltons' car and of course had to travel back with them.... Early to bed, dead tired with talk and lack of ventilation. I found my mind was crumbling into the state which this place always produces; I have gone back six years to be flabby, sensual, unambitious. Headache again.

11 January 1923

After this I read Macdonald's *Phantastes* over my tea, which I have read many times and which I really believe fills for me the place of a devotional book....

25 January 1923

I went to Schools at 10 o.c. to hear Onions on Middle English.... Onions gave a delightful lecture; the best part being the quotations, which he does inimitably. Once he repeated nearly a whole poem with much relish, and then observed, 'That wasn't what I meant to say'. A man after my own heart....

26 January 1923

I was just sitting down again after supper when I heard a knock and going out, found Barfield. The unexpected delight gave me one of the best moments I have had since the even better ones of leaving Belfast and arriving home. . . . We went at our talk like a dogfight; of Baker, of Harwood, of our mutual news. . . . Barfield is working with Pearsall Smith, who is genuinely *triviosus* and a complete materialist. He (Smith) and de la Mare are fast friends. Barfield sees Squire fairly often. He says Squire is a man who promises more than he can perform, not through flattery but because he really believes his own influence to be greater than it is. . . . He went on to a very serious and honest review of my work in general. He said it always surprised him that my things were as good as they were, for I seemed to work simply on inspiration and did no clipping. I thus wrote plenty of good poetry, but never one perfect poem. He said that the 'inspired' percentage was increasing all the time, and that might save me in the end. . . . I thought his insight was almost uncanny, and agreed with every word. . . . I walked back to Wadham with him in the moonlight. . . .

4 February 1923

I found Miss Wardale alone. After a few minutes I was pleasantly surprised by the arrival of Coghill. . . . Miss Wardale, apart from a few sensible remarks on Wagner, was content to sit back in a sort of maternal attitude. . . . Coghill did most of the talking, except when contradicted by me. He said that Mozart had remained a boy of six all his life. I said nothing cd. be more delightful; he replied (and quite right) that he could imagine many things more delightful. He entirely disagreed with my love of Langland and of Morris. . . . He said that Blake was really inspired. I was beginning to say, 'In a sense——' when he said 'in the same sense as Joan of Arc'. I said, 'I agree. In exactly the same sense. But we may mean different things'. He: 'If you are a materialist'.

When I rose he came with me, and we walked together as far as Carfax. . . . He said (just like Barfield) that he felt it his duty to be a 'conchie' if there was another war, but admitted that he had not the courage. I said Yes, unless there was something really worth fighting for. He said that the only thing he would fight for was the monarchy. . . . I said I didn't care twopence about the monarchy—the only real issue was civilization against barbarism. He agreed, but thought with Hobbes that civilization and monarchy went together. . . . Before parting, I asked him to tea; he said he had just been going to ask me, and finally we arranged that I should go to him on Friday. . . . I thought Coghill a good man, quite free from our usual Oxford flippancy and fear of being crude. . . .

9 February 1923

On getting into bed I was attacked by a series of gloomy thoughts about professional and literary failure—what Barfield calls 'one of those moments when one is afraid one may not be a great man after all'.

13 February 1923

Again today—it is happening much too often now—I am haunted by fears for the future, as to whether I will ever get a job, and whether I shall ever be able to write good poetry. . . .

22 March 1923

I told Mrs. Moore that I didn't feel very happy about the plan of staying on here as a more or less unattached tutor. I did not want to join the rank of advertisements in the Union—it sounds so like the prelude to being a mere grinder all my days. If it wasn't for Maureen I think I should plump for a minor university if possible. We had a rather dismal conversation about our various doubts and difficulties. . . . I then went and saw Stevenson. . . . I asked him what prospects there were of my being able to exist as a freelance tutor until something turned up. He said there was practically no such work to be had in my subject. . . . He said he thought I was pretty sure to get a Fellowship soon. . . . In the meantime he advised me to get a job at a minor university. . . . I then came home and discussed the situation with Mrs. Moore. We were both greatly depressed. If one could be sure of coming back to a Fellowship after a term or two at some minor university we could take the Woodstock Rd. house—but if not? . . . It was certainly a damnably difficult situation. Thence we drifted into the perennial difficulty of money, which would be far more acute if we had to separate for a time. . . .

1 June 1923

A cold day. I spent the morning working on my essay. . . . Coming back to College I heard with interest what I suppose is my nickname. Several Univ. men whom I don't know, passed me. One of them, noticing my blazer, must have asked another who I was, for I heard him answer 'Heavy Lewis'. . . .

20 June 1923

Rode home and found Mrs. Moore and Dorothy polishing in Mrs. Moore's room. Had hardly left them when I heard an awful crash. . . . Mrs. Moore had fallen and hurt her elbow; all attempts to get her to stop polishing were treated in the usual way. . . . This put me into such a rage against poverty and fear and all the infernal net I seemed to be in that I went out and mowed the lawn and cursed all the gods for half an hour. . . .

22 June 1923

In the morning I read *Venice Preserved* which contains more loathsome sentimentality, flat language, and bad verse than I should have imagined possible. Later I scraped and began to stain the exposed passages of the floor in the hall, which was work both hot and hard. After lunch I finished the hall and did the same for the drawing room and helped Mrs. Moore with some changes of furniture in the dining room. . . . At six I walked out to find a new field path. . . . This brought me up a hill beside a very fine hedge with wild roses in it. This, in the cool of the evening, together with some curious illusion of being on the slope of a much bigger slope than I really was, and the wind in the hedge, gave me intense pleasure with a lot of vague reminiscences. . . . I got back about 8 and watered the garden. . . .

TO HIS FATHER, *after taking Schools in English Literature.*

1 July 1923

Before anything else, let me thank you very heartily. . . . I hope some day to repay these long years of education in the only way in which they can be repaid—by success and distinction in the kind of life I aim at. But . . . the thought of how much you are doing for me is often, even insistently, in my mind. . . . I should not be a son of yours if the prospect of being adrift and unemployed at thirty had not been very often present to my mind; for of course the worrying temperament of the family did not end with your generation. . . .

I can only put the situation thus. I have, and of course always shall have, qualifications that should, by all ordinary probability, make a tolerable schoolmastering job practically certain whenever we decide to give up Oxford as hopeless. The same qualifications also put me fairly high in the rank of candidates for academic jobs here. . . . What it comes to is that there is a pretty healthy chance here which would, on the whole, be increased by a few years more residence in which I should have time to make myself more known, and to take some research degree, and which would be, perhaps, permanently or indefinitely lost if I now left. . . . Speaking, for the moment, purely for myself, I should be inclined to put three years as a suitable term for waiting before beating a retreat. . . .

From his journal.

7 July 1923

I went to the station where I met Harwood . . . and thence bussed up to Headington . . . we lay under the trees and talked. He told me of his new philosopher, Rudolf Steiner, who has 'made the burden roll from his back'. Steiner seems to be a sort of panpsychist, with a vein of posing superstition, and I was very much disappointed to hear that both Harwood and Barfield were impressed by him. The comfort they got from him (apart from the sugar plum of promised immortality, which is really the bait with which he has caught Harwood) seemed something I could get much better without him. I argued that the 'spiritual forces' which Steiner found everywhere were either shamelessly mythological people or else no-one-knows-what. Harwood said this was nonsense and that he understood perfectly what he meant by a spiritual force. I also protested that Pagan animism was an anthropomorphic failure of imagination and that we should prefer a knowledge of the real unhuman life which is in the trees etc. He accused me of a materialist way of thinking when I said that the similarity of all languages probably depended on the similarity of all throats. . . . The best thing about Steiner seems to be the Goetheanum which he built up in the Alps. . . . Unfortunately the building has been burned down by the Catholics. . . .

10 July 1923

Up betimes and dressed in subfusc and white tie. . . . At 9.30 we entered the viva room and after the names had been called, six of us were told to stay, of whom I was one. I then sat in the fearful heat, in my gown and rabbit skin on a hard chair, unable to smoke, talk, read, or write until 11.50. . . . Most of the vivas were long and discouraging. My own—by Brett-Smith—lasted about two minutes. I was asked my authority—if any—for the word 'little-est'. I gave it—the Coleridge-Poole correspondence in 'Thomas Poole and his friends'. I was then asked if I had not been rather severe on Dryden and after we had discussed this for a little, Simpson said that they need not bother me any more.

I came away much encouraged, and delighted to escape the language people—one of whom, not a Don, was a foul creature, yawning insolently at his victims and rubbing his small puffy eyes. He had the face of a pork butcher and the manners of a village boy on a Sunday afternoon, when he has grown bored but not yet quite arrived at the quarrelsome stage. . . .

TO HIS FATHER, *after taking a First in English Literature.*

22 November 1923

I have a certain amount of news to give you, all of an inconclusive character. To get the least agreeable item over first, I am afraid old Poynton has proved a broken reed in the matter of pupils; I believe because he put the job off too long. I have got quite recently *one* pupil, a youth of eighteen who is trying to get a Classical Scholarship. . . . I fear we shall win no laurels by him. I questioned him about his classical reading, and our dialogue went something like this:—

SELF 'Well S., what Greek authors have you been reading?'
S. (*cheerfully*) 'I can never remember. Try a few names and I'll see if I get on to any.'
SELF (*a little damped*) 'Have you read any Euripides?'
S. 'No'.
SELF 'Any Sophocles?'
S. 'Oh yes'.
SELF 'What plays of his have you read?'
S. (*after a pause*) 'Well—the Alcestis'.
SELF (*apologetically*) 'But isn't that by Euripides?'
S. (*with the genial surprise of a man who finds £1 where he thought there was only a 10/- note*) 'Really. Is it now? Then by Jove I *have* read some Euripides'.

What idiots can have sent him in for a Scholarship? However, he is one of the cheeriest, healthiest, and most perfectly contented creatures I have ever met with. . . .

From his journal.

(Undated)

It was shortly before this that I read Flecker's 'Hassan.' It made a great impression on me and I believe it is a really great work. Carritt (whom I met at the Martlets shortly after) thinks that its dwelling on physical pain puts it as much outside literature as is pornography; that it works on the nervous system rather than the imagination. I find this hard to answer, but I am almost sure he is wrong. . . .

TO HIS FATHER.

(Undated: February 1924)

As soon as I met people here I heard of a new will-of-the-wisp, a poor Fellowship at St. John's now vacant and calling out for a candidate. The warning that preference would be given to 'founder's kin and persons born in the County of Stafford' did not seem sufficient to deter me from trying my luck. . . . I had supposed that the preference for natives of Staffordshire etc., meant only a preference, other things being equal. I find however that if any candidate who claims such preference, and who has in addition either a *Second* in Greats or a First in any other final School, he must be elected. I do not of course know whether there is any such candidate in the field, but Stafford is a large county, and we may be sure that the founder was some philo-progenitive old fellow who, like Charles II in Dryden, 'scattered his Maker's image through the land'. In short, we may expect a defeat with almost complete certainty. . . .

From his journal.

29 February 1924

Shortly after tea, which was very late, I went up to dress preparatory to dining with Carritt. . . . At dinner he put into my hand the notice of the vacancy at Trinity—an official Fellowship in Philosophy worth £500 a year. . . . I walked home, looking at the details of the Trinity Fellowship as I passed the lamps. For some reason the possibility of getting it and all that would follow if I did, came before my mind with unusual vividness. I saw it would involve living in, and what a break up of our present life that would mean, and also how the extra money would lift terrible loads off us all. I saw that it would mean pretty full work and that I might become submerged and poetry crushed out. I suddenly had a vision of myself, God knows when or where, in the future, looking back on these years since the war as the happiest or only really valuable part of my life, in spite of all their disappointments and fears. Yet the longing for an income that would free us from anxiety was stronger than all these feelings. I was in a strange state of excitement—and all on the mere hundredth chance of getting it. . . .

17–25 March 1924

During this time it was unfortunate that my first spring flood of *Dymer* should coincide with a burst of marmalade-making and spring-cleaning on Mrs. Moore's part, which led without intermission into packing. I managed to get through a good deal of writing in the intervals of jobbing in the kitchen and doing messages in Headington. . . . I also kept my temper nearly all the time. Domestic drudgery is excellent as an alternative to idleness or to hateful thoughts—which is perhaps poor Mrs. Moore's reason for piling it on all the time; as an alternative to the work one is longing to do and able to do (*at that time* and heaven knows when again) it is maddening. No one's fault; the curse of Adam.

TO HIS FATHER.

27 April 1924

I have been exercised in the slightly unpleasant duty of getting all things in readiness for my application for the Trinity Fellowship—getting testimonials and talking to one or two people who will write unofficially for me. I also went to a dinner where I met the present philosophy man from Trinity whose successor I should become if I were elected. This was done no doubt to give me an opportunity of impressing him with my unique social and intellectual qualifications. Unhappily the whole conversation was dominated by a bore who wanted to talk (and *did* talk) about the state of India, and I suppose I hardly exchanged ten words with the Trinity man. However, it may have been just as well. A man who knows he is on show can hardly be at his best, and I am told that this Trinity man is a very shy, retiring, moody old man and difficult to talk to. In the meantime I send in my application and wait....

TO HIS FATHER.

(Undated: May or June 1924)

I have a bit of good—or fairly good—news.... Carritt (of Univ.) it appears is going for a year to teach philosophy in the University of Ann Arbor, Michigan, and it was suggested that I should undertake his tutorial duties during his absence and also give lectures. As soon as I heard the proposal I said that I was already a candidate for the vacancy at Trinity. To this they replied that they had no intention of asking me to sacrifice the possibility of a permanent job; it would be understood that if I were elected to Trinity I should be released from my engagement to Univ.—unless indeed Trinity were willing to let me do both tasks and I felt able to do so. This being settled I of course accepted the offer. I was a little disappointed that they only offered me £200—specially as I anticipate that when living in and dining at high table I shall hardly be able to economize as much as I do now.... Well, it's poorly paid and temporary ... but it is better to be inside than out, and it is always a beginning. The experience should be valuable.

You may imagine that I am now pretty busy. I must try to get through most of the Greats reading before next term, and do it more thoroughly than ever I did when I was a candidate myself. . . . There can be no throwing dust in the examiner's eyes this time. . .

As a prospective candidate I dined at Trinity the other night. . . . I was very favourably impressed with the Trinity people. In the smoking room after dinner we were just of a number for conversation to be general and I had one of the best evenings imaginable. . . . So if Trinity don't give me a Fellowship, at least they gave me a very good time. . . .

From his journal.

15 June 1924

M. told us a good story of how H. G. Wells had dined at All Souls and said that Oxford wasted too much time over Latin and Greek. Why should these two literatures have it all to themselves? Now Russian and Persian literature were far superior to the classics. Someone (I forget the name) asked a few questions. It soon became apparent that Wells knew neither Greek, Latin, Persian, or Russian. 'I think,' said someone, 'I am the only person present here tonight who knows these four languages; and I can assure you, Mr. Wells, that you are mistaken; neither Russian nor Persian literature are as great as the literatures of Greece or Rome'. . . .

3 July 1924

Today I went to Colchester in order to travel back in Warnie's sidecar. . . . A brisk shower of rain came down as I reached Colchester, where I was met by Warnie and driven to the Red Lion where we had tea. This is one of the oldest hotels in England, curiously and beautifully beamed. . . . Warnie had just been reading *Puck of Pook's Hill* for the first time; he praised it highly and I agreed with him.

While we were sitting under the roof of a kind of courtyard after tea waiting for the rain to stop, a Major came up, to whom Warnie introduced me, telling me afterwards that he was a very well preserved specimen of the real old type of army bore.

When it cleared a little we walked out to see the town, which is a very pleasant, sprawling, old-world place, not unlike Guildford. The Roman castle is very fine in a kind quite new to me, as also the remains of the old gate of Camolodunum. There is also a pleasant old house (now an office but it ought to be a pub) bullet marked from the civil wars. After this we motored up out of the town to a higher, windy land, full of camps. Warnie's camp consists of a small old country house ('a Jorrocks house' he called it), and its park, now filled with huts. The C.O. lives in the Jorrock house.

I was taken into the Mess (Lord, how strange to be in such a place again!) and of course given a drink. The 'Orficers' were really very nice to me. It was odd to see a Mess full of people in mufti. We then motored back to town to a civilian club of which Warnie is a member, where he had provided a royal feast of the sort we both like; no nonsense about soup and pudding, but a sole each, cutlets with green pease, a *large* portion of strawberries and cream, and a tankard of the local beer, which is very good. So we gorged like Roman emperors in a room to ourselves and had good talk. . . .

We drove back to camp. Warnie had turned out into another hut and I had his bedroom. He has two rooms for his quarters. The sitting room, with stove, easy chair, pictures, and all his French books, is very snug. I notice that a study in a hut, or a cave, or the cabin of a ship can be snug in a way that is impossible for a mere room in a house, the snugness being a *victory*, a sort of defiant comfortableness—whereas in a house of course, one demands comfort, and is simply annoyed at its absence. He 'put into my hands' Anatole France's 'Revolt of the Angels' in a translation, which seems an amusing squib.

4 July 1924

We started on our Oxford journey after breakfast in the Mess. The day looked threatening at first, but we had fair weather. I do not remember the names of the villages we passed, except Braintree and Dunmow (where the flitch lives). At St. Albans we stopped to see the Cathedral; I had been there once before in [Belsen] days about 1909 or 1910 to sit and kneel for three hours watching Oldie's son (whom God reject) ordained a deacon or a priest, I forget which. Yet in those days, that day without work, the journey to St. Albans, the three-hour service, and a lunch of cold beef and rice in an hotel was a treat for which we counted the days beforehand. . . .

I was rather relieved to find the Cathedral quite definitely the poorest English Cathedral I have yet seen. In the town we bought two pork pies to supplement what Warnie considered the Spartan allowance of sandwiches given us by the Mess, and drank some beer. I think it was here that Warnie formed the project of going far out of our way to eat our lunch at Hunton Bridge on the L.N.W.R. where we used to sit and watch the trains when out on our walks from [Belsen]. I assented eagerly. I love to exult in my happiness at being for ever safe from at least one of the major ills of life—that of being a boy at school.

We bowled along very merrily in brilliant sunshine, while the country grew uglier and uglier at every turn, and therefore all the better for our purpose. We arrived at the bridge and devoured the scene—the two tunnels, which I hardly recognised at first, but memory came back. Of course things were changed. The spinney of little saplings had grown quite high. The countryside was no longer the howling waste it had once looked to us. We ate our egg sandwiches and pork pies and drank our bottled beer. In spite of Warnie's fears it was as much as we could do to get through them all. But then, as he pointed out, this was appropriate to the scene. We were behaving just as we would have done fifteen years earlier. 'Having eaten everything in sight, we are now finished'. We had a lot of glorious reminiscent talk. We developed our own version of *si jeunesse savait*; if we could only have seen as far as this out of the hell of [Belsen]. I felt a half comic, half savage pleasure (Hobbes's sudden glory) to think how by the mere laws of life we had completely won and Oldie had completely lost. For here were we, with our stomachs full of sandwiches, sitting in the sun and the wind, while he had been in hell these ten years.

We drove on and had tea at Aylesbury—dizzy now and stupid with fresh air—and got to Oxford before seven. . . . On Saturday . . . Warnie and I motor biked to Wantage Road where he wanted to take a photo of the fastest train in England. We did this successfully and looked out for a suitable place for tea on the return journey. A countryman told us that there was no pub near, but that we could get tea at the — it sounded like dog house. We both felt sure that there could be no places called the dog house, yet presently found it. Here we had strange adventures. I rang at the closed door—it is a little red house under a woodside—and waited for ten minutes; then rang again. At last a very ancient beldame appeared. I asked if we could have some tea. She looked hard at me and asked, 'Are you golfers?'; on my answering no, she shut the door softly and I could hear her hobbling away into the bowels of the house. I felt like Arthur at Orgoglio's castle. Anon the ancient appeared again, and looking even harder at me, asked me a second time what I wanted. I repeated that we wanted some tea. She brought her face closer to mine and then with the air of one who comes at last to the real point, asked, 'How long do you want it for?' I was quite unable to answer this question, but by God's grace the witch left me and hobbled away once more. This time she left the door open and we walked in and found our way to a comfortable dining room where a plentiful and quite unmagical tea was presently brought us. We sat there for a very long time. A storm of wind got up (raised, I have no doubt, by our hostess) and the ivy lashed the windows. On the next day, Sunday, we went to bathe at Parson's Pleasure. . . . Warnie left us on Monday. . . .

9–16 July 1924

Looking up the books I was to examine in. . . . This was the first time I had looked into Macaulay for many a year; I hope it will be many years before I read him again. It's not the style that's the trouble; it's a very good style within its own limits. But the man is a humbug—a vulgar, shallow, self-satisfied mind, absolutely inaccessible to the complexities and delicacies of the real world. He has the journalist's air of being a specialist in everything, of taking in all points of view, and being always on the side of the angels; he merely annoys a reader who has had the least experience of *knowing* things, of what knowing is like. There is not two pence worth of real thought or real nobility in him. But he isn't dull. . . .

TO HIS FATHER.

(Undated: July 1924)

To examine is like censoring letters in the army or (I fancy) like hearing confessions if you are a priest. Beforehand it seems interesting . . . but it turns out to be cruelly dull. As the censoring subaltern finds that every man in his platoon says the same things in his letters home, and as the priest, no doubt, finds that all his penitents confess the same sins, so the examiner finds that out of hundreds of girls and boys of all social classes from all parts of England, scarcely a dozen make themselves memorable either for original ideas or amusing mistakes.

The paper which I corrected most of was on *David Copperfield* and Kinglake's *Eothen*; and the first question was, 'Contrast the characters of Uriah Heep and Mr. Micawber'. So one takes up one's first sheet of answers and reads, 'Uriah Heep is the finished type of a rogue; Mr. Micawber on the other hand is the portrait of a happy-go-lucky debtor'. Then one plods on to the same question answered by the next candidate and reads, 'Mr. Micawber is the finished portrait of a happy-go-lucky debtor, while Uriah Heep is a typical (or perhaps 'typicle') rogue'. And so it goes on through all the weary hours of the day till one's brain reels with Uriah Heep and Mr. Micawber and one would willingly thrash the editor or whoever it is who has supplied them with that maddening jargon about 'the finished portrait of a rogue'.

I must set down on the credit side the fact of having been thus forced to read *Eothen*. . . . I most strongly advise you to give yourself a very pleasant evening by taking down Kinglake. If you don't feel a stomach for the whole thing, at least read the interview between the Pasha and the 'possible policeman of Bedfordshire'. . . . Warnie was over here shortly before my durance began and I have converted him to my idol. . . . His new bike is a noble machine, and we stopped to eat our lunch at a railway bridge . . . which used to be the regular goal of our walks when we were at [Belsen]. . . . We were puzzled for some time as to why the line was invisible from a fence on which we used to sit and watch it; until Warnie hit on the simple truth that some trees which had been little trees in 1909 had become big trees by 1924. That's the sort of moment that makes the youngest of us feel old. . . .

TO HIS FATHER.

(Undated: postmarked 28 August 1924)

I am plodding on with my fourteen lectures. . . . I think I said before that I am not writing them *in extenso*, only notes. The extemporary element thus introduced is dangerous for a beginner, but *read* lectures send people to sleep, and I think I must make the plunge from the very beginning and learn to *talk*, not to recite. . . . Hitherto I have always talked or read to people to whom I could say, 'You remember Bradley's stunt about judgment' or 'The sort of business you get at the beginning of Kant'. But of course this won't do now—and the deuce of it is that when you actually look up the passage you always find that they either say more or less than you want. . . .

The photo of Warnie bathing I take it is the one of him floating which he showed me—telling me at the same time that one of his colleagues had remarked, 'It is one of the sights of the summer to see Lewis *anchored* off the coast'. . . .

TO HIS FATHER.

(Undated: April or May 1925)

My Easter was redeemed by a glorious two days trip with Warnie. . . . I was pleased to revisit Salisbury and see it more thoroughly.

I well remembered my former visit . . . we stopped for a few minutes in Uncle Hamilton's headlong career and heard morning prayers going on in the Cathedral. At that time I did not agree with you, and cared for it less than Wells or Winchester. This time, as we came into sight of Salisbury, where, on those big rolling downs that spire can be seen from fifteen miles away, I began to have my doubts. Later, when we had had tea and strolled into the Close I decided that it was very good in its own way but not in my favourite way. But when we came out again and saw it by moonlight after supper, I was completely conquered. It was a perfect spring night, with the moon nearly full and not a breath of wind stirring nor a sound from the streets. The half light enhanced its size, and the sharp masses of shadow falling in three great patches from the three main faces of one side emphasized the extraordinary simplicity in which it differs from Wells.

That is the real difference I think, and what repelled me at first; the others, mixed of a dozen styles, have grown from century to century like organic things and the slow history of secular change has been built into them. One feels the *people* behind them more; the nameless craftsmen in this or that gargoyle which is different from any other. Salisbury, on the other hand, is the idea of a master mind, struck out at once for ever. Bating mechanical difficulties it might have been built in a day. . . . One might say that Wells is an age made into stone and Salisbury is a petrified moment. But what a moment! The more one looks, the more it satisfies. What impressed me most was the force of Mind; the thousands of tons of masonry held in place by an idea, a religion; buttress, window, acres of carving, the very lifeblood of men's work, all piled up there, and gloriously *useless* from the side of the base utility for which alone we build now. It really is typical of a change—the mediaeval town where the shops and houses huddle at the foot of the Cathedral, and the modern city where the churches huddle between the sky-scraping offices and the appalling 'stores'. We had another good look at it in the morning light after breakfast—when the plump and confident members of the feathered chapter cooing in the porch added a new charm. Warnie says that Salisbury is Barset; if so, we must have been standing near where the Warden said, 'I'm afraid I shall never like Mrs. Proudie', and the Archdeacon took off his hat to 'let a cloud of steam escape'.

On our run that day we stopped at Stonehenge—a very fine morning and intensely quiet except for a battery practising over the next ridge. It was the first time I had heard a gun fired since I left France, and I cannot tell you how odd the sensation was. For one thing it seemed much louder and more sinister and generally unpleasant than I had expected; as was perhaps natural from the general tendency of memory to minimize, and also from the solitude and quiet of the place. . . .

A Fellowship in English is announced at Magdalen and of course I am putting in for it, but without any serious hopes as I believe much senior people . . . are in for it. . . . These continued hopes deferred are trying, and I'm afraid trying for you too. . . .

I have been into Hall and Common Room afterwards and heard an interesting thing. Do you remember Mrs. Asquith's saying in that detestable autobiography that she once asked Jowett if he had ever been in love? He replied, 'Yes', and being asked what the lady was like, replied, 'Violent, very violent'. Apparently the lady was really Florence Nightingale. X and Y both knew of it. For her 'violence' see Strachey in *Eminent Victorians*. The story—a strange tragi-comedy—seems to have been common property. Both the parties were irascible and opinionated and quarrelled nearly as often as they met; and yet the affair hung on for a long time. . . .

TO HIS FATHER, *on election to a Fellowship at Magdalen.*

26 May 1925

First, let me thank you from the bottom of my heart for the generous support, extended over six years, which alone has enabled me to hang on till this. In the long course I have seen men at least my equals in ability and qualifications, fall out for the lack of it. 'How long can I afford to wait?' was everybody's question; and few of them had at their back those who were both able and willing to keep them in the field so long. You have waited, not only without complaint but full of encouragement, while chance after chance slipped away and when the goal receded farthest from sight. Thank you again and again. It has been a nerve-racking business, and I have hardly yet had time to taste my good fortune with a deliberate home-felt relish. . . .

I had an invitation to dine at Magdalen on Sunday a fortnight ago. This showed only that I was one of the possibles. Then came the *little* problems which seem so big at the time. Was Magdalen one of the Colleges where they wore white ties and tails, or did they wear dinner jackets and black ties? I asked the Farq. and he advised white tie and tails; and of course when I got there I found everyone in black ties and dinner jackets. These dinners for inspection are not exactly the pleasantest way of spending one's evening—as you may imagine. . . . But I must say they carried off as well as could be asked a situation which must be irksome to the hosts as well as to the guest. So far so good. . . .

On the Saturday the President met me in the street and had a vague tho' kindly conversation with me. On Monday I had a very abrupt note from him asking me to see him on Tuesday morning, with the curious addition, 'it is most important'. I didn't like it at all; it suggested some horrible hitch. Was I going to be viva-d on Anglo-Saxon verbs, or asked my views on the Thirty-Nine Articles? . . . I got to Magdalen, and would you believe it, he kept me waiting for half an hour before he saw me. When he did see me it turned out to be all formalities. . . . Now *if* I were elected would I agree to this, would I be prepared to do that, and did I understand what the terms of the Fellowship implied? The only thing of the slightest importance was 'would I be prepared, in addition to the English pupils, to help with the philosophy?' I need hardly say that I would have agreed to coach a troupe of performing bagbirds in the quadrangle; but I looked very wise and thought over all his points and I hope let no subservience appear. He then gave me a long talk about the special needs of Magdalen undergraduates—as if they differed from any others!—all as if I had been elected but without saying I had been. During the whole interview he was cold and dry, and not nearly so agreeable as he had been on Saturday. He finally dismissed me with a request that I would hang about Univ. the following afternoon in case I was called for.

And then next day—about 2.30—they telephoned for me and I went down. Warren saw me, told me I had been elected, and shook hands; since, he has written me a very nice letter of congratulations, saying that he believes they may congratulate themselves. It is a fine job as our standards go; starting at £500 a year with 'provision made for rooms, a pension, and dining allowance'. The election for five years only in the first case of course means only that in five years they have the chance of getting rid of you if you turn out 'hardly one of our successes'. One hopes in the ordinary course of events to be re-elected. . . .

TO HIS FATHER.

14 August 1925

The only other event of importance since I last wrote has been my formal 'admission' at Magdalen. It was a formidable ceremony, and not entirely to my taste. Without any warning of what was in store for me, the Vice-President ushered me into a room where I found the whole household—it is large at Magdalen. Warren (the President) was standing, and when the V.P. laid a red cushion at his feet I realized with some displeasure that this was going to be a kneeling affair. Warren then addressed me for some five minutes in Latin. I was able to follow some three quarters of what he said; but no one had told me what response I was to make, and it was with some hesitation that I hazarded *do fidem* as a reply. . . . This appeared to fill the bill. I was then told in English to kneel. When I had done so, Warren took me by the hand and raised me with the words, 'I wish you joy'. It sounds well enough on paper, but it was hardly impressive in fact; and I tripped over my gown in rising. I now thought my ordeal at an end; but I was never more mistaken in my life. I was sent all round the table and every single member in turn shook my hand and repeated the words: 'I wish you joy'. You can hardly imagine how odd it sounded by the twenty-fifth repetition. English people have not the talent for graceful ceremonial. They go through it lumpishly and with a certain mixture of defiance and embarrassment, as if everyone felt he was being rather silly, and was at the same time ready to shoot down anyone who said so. In a French now, or an Italian university, this might have gone off nobly. . . .

TO HIS FATHER, *after a visit home.*

21 October 1925

When we discussed the question of furnishing my rooms before I left, I thought it a very remote contingency. It was rather a crushing blow to find that I had to get everything—and for three spacious rooms; the extent of College's bounty being some linoleum in the smaller sitting room and a washstand in the bedroom. It is hard to say on what principle Fellows are provided with washstands but left to provide their own beds. . . . Carpets, tables, curtains, chairs, fenders, fire irons, coal boxes, table covers —everything—had to be bought in haste. It has cost me over £90, although I was able to pick up a few things second-hand. It sounds an alarming total, but I do not think I have been extravagant; the rooms certainly do not look as if they had been furnished by a plutocrat. . . .

My external surroundings are beautiful beyond compare. To live in the Bishop's Palace at Wells would be good, but could hardly be better than this. My big sitting-room looks north and from it I see nothing, not even a gable or a spire, to remind me that I am in a town. I look down on a stretch of level grass which passes into a grove of immemorial forest trees, at present coloured autumn red. Over this stray the deer. They are erratic in their habits. Some mornings when I look out there will be half a dozen chewing the cud just underneath me, and on others there will be none in sight—or one little stag (not much bigger than a calf and looking too slender for the weight of his antlers) standing still and sending through the fog that queer little bark which is these beasts' 'moo'. It is a sound that will soon be as familiar to me as the cough of the cows in the field at home, for I hear it day and night. On my right hand as I look from these windows is 'his favourite walk' (Addison's). My smaller sitting room and bed-room look out southwards across a broad lawn to the main buildings of Magdalen with the tower beyond it. . . .

As to the 'College' in the other sense—as a human society —I can say little yet. One's first impressions of a new set are changed many times in the first month. They are all very nice to me. The general tone of the place strikes me as rather slack and flippant—I mean among the Dons—but I may well be mistaken. . . . The most surprising thing is that they are much less formal than Univ. They don't dress for dinner except when the President dines, on which occasions a warning notice is sent round to our rooms. Again, there are an enormous number of us as compared with Univ., and we meet much more often. Thus we breakfast and lunch in Common Room; meals in your own rooms (which I had thought universal at Oxford) being unknown here, either for Dons or undergraduates. The latter are a little aloof from the rest of Oxford; not entirely through affectation but because as a matter of geography we are 'at the town's end'; or as someone said, we are at the beginning of Suburbia. . . .

TO HIS FATHER.

4 December 1925

I have had a nasty blow—don't be alarmed, it concerns neither life, limb, or reputation. I was already rather worried about the difficulty of preparing an English Lecture in the short time at my disposal, but by dint of choosing a short subject which I know well (XVIII century precursors of the Romantic movement) I hoped to be able to acquit myself well enough. What was my displeasure on finding, when the rough draught of next term's lecture list was sent me, that —— is lecturing on 'English poetry from Thompson to Cowper'. Now of course my 'precursors', with the exception of some critics and other prose writers, are just the poets from Thompson to Cowper. It is in fact the same subject under a different name. This means that, being neither willing nor able to rival —— I am driven to concentrate on the prose people, of whom at present I know very little. I have as hard a spell cut out for me between now and next term as I have ever had. Of course all the more easy and obvious subjects which will leap to your mind, are long since occupied by the bigwigs. The immediate consequence is that I am afraid I shall scarcely be able to take more than a week at home this Christmas. To compensate for this I shall try to get across at Easter. . . .

TO HIS FATHER, *after a Christmas visit home.*

5 January 1926

Warnie and I had rather an interesting journey back. Firstly there was the episode of the friendly and intoxicated stranger in the smoking room of the Liverpool boat; but I feel that Warnie's pen will do that story more justice than mine.

Secondly there was the amazingly erudite traveller in the train. I suppose he had gathered from our conversation—Warnie was reading Evelyn's diary—that we were bookish people, but he let several hours pass by before he suddenly chipped in in rather an apologetic manner. I surmise that he lives among people who do not share his tastes, and that it was a relief to him to talk about them. He did not speak with the voice of an educated man, but his reading was curious; Pepys, Evelyn, Burney, Boswell, Macaulay, Trollope, Thackeray, Ruskin, Morris and *The Golden Bough*. He seemed to be some sort of architect or decorator. Now this is the sort of thing I like. To have a literary conversation in the common room at Magdalen is (by comparison) nothing because one remains in the charmed circle of one's own set and caste; there is nothing to refute the accusation of being out of the world, of playing with things that perhaps derive a fictitious value from the chatter of specially formed groups. But to talk over the same things with a man whose aitches are uncertain, in a third class carriage—this restores one's faith in the value of the written word and makes one feel suddenly at home in one's country....

The other interesting thing in our journey was the new scenery produced by the floods. Round about Warwick for miles at a time there was nothing but water between one hedgerow and the next—and then the little hills made into islands—you can imagine what a magnificent view I now have when the (Magdalen) park has been converted into a lake. On a fine day when the sky makes the water blue and the wind fills it with ripples, one might almost take it for an arm of the sea. Of course I'm not forgetting the serious side of the floods....

TO HIS FATHER.

(Undated: postmarked 25 January 1926)

As to the German measles—you will think me affected if I number a small illness among the minor pleasures of Life? The early stages are unpleasant but at least they bring you to a point at which the mere giving up and going to bed is a relief. Then after twenty-four hours the really high temperature and the headache is gone; one is not well enough to get up, but then one is ill enough not to want to get up. Best of all, work is impossible and one can read all day for mere pleasure with a clear conscience. I re-read some of my favourite Jane Austens and read for the first time that jolly, unexacting tale *Quentin Durward*. I even took a chance of going on with my neglected Italian. . . . One returns to a primitive and natural life as regards sleeping and waking. One dozes when the doze comes unsought, and if one lies castle building at night one does not mind because there is no getting up in the morning. But of course all these delights have to be paid for; the first few days back to work when the legs still ache and the hours are long, are an unwelcome shock of earth—and that I think is the really bad part of it. . . .

I have given my first lecture. I suppose my various friends in the English Schools have been telling their pupils to come to it; at any rate it was a pleasant change from talking to empty rooms in Greats. I modestly selected the smallest lecture room in College. As I approached, half wondering whether anyone would turn up, I noticed a crowd of undergraduates coming in to Magdalen, but it was no mock modesty to assume that they were coming to hear someone else. When however I actually reached my own room it was crowded out and I had to sally forth with the audience at my heels to find another. The porter directed me to another one which we have in another building across the street. So we surged over the High in a disorderly mass, suspending the traffic. It was a most exhilarating scene. Of course their coming to the first lecture, the men to see what *it* is like, the girls to see what *I* am like, really means nothing; curiosity is now satisfied—I have been weighed with results unknown—and next week I may have an audience of five or none. Still, it is something to be given a chance. . . .

From his journal.

27 May 1926

Betjeman and Valentin came for O.E. (i.e. tuition in Old English). Betjeman appeared in a pair of eccentric bedroom slippers and said he hoped I didn't mind them as he had a blister. He seemed so pleased with himself that I couldn't help saying that I should mind them very much myself, but that I had no objection to *his* wearing them—a view which I believe surprised him. . . .

TO HIS FATHER.

5 June 1926

A heavy responsibility rests on those who forage through a dead man's correspondence and publish it indiscriminately. In those books of Raleigh's we find as you say, letters 'like a glass of good champagne' side by side with mere squibs thrown off in high spirits, or mere grumbles written when he was liverish. . . . On the whole I must confess that the reading of the letters, much though I enjoyed them, did not raise my opinion of Raleigh . . . there must be some flaw in a man who is always blessing or damning something or other. . . . I have been bothered into the last job I ever expected to do this term; taking a class of girls once a week at one of the women's Colleges. However, I am not engaged to be married yet, and there are always seven of them there together, and the pretty ones are stupid and the interesting ones are ugly, so it is all right. I say this because as a general rule, women marry their tutors. I suppose if a girl is determined to marry and has a man alone once a week to whom she can play the wrapt disciple (most fatal of all poses to male vanity) her task is done. . . .

The best strike story I have heard is about engines. A train (with amateur driver) set out from Paddington for Bristol, first stop Bath. When it reached Bath *half an hour* earlier than normal express time, every single passenger got out of that train and refused to enter it again. Apparently the genius on the engine had just opened the throttle full, said to the stoker, 'carry on', and left the rest to fate. . . .

From his journal.

6 June 1926

As H. and I were coming across to New Building we were overtaken by J. A. who proposed a stroll in the walks. . . . He was very great, telling us about his travels in the Balkans. The best things were, (a) the masterful ladies (English of course) on a Greek steamer who made such a nuisance of themselves that the Captain said, 'Have you no brothers? Why have they not got someone to marry you?' and went on muttering at intervals for the rest of the evening, 'It ought to have been possible to get *someone*!' (b) The Austrian minister at some unhealthy town who took J. A. and his party out for a walk on the railway line, which was the only place level enough to walk on, and beginning to balance himself on the rails, remarked sadly, 'C'est mon seul sport'. (c) The Greek clergyman who asked J. A. and his sister to tea and when they departed, accompanied them back to their hotel repeating, 'You will remember me?' 'Yes, certainly', said J. A. The clergyman repeated his touching request about fifteen times and each time J. A. (tho' somewhat surprised) assured him with increasing warmth that he would never forget him. It was only afterwards that they realized that the reverend gentleman was asking for a tip. . . .

13 June 1926

The chief excitement today was over Henry, Dotty's tortoise, who was discovered about two hundred yards from the gate, working his passage to the London Rd. He was brought back and tethered by a cord across his body, and supplied with lettuce leaves and snails, in which he took no interest. He escaped repeatedly during the day. When I buy a tortoise I shall say I want a quiet one for a lady. . . .

4 July 1926

Beginning to re-read *The Well at the World's End*. I was anxious to see if the old spell still worked. It does—rather too well. This going back to books read at that age is humiliating; one keeps on tracing what are quite big things in one's mental outfit to quite small sources. I wondered how much my feeling for external nature comes out of the brief, convincing little descriptions of mountains and woods in this book.

6 July 1926

After tea I went over the revised proofs of *Dymer* which arrived today, from 1.30 to the end of the whole. I never liked it less. I felt that no mortal could get any notion of what the devil it was all about. I'm afraid this sort of stuff is very hit or miss, yet I think it is my only real line. . . .

10 January 1927

A most extraordinary afternoon. Most of the sky was very pale creamy blue and there were clouds about, of the coldest shade of dark blue I have ever seen. The further hills were exactly the same as the clouds in colour and texture. Then near the sun the sky simply turned white and the sun itself (its outline was invisible) was a patch of absolutely pure white light that looked as if it had no more power of heating than moonlight. . . . I got into a tremendously happy mood. . . .

3 February 1927

Dined in, and sat beside J. A. in Common Room who told me of a lady who had long worried him by coming up at the end of lectures to ask questions; and finally wrote offering him her hand. 'She pretended it was a joke afterwards' he said, shaking his white head, 'but it wasn't. And she wasn't the only one either. A man who lectures to women takes his life in his hand' . . .

8 February 1927

Spent the morning partly on the Edda. . . . An exciting experience when I remember my first passion for things Norse under the initiation of Longfellow at about the age of nine; and its return, much stronger, when I was about 13, when the high priests were M. Arnold, Wagner's music, and the Arthur Rackham *Ring*. It seemed impossible then that I should ever come to read these things in the original. The old authentic thrill came back to me once or twice this morning; the mere names of god and giant catching my eye as I turned the pages of Zeega's dictionary was enough.

9 February 1927

He (Carlyle) told me a lot more about the murderer of Rasputin (Prince Youssepoff) who had been incapable of passing an exam, and had suggested to the Farq. that 'of course he presumed that there would be no difficulty in arranging these things in the case of a person of quality'. Being told that the organization of our exams was inflexibly democratic, he exclaimed, 'But what am I to do? My parents will not let me marry unless I get some sort of certificate or diploma. They will only send me to some other university'. Finally Farq. and Carlyle made him out a parchment very solemnly, a sort of certificate of their own. . . .

10 February 1927

I went on to Corpus. . . . We had an evening of pleasant and desultory tomfoolery, enriched later on by the arrival of Weldon. Someone started the question 'whether God can understand His own necessity'; whereupon Hardie got down St. Thomas's *Summa* and after ferreting in the index pronounced, without any intention of being funny, 'He doesn't understand anything'. This led to great amusement, the best being an imaginary scene of God trying to explain the theory of vicarious punishment to Socrates. We left Hardie at about 10 to 12, and found Corpus in total darkness. Escaped in the end with difficulty.

15 February 1927

Spent the morning reading Gower, a poet I always turn to for pure, tho' not for intense pleasure. It's a rum thing that Morris should have wanted so desperately to be like Chaucer and succeeded in being so exactly like Gower. . . .

After dinner to meet Mrs. Moore and Maureen at the theatre, where the OUDS were doing *Lear*. We decided that we would give up going to them hereafter. It was all that sort of acting which fills one at first with embarrassment and pity, finally with an unreasoning personal hatred of the actors. 'Why should that damned man keep on bellowing at me?' They nearly all shouted hoarsely and inarticulately. . . . All very cheery in spite of our wasted evening. . . .

1 April 1927

I am entertaining the —— Society tonight, drat 'em. They are nothing but a drinking, guffawing cry of barbarians with hardly any taste among them, and I wish I hadn't joined them; but I don't see my way out now. . . . Back to College and had to spend most of the time getting things ready for the sons of Belial. The evening passed off alright I think; Tourneur's *Revenger's Tragedy* was read, a rotten piece of work whose merits, pretty small to begin with, were entirely lost in the continual cackling which greeted every bawdy reference, however tragic. . . . If one spent much time with these swine one would blaspheme against humour itself as being nothing but a kind of shield with which (the) rabble protect themselves from anything which might disturb the muddy puddle inside them. . . .

TO HIS FATHER.

30 March 1927

Here is the President's latest exploit when we met to elect a Proctor. . . . When the election had been made he said that a formal notice had to be sent to the Vice-Chancellor at once, 'so perhaps Mr. Benecke' (Benecke is about 60 years of age) 'you wouldn't mind going round; and then you must ring at the door and hand it to the maid'. As someone said, it only needed the additional injunctions, 'and remember to wipe your feet and take a clean handkerchief' to make it really complete. While I'm on this I must tell you another. We are putting up some new buildings. In the committee which met to discuss this, someone suggested an architect's name, adding by way of explanation, "That's the man who built Liverpool Cathedral'. To which the President at once retorted with an air of closing the matter, 'Oh I don't think we want anything as large as that'. He has at last announced his intention of retiring, so I suppose we shall live in the excitement of an election for the next year. He has certainly had a wonderful run for his money, and tho' a very laughable, is also a very loveable old fellow. He had the ludicrous without the odious side of snobbery. He may have reverenced a Prince or a Duke too much, but never in his life did he despise or snub a poor scholar from a Grammar School. When snobbery consists *only* of the admiring look upward and *not* of the contemptuous look downward, one need not be hard on it. A laugh—no unfriendly laugh—is the worst that it deserves. After all, this kind of snobbery is half of it mere romance. . . .

We live in the most absurd age. I met a girl the other day who had been teaching in an infant school (boys and girls up to the age of six) where these infants are taught the theory of evolution. Or rather the Headmistress's version of it. Simple people like ourselves had an idea that Darwin said that life developed from simple organisms up to the higher plants and animals, finally to the monkey group, and from the monkey group to man. The infants seem to be taught however that 'in the beginning was the Ape', from whom all other life developed, including such dainties as the Brontosaurus and the Iguanadon. Whether the plants were supposed to be descendants of the apes I didn't gather. And then people talk about the credulity of the Middle Ages! Apropos of this, can you tell me who said, 'Before you begin these studies, I should warn you that you need much more *faith* in science than in theology'. It was Huxley or Clifford or one of the nineteenth century scientists I think. Another good remark I read long ago in one of E. Nesbitt's fairy tales—'Grown ups know that children can believe almost anything; that's why they tell you that the earth is round and smooth like an orange when you can see perfectly well for yourself that it's flat and lumpy'. . . .

I dined the other night at an Italian Professor's . . . and sat next to a Frenchwoman who has met Mussolini. She says he is a rhetorician and escapes from questions he doesn't want to answer into a cloud of eloquence. I asked if she thought him a charlatan. She said no: he quite believes all his own gas, like a schoolboy, and is carried away by it himself. It interested me very much as being true to type—Cicero must have been just that sort of man. . . .

TO HIS BROTHER.

26 April 1927

I thought we had mentioned Squire Western's table talk before. . . . I have never been able to share that popular feeling about Western as a fine type of bluff, honest, genial Englishman; he seems to me to be one of the four or five most intolerable characters in fiction (I mean to meet: of course he is excellent in a book). *Tom Jones* goes far to explain why Johnson and his set didn't like the country. I can quite imagine that a countryside of highwaymen and the rural jokes of the period, inhabited by Westerns and Blifils would have led him to 'abstract his mind and think of Tom Thumb'; for one can hardly imagine him knocking them down with folios. At least if he had made the attempt, he would have liked the country even less after it than before it. He would have dismissed Mr. Square as an infidel dog, and I don't feel that he would have got on with Thwackum. Sophia is good. She comes during that lucid interval when good heroines were possible in books written by men, when the restoration tradition by which the heroine must be a whore was dead and the Victorian tradition that she must be a fool had not yet been born.

Now for my own adventures. I was joined at Oxford station by two others and we proceeded together to Goring . . . our fourth joined us at Goring station. . . . We set out N.N.W. . . . on the broad grass track of the Icknield Way, the grass very short and fine and perfectly dry, as it is nearly all the year round in these chalk hills. It was an afternoon of lovely sunshine, with a pleasant light wind and a lark overhead. . . .

That night we slept at East Ilsley. . . . We spent nearly the whole of Wednesday following the Icknield Way along the northern edge of the Downs, overlooking the Wantage valley on our right. Around us and to our left the country had all the same character; close, smooth grass, deliciously springy to the foot; chalk showing through here and there and making the few ploughed places almost cream colour; and, about three to the mile, clumps of fir whose darkness made them stand out very strikingly from the low tones of the ground. The extent of prospect was (or seemed to be) larger than any I have ever seen, even from the highest hills I have been on—just wave after wave of down, and then more of them, for ever. . . . We had tea at Lambourn and slept at Aldbourne.

Thursday opened with discussions. A survey of the maps showed a lamentable discrepancy between the route we wanted to follow and the possible places for lunch. Then emerged the dark and hideous prospect of 'taking' lunch. Perfectly simple, you know. Buy some bread and cheese before we start and have lunch where we like. Makes you independent you know. Drinks? Oh get a few oranges. . . . I of course, who have seen days spoilt like this before, was the head of the opposition. The wrong party won. We stuffed our packs with bread, cheese, butter and oranges. The only thing I look back on with satisfaction was that the butter was not in my pack. Then we set off.

The first mile made us thoroughly aware of the fact that the wind had risen to a gale. The next three miles left no one in any doubt of the fact that when a strong wind blows in your face all day, it parches your throat and chaps your lips without cooling your body. We were now in sight of 'Barberry Castle', a Roman camp, for the sake of seeing which all this folly had started. The exponents of the 'carry your lunch' school had now reached the stage of indulging in a quite unusual degree of praise of the scenery and the pleasures of walking tours. . . . But long before we had reached the top of that disastrous camp they slunk into silence, and only the malcontents (Barfield and myself) felt inclined to talk. In fact we talked quite a lot.

When we reached the top we found ourselves in one of those places where you can neither speak for the hurricane nor open your eyes for the sun. . . . We were silent here. Turning up our collars and pulling our hats hard down on our heads, we couched under a scrannel gorse bush wherever prickles and sheep dung left a space, and produced our scanty and squalid meal. The appearance of the butter faintly cheered us (all of us except the man among whose socks and pyjamas it had travelled), but it was a sight that moved mirth, not appetite. The last straw was the oranges, which proved to be of the tough, acrid, unjuicy type which is useless for thirst and revolting to taste. The midday siesta (that great essential of a day's walking) was out of the question in that abominable camp, and we set off gloomily S.W. . . .

Five o'clock found us descending a slope full of druidical stones . . . into the village of Avebury. Avebury overwhelmed me and put me into that dreamlike state which is sometimes the reward of being very tired. Imagine a green ancient earthwork with four openings to the four points of the compass, almost perfectly circular, the wall of a British city, large enough to contain broad fields and spinneys inside its circuit, and in the middle of them, dwarfed by its context, a modern village. . . . Here we had tea gloriously, in the orchard of an inn; and took off our shoes and ordered a fresh pot and more hot water, lay on our backs and talked Oxford reminiscences and smoked pipes. Then Woff, returning after a moment's absence, said, 'If you are not very keen on *walking* into Marlborough, there's a man here with a milk cart who will take us in'. So we sat among milk cans (which are just the right angle to lean against) and bumped and rattled along the Bath road . . . into Marlborough. . . .

Next day we walked about four miles into Savernake Forest. It is not to be compared with the Forest of Dean, but well worth an hour or so. It is the typically English kind of wood—nearly all big oaks with mossy spaces between them, and deer flitting about in the distance. . . . We lunched admirably in the village of Ocue . . . and shortly after lunch had the best 'easy' I've ever had in a walk, by turning out of a little grassy lane into a wood where the grass grew soft and mossy, and there were solid clumps of primroses the size of dinner plates; not to mention a powdering of wood anemones. We laid ourselves flat on our backs, with our packs for pillows; some rash attempts at conversation were ignored and we spent an hour and a half with half shut eyes, listening to the burring of the wind in the branches, and an occasional early bumble bee. . . .

We lay at Devizes, and next day struck south across the vale of Pewsey. We expected to be bored in this low ground . . . but it turned out a pleasant morning's tramp. . . . Even if it had been dull, who would not make sacrifices to pass through a place called Cuckold's Green (we had passed Shapely Bottom two days before). I myself was for tossing a pot of beer at Cuckold's Green . . . but the other two, being married men, ruled that this was no place to rest a moment longer than we need. . . . In passing, if one had lived in the 17th century, what a horrible fate it would have been to live at Cuckold's Green. 'Your servant Sir. Your wife tells me that you are carrying her to the country in a few days. Pray Sir where do you live?' By the age of forty one would be quite definitely tired of the joke. . . .

No one can describe the delight of coming to a sudden drop and looking down into a rich wooded valley where you see the roofs of the place where you're going to have supper and bed; especially if the sunset lies on the ridge beyond the valley. There is so much mixed in it; the mere physical anticipation, as of a horse nearing his stable, the sense of accomplishment and the feeling of 'one more town', one further away into the country you don't know, and the old, never hackneyed romance of travelling. It always seems to sum up the whole day that is behind you—give it a sort of climax, and then stow it away with the faintly melancholy feeling of things going past. . . . Next day we all returned home by train. . . .

TO HIS BROTHER.

9 July 1927

The Term has been over for some weeks, for which I am not sorry. It produced one public event of good omen—the carrying in Congregation of a Statute limiting the number of wimmen at Oxford. . . . There was fierce opposition of course . . . but the question of the age of the anti-feminists is an interesting one; and the voting (we have no secret franchise) revealed very consolatory facts. First came the very old guard, the octogenarians and the centurions, the full fed patriarchs of Corpus, the last survivors of the days when 'women's rights' were still new fangled crankery. They were against the women. Then came the very-nearly-as-old who date from the palmy days of J. S. Mill, when feminism was the new, exciting, enlightened thing—people representing the progressiveness of the 'eighties. They voted for the women. Then came the young and the post-war who voted *against*. Quite natural when you think it out. The first lot belong to the age of innocence when women had not yet been noticed; the second, to the age when they had been noticed and not yet found out; the third to us. Ignorance, romance, realism. . . .

I have just been reading Smollett's *Roderick Random*. . . . Can you suggest why it is that when you read Boswell, Walpole's letters, or Fanny Burney's diary, you find the 18th century a very delightful period, differing from ours chiefly by a greater formality and 'elegance' of manners, whereas when you turn to the novel (including *Evelina*) you suddenly step into a world of full-blooded, brutal, strident, pull-away-the-chair barbarity? . . . What is the common denominator between this and Johnson's circle? And which is true? Perhaps both are, and one sees what the Doctor meant when he said that the society in a jail was commonly better than at sea. . . .

I have a ludicrous adventure of my own to tell. Mme Balot is the widow of a M. Balot who died recently. She had been temporarily insane once during his lifetime; and tho' there was no serious fear of a relapse, her state of mind after his death . . . led most of her friends to keep an eye on her. Mrs. Moore went to see her pretty regularly. So did the heroine of my story, Mrs. Moreton. She is what is called 'a brave little woman', tho' it is not known what danger she ever had to encounter. She is a spiritualist, she weighs the babies of poor women, her business is universal benevolence. . . .

Well, the other night Mrs. Moore suddenly called me out of the dining room and said, 'Mrs. Moreton is here. She says that Mme Balot twice tried to commit suicide today. She has got a taxi here and wants me to go and see the doctor at the Warneford. We shall have to get a nurse for Mme Balot'. I said I'd come along. . . . I stayed in the taxi while the two ladies went in to see the doctor. . . . They emerged at last with a Nurse Jackson and we started off for the Balots' house. But now the question was what to do? Madame would certainly refuse to have a strange young woman thrust upon her for the night for no apparent reason . . . no one had any authority over her . . . no doctor would certify her as insane on the evidence of a child. Mrs. Moreton said it was all perfectly simple. She would stay hidden in the Balot garden all night. Nurse could be put up in the bungalow of a stranger opposite to Madame's house. . . . If only she could have a *man* with her, she confessed she would feel less nervous about it. I began to wish I'd stayed at home; but in the end of course I had to offer. No one raised the question as to why the Nurse had been prevented from going to bed in her hospital in order to be carried half a mile in a taxi and immediately put to bed in another house totally unconnected with the scene of action, where she could not possibly be of the slightest use. The nurse herself, who was possibly in some doubt as to who the supposed lunatic might be, maintained a stupefied silence. I now suggested as a last line of defence that nothing would be more likely to upset Mme Balot than to find dim figures walking about her garden all night; to which Mrs. Moreton replied brightly that we must keep out of sight and go very quietly. 'We could put our stockings on outside our boots, you know'. We were whispering outside a house just down the street, and at this stage a window opened overhead and someone asked me rather curtly if we wanted anything, and if not would we kindly go away. This restored to me some of the sanity which I was rapidly losing, and I determined that whatever else happened, four o'clock should not find me 'with my stockings over my boots' in someone else's garden for fear the owner might commit suicide, explaining this to a policeman.

I therefore ruled that we must keep our watch in the road, where, if we sat down, we should be hidden from the windows by the paling (and, I added mentally, would be open to arrest for vagabondage, not for burglary). Several neighbours had now turned up—all women, and nearly all vulgar—to revel in the excitement and Mrs. Moreton (while insisting on the absolute necessity of letting no one know) gave each newcomer a full account of the situation. . . . I came home, drank a cup of tea, put on a greatcoat, took some biscuits, smokes, a couple of apples, a rug, a waterproof sheet, and two cushions and returned to the fatal spot. . . . Someone had had the rare good sense to leave some sandwiches and three thermos flasks, and I found the brave little woman actually eating and drinking when I arrived. Hastily deciding that if I was to lie under the obligations of a *man* I would assume his authority, I explained that we would be really hungry later on and authoritatively put a stop to that nonsense. . . .

I settled down. There had been some attempt at moonlight earlier, but it had clouded over and a fine rain began to fall. Mrs. Moreton's feminine and civilian vision of night watches had evidently not included this. She was surprised at it. She was also surprised at its getting really cold; and most surprised of all to find that she was getting really sleepy. . . . If I could have been quit of her society I should have found my watch just tolerable—despite the misfortune of finding my greatcoat pockets stuffed with camphor balls which I flung angrily on the road, and then some hours later forgetting this and trying to eat one of the apples. The taste of camphor is exactly like the smell. . . . However, my story is over now, and when I have added that the crows had been 'tuning up for their unseasonable matins' a full half hour before any other bird squeaked (a fact of natural history which I never knew before) I may dismiss Mrs.-Ruddy-Moreton from my mind. . . .

TO HIS FATHER.

29 July 1927

I am just in the few days' lull between two fits of examining. . . . My labours were rewarded by some good things from the candidates, who are schoolboys under sixteen. . . . In answer to the question, 'Would you have liked Colonel Mannering as a father?' one youth sagely replied that he would. It was true that Mannering was cold, suspicious, autocratic etc. 'but he was very rich and I think he would have made an excellent father'. That boy should be sent to the City at once; he has the single eye. . . .

I have been reading *The Woman in White*, a book of course now practically unknown to anyone under forty. I thought it extremely good of its kind, and not a bad kind. But what spacious days those were! The characters, at least all the wicked ones, flame in jewels and the hero is so poor that in one place he actually had to travel *second class* on the railway. . . . Another curious thing is the elaborate descriptions of male beauty, which I hardly remember to have seen since Elizabethan poetry; or do the 'noble brow', the 'silky beard' and the 'manly beauty' still flourish in fiction I don't happen to have read? Of course only third-rate people write that kind of novel now, whereas Wilkie Collins was clearly a man of genius; and there is a good deal to be said for his point of view (expressed in the preface) that the first business of a novel is to tell a story and that characters etc. come second. . . .

TO HIS BROTHER.

3 September 1927

The only Cornish city I have been to is Truro. The town is an ordinary little market town, much less pleasing than any in the 'homely' counties . . . the cathedral the poorest almost that I have ever seen. . . . The main object of my visit was to get a book, having finished *Martin Chuzzlewit* which I had brought down. And here let me make a digression for a moment to advise you strongly to make one more effort with Dickens and make it *Martin Chuzzlewit*, if only for the account of 19th century America. . . . Of course to enjoy it, or any other Dickens, you must get rid of all idea of realism—as much as in approaching Morris or the music hall. In fact I should say he is the real thing of which the Grand Xmas Panto. is the degeneration and abuse; broadly typical sentiment, only rarely intolerable if taken in a jolly after dinner pantomime mood, and broadly effective 'comics'; only all done by a genius. . . .

But this is all by the way. I had assumed that as Truro was a cathedral city, it must have at least a clerical intelligentsia; and if that, a decent bookshop. It appeared only to have a Smith's and a faded looking place that seemed half a newsagent's. At the door of this I stopped an elderly parson and asked him whether this and Smith's were the only two booksellers. He said they were: then a few moments later came back walking on tiptoe as some parsons do, and buzzed softly in my ear, 'There is an S.P.C.K. depot further down this street'. This almost adds a new character to my world; henceforward among my terms of abuse none shall rank higher than 'he's the sort of man who'd call an S.P.C.K. depot a bookshop'. . . .

I discovered however that my unpromising bookshop had a second-hand room upstairs. . . . I got the poetical works of 'Armstrong, Dyer, and Green'. Armstrong wrote a poem in Miltonic blank verse on 'The Art of Preserving Health' which I have read with huge enjoyment. It is beyond all parody as a specimen of the noble art of making poetry by translating ordinary sentences into Miltonic diction. Thus 'some people can't eat eggs' is rendered,

Some even the generous nutriment detest
Which in the shell, the sleeping embryo rears.

If one eats too much fat,

The irresoluble oil
So gentle late and blandishing, in floods
Of rancid bile o'erflows; what tumults hence
What horrors rise, were nauseous to relate.

I enclose some photos and good wishes from all.

TO HIS BROTHER.

12 December 1927

I have done very little reading outside my work these last months. In Oman's *Dark Ages* I have come up against a thing I had almost forgotten since my school days—the boundless self-assurance of the pure text book. 'The four brothers were all worthy sons of their wicked father—destitute of natural affection, cruel, lustful, and treacherous'—Louis the Pious was 'a man of blameless and virtuous habits'—tho' every other sentence in the chapter makes it clear that he was a four letter man. 'Charles had one lamentable failing—he was too careless of the teachings of Christianity about the relations of the sexes'. It is so nice too, to be told without a hint of doubt who was in the right and who was in the wrong in every controversy, and exactly why everyone did what he did. Yet Oman is quite right; that is the way—I suppose—to write an *introduction* to a subject. . . . I am almost coming to the conclusion that all histories are bad. Whenever one turns from the historian to the writings of the people he deals with, there is always such a difference.

What a wonderful conceit of Thomas Browne's referring to the long-lived antediluvians—'an age when living men might be antiquities'. Query:—*Would* a living man a thousand years old give you the same feeling that an old building does? I think there is a good deal to be said for Alice Meynell's theory that one's idea of antiquity and the standard one measures it by, is derived entirely from one's own life. Certainly 'Balbec and Tadmor' (whoever they may be) could hardly give one a more weird sense of 'ages and ages ago' than some early relic discovered in the drawers of the little end room often does. One has one's own 'dark ages'. But I daresay this is not so for everyone; it may be that you and I have a specially historical sense of our own lives. Are you often struck, when you become sufficiently intimate with other people to know something of their development, how *late* their lives begin, so to speak? . . .

TO HIS BROTHER.

(Undated)

A man who was up with me was the only genuine maker of malapropisms I ever met; but this one I never heard until the other day. It appears that while having tea with the Mugger he conducted a long conversation with the ladies, chiefly re places to stay for one's holidays, under the impression that the word 'salacious' meant 'salubrious'. You can imagine the result. But what you can't imagine is that when the Mugger himself, whose brow had been steadily darkening for some minutes (during which he had heard his daughters told that they wouldn't like Devonshire very much because it wasn't very salacious) finally decided to cut it short and broke in with, 'Well Mr. ——, and how do you like Oxford?' Mr. —— turned to him with imperturbable good humour and said, 'Well sir, it isn't as salacious as I had hoped'. This fellow indulged also—as I well remember—in a kind of complicated misfire of meaning. When arriving with me late somewhere, he observed, panting, 'We might have known that it would take us longer than it did'....

TO HIS FATHER.

25 February 1928

The night before last I exercised for the first time my newly acquired right of dining at Univ.... and it was delightful to revisit the whimsical stateliness of that particular common room. There's no getting away from the fact that we at Magdalen are terribly 'ordinary' beside it. We are just like anyone else; there, every single one of them is a character part that could be found nowhere outside their own walls. I wonder is there some influence abroad now-a-days that prevents the growth of rich, strongly marked personal peculiarities. Are any of our contemporaries 'characters' as Queen Victoria or Dizzy or Carlyle were 'characters'? I am not asking the ordinary question whether we produce smaller or greater men. To be a 'character' in this sense is not the same thing as to 'have character'. For instance I suppose Abraham had 'character' but no one ever thought of calling him 'a character'.... But all this is from the purpose. What I began on was the difficulty of letter-writing. But I fear the fault is in myself, for the born letter writer is quite independent of material. Have you ever read the letters of the poet Cowper? He had nothing—literally nothing—to tell anyone about; private life in a sleepy country town where Evangelical distrust of 'the world' denied him even such miserable society as the place would have afforded. And yet one reads a whole volume of his letters with unfailing interest. How his tooth came loose at dinner, how he made a hutch for a tame hare, what he is doing about his cucumbers—all this he makes one follow as if the fate of empires hung on it....

TO HIS FATHER.

31 March 1928

My studies in the XVIth century—you will remember my idea of a book about Erasmus—have carried me much further back than I anticipated. Indeed it is the curse and the fascination of literary history that there are no real beginnings. Take what point you will for the start of some new chapter in the mind and imaginations of man, and you will invariably find that it has always begun a bit earlier; or rather, it branches so imperceptibly out of something else that you are forced to go back to the something else. The only satisfactory opening for any study is the first chapter of Genesis. . . .

I spend all my mornings in the Bodleian. . . . If only one could smoke and if only there were upholstered chairs, this would be one of the most delightful places in the world. I sit in 'Duke Humphrey's Library', the oldest part, a Fifteenth Century building with a very beautiful wooden painted ceiling above me and a little mullioned window on my left hand through which I look down on the garden of Exeter, where these mornings I see the sudden squalls of wind and rain driving the first blossoms off the fruit trees and snowing the lawn with them. At the bottom of the room the gilt bust of Charles I, presented by Laud, faces the gilt bust of Strafford—poor Strafford. The library itself—I mean the books—is mostly in a labyrinth of cellars under the neighbouring squares. This room however is full of books which stand in little cases at right angles to the wall, so that between each pair there is a kind of little 'box'—in the public-house sense of the word—and in these boxes one sits and reads. By a merciful provision, however many books you send for, they will be left on your chosen table at night for you to resume work next morning; so that one gradually accumulates a pile as comfortably as in one's own room. There is not, as in modern libraries, a forbidding framed notice to shriek 'Silence'; on the contrary the more moderate request, 'Talk little and tread lightly'. There is indeed always a faint murmur going on of semi-whispered conversations in the neighbouring boxes. It disturbs no one. I rather like to hear the hum of the hive. . . .

As you may imagine, one sees many oddities amongst one's fellow readers—people whom I have never met elsewhere and who look as if they were shut up with the other properties every night. Positively the only drawback is that beauty, antiquity and overheating weave a spell very much more suited to dreaming than to working. But I trust in time to become inoculated. (The practice of opening the window in one's box is not, I need hardly say, encouraged.)

There is a religious revival going on amongst our undergraduates . . . run by a Dr. Buchman. He gets a number of young men together (some reports say women too, but I believe not) and they confess their sins to one another. Jolly, ain't it? But what can you do? If you try to suppress it you only make martyrs. . . .

TO HIS BROTHER.

1 April 1928

I have a new 'holiday' period to record, which was almost barren in events. Our father's conversation was singularly poor in those 'anfractuosities' which so delight us. The only item worth remembering was his curious contribution to the problem of venereal disease, to the effect that obviously it must have begun with women and spread thence to men. Being asked why, he replied, 'Sure how could a man have given it to a woman if he hadn't got it from a woman himself?' This is unanswerable. Another illuminating remark was made in answer to some casual remark of mine as to the control of one's imagination—I was talking I think about not letting one's mind brood on fears or grievances. He replied, 'What on earth do you mean by controlling the imagination? One controls one's appetites'. That is the whole psychology of his generation in a nutshell, isn't it? A man sits thinking of whiskey and making 'iron rules' not to drink any, with much contortion of the face and 'Oh Lords' until the inevitable moment when he finds some excellent reason for breaking the iron rule. The idea of a simpler method—that of applying his mind to something else and using a little concentration—would never occur.

The discussion ended (of course) with the infuriating statement that we were not *ad idem* on the connotation of the word control. . . . Apart from these, there is little to record. We had the usual regrets that you were in the army, and the usual astonishment that you didn't appear to be nearly as unhappy as a man of your income ought by all reason to be. We had the usual discussions on theology, drifting off into something else as soon as one had cleared one's ground to begin. His health was tolerable, I thought. . . .

TO HIS FATHER, *with an early reference to what became* The Allegory of Love, *which was published in 1936.*

10 July 1928

I have actually begun the first chapter of my book. This perhaps sounds rather odd since I was working at it all last Vac., but you will understand that in a thing of this sort the collection of the material is three quarters of the battle. Of course like a child who wants to get the painting before he has really finished drawing the outline, I have been itching to do some actual *writing* for a long time. Indeed—you can imagine it as well as I—the most delightful sentences would come into one's head; and now half of them can't be used because, knowing a little more of the subject, I find they aren't true. That's the worst of facts—they do cramp a fellow's style. If I can get it—the first chapter—to the stage of being typed, I shall bring a copy home for your amusement.

I should warn you, by the by, that Erasmus and all that has had to be postponed to a later book. The actual book is about mediaeval love poetry and the mediaeval idea of love, which is a very paradoxical business indeed when you go into it; for on the one hand it is extremely super-sensual and refined, and on the other it is an absolute point of honour that the lady should be someone else's wife, as Dante and Beatrice, Launcelot and Guinevere etc. . . .

I am intending by the way to pay my summer visit in *August* this year instead of at the usual time. This is because the whole of the latter part of the Long (Vacation) will be occupied with the preliminary stages of the Presidential election, specially the informal conversations which matter most. I am particularly anxious to be there, with one or two others, at the early parts and see what is going on....

TO HIS BROTHER.

2 August 1928

I'm glad you like the *Lives of the Poets*. There is no subject on which more nonsense has been talked than the style of Johnson.... I don't know anyone who can settle a thing so well in half a dozen words. I read a good deal of the *Rambler* last term, which is supposed to be more Johnsonian than the *Lives*.... You know that the *Rambler* is a mass of moral platitudes—and infuriates the French critics who say that they haven't come to their time of life to be told that life is short and that wasted time can never be recovered. Johnson, anticipating that kind of objection, simply remarks, 'People more frequently require to be reminded than instructed'. What more is there to say? Or again, 'The natural process of the mind is not from enjoyment to enjoyment but from hope to hope'. That would be a page of whining and snivelling in Thackeray—ah, which of us, dear reader, has his heart's desire, etc., etc. Better still, this on marriage, 'Marriage is not otherwise unhappy than as life is unhappy'. I can't say that would be a whole novel with the moderns, because the whole novel would not get as far as that. The author would make a great fuss about how Pamela got on Alan's nerves ... and would be praised for his fearless criticism of the institution of marriage, without ever getting one glimpse of the fact that he was merely describing the *general* irritatingness of daily life, as it happens in the case of married people....

Earlier in the year I had a delightful week end in a farm house in the Forest of Dean.... I think it is the most glorious *inland* place I know ... almost untouched by trippers, and excellently solitary; almost uncannily so on an all day walk if one gets into the fir districts where birds don't sing, and happens for the moment to be out of sound of a stream (Pat by the way decided at once that the whole forest was a dangerous place, and always kept close to heel). Here and there in the woods you come on a little old farmhouse with a few acres of clearing, surrounded by a hedge and approached by a road so desolate that it is hardly different from the green 'rides' that pierce the wood in every direction. In these 'islands' of farms—in one of which we stayed—there is the most comfortable sense of being tucked away miles deep from the world, of being snugged down in a blanket. We lived in a world of country butter and fresh eggs and boiled fowl, of early hours and hens lazily squawking (*not* crowing, just making that long drawling sound they make). The nights were noisy with the sounds that keep no right thinking man awake—owls, a very good nightingale, and once the barking of a fox. 'A pleasant land of drowsihead it was. . . .'

It sounds astonishing but English poetry is one of the things that you can come to the end of. I don't mean of course that I shall ever have read everything worth reading that was ever said in verse in the English language. But I do mean that there is no longer any chance of discovering a long poem in English which will turn out to be just what I want and which can be added to the *Faerie Queene*, the *Prelude*, *Paradise Lost*, *The Ring and the Book*, the *Earthly Paradise* and a few others—because there aren't any more. I mean, in the case of poems one hasn't read, one knows pretty well what they're like, and knows too that tho' they may be worth reading they will not become part of one's permanent stock. In that sense I may be said to have come to the end of English poetry—as you may be said to have come to the end of a wood, not when you have actually walked every inch of it, but when you have walked about in it enough to know where all the boundaries are and to feel the end near even when you can't see it; when there is no longer any hope (as there was in the first few days) that the next turn of the path might bring you to an unsuspected lake or cave or clearing on the edge of a new valley—when it can no longer conceal anything. . . .

TO HIS FATHER.

(Undated)

They had great fun at the Union last week. Birkenhead came to speak. The first thing that worried him was the private business in which two gentlemen got up and discussed the library list—additions to the library of the Union being naturally a subject which comes up in private business. On this occasion the merits of *Psmith Journalist* by P. G. Wodehouse, *That Ass Psmith* by the same author, and *The Wreck of the Birkenhead* were hotly canvassed. The noble lord was understood to make some observation to those around him in which the word 'schoolboys' figured. Then the debate began. The first speaker produced the good old Wadham story of how Smith and Simon had decided what parties they were to follow in their political careers by the toss of a coin the night before they took Schools. You will hardly believe me when I tell you that Smith jumped up—'Baseless fabrication'—'Silly, stale story'—'hoped that even the home of lost causes had abandoned that chestnut' etc. etc.—and allowed himself to be sidetracked and leg-pulled to such an extent that he never reached his real subject at all. It seems impossible that a man of his experience could fall to such frivolous tactics; unless we accept the accompanying story that he was drunk at the time, or even the subtler explanation that he was *not*. . . .

TO HIS FATHER, *at the time of an election to the Presidency of Magdalen.*

(Undated: November 1928)

Thank heavens our electioneering troubles are nearly over. This day fortnight we shall all be locked into Chapel like so many Cardinals and proceed to make a President, and then good-bye to the endless talk and agreements and disagreements and personalities that I have lived in since term began. A subject of this sort hanging in the air manifests itself chiefly by a plethora of informal meetings which naturally spring up on those few hours and days when the ordinary routine has left one a little freedom. . . .

At the same time I have added to my occupations in other

and I hope more hopeful ways. Two or three of us who are agreed as to what a College should be, have been endeavouring to stimulate the undergraduates into forming some sort of literary society. In any other college the idea that undergraduates should require, or endure, stimulus in that direction from the Dons, would be laughable. But this is a very curious place. All College societies whatsoever were forbidden early in the reign of the late President—an action which was then necessitated by the savagely exclusive clubs of rich dipsomaniacs which really dominated the life of the whole place. This prohibition succeeded in producing decency, but at the cost of all intellectual life. When I came, I found that any Magdalen undergraduate who had interests beyond rowing, drinking, motoring, and fornication, sought his friends outside College, and indeed kept out of the place as much as he could. They certainly seldom discovered one another, and never collaborated so as to resist the prevailing tone. This is what we wish to remedy; but it has to be done with endless delicacy, which means as you know endless waste of time.

First of all we had to make sure that our colleagues would agree to the relaxation of the rule against societies. Then we had to pick our men among the undergraduates very carefully. Luckily I had been endeavouring for a term or two to get a few intelligent men to meet one another in my rooms under the pretext of play-reading or what not, and that gave us a lead. Then we had to try to push these chosen men very gently so that the scheme should not appear too obviously to be managed by the Dons. At present we are at the stage of holding a preparatory meeting 'at which to discuss the foundation of a society' next Monday—so the whole show may yet be a dismal failure. I hope not; for I'm quite sure that this College will never be anything more than a country club for all the idlest 'bloods' of Eton and Charterhouse as long as undergraduates retain the schoolboy's idea that it would be bad form to discuss among themselves the sort of subjects on which they write essays for their Tutors. Ours at present are all absolute babies and terrific men of the world—the two characters I think nearly always go together . . . the cynicism of forty, and the mental crudeness and confusion of fourteen.

I sometimes wonder if this country will kill the Public Schools before they kill it. My experience goes on confirming the ideas about them that were first suggested to me at Malvern many years ago. The best men, the best scholars and (properly understood) the best gentlemen seem now to be wafted up on county scholarships from secondary schools. Except for pure classics (and that only at Winchester, and only for a few boys even there) I really don't know what gifts the Public Schools bestow on their nurslings, beyond the mere surface of good manners; unless contempt for the things of the intellect, extravagance, insolence, and self-sufficiency are to be called gifts. . . .

TO HIS BROTHER.

(Undated: postmarked 13 April 1929)

I am moved to write at this moment by the selfish consideration that I heard last night a thing which you of all people ought to hear—you know how one classifies jokes according to the people one wants to tell them to—and am therefore uneasy until I have unloaded. The other night an undergraduate, presumably drunk, at dinner in the George covered the face of his neighbour with potatoes, his neighbour being a total stranger. Whether this means simply that he flung the contents of the potato dish at him or (as I prefer to think) that he seized him firmly by the short hairs and systematically lathered him with warm mash, my informant could not say. But that is not the point of the story. The point is that, being haled before the Proctors and asked why he had done so, the culprit very gravely and with many expressions of regret, pleaded in so many words, 'I couldn't think of anything else to do'. I am sure you will share my delight at this transference of the outrage from the class of *positive* to that of *negative* faults; as though it proceeds entirely from a failure of the inventive faculty or a mere poverty of the imagination. One ought to be careful of sitting near one of these *unimaginative* men. The novel idea can be worked equally well from either end; whether one thinks of the mohawk bashing your hat over your eyes with the words, 'Sorry old chap, I know it's a bit hackneyed, but I can't think of anything better'—or of some elderly gentleman exclaiming testily, 'Ah what all these young men lack now-a-days is initiative' as he springs into the air from the hindward pressure of a pin. . . .

By the way I thoroughly agree with you about Scott; in fact I think even his most fanatical admirers have 'given up' his heroines (with the exception of Di Vernon and Jeanie Deans) and his love scenes. But then one gives *that* up in all XIX century novels; certainly in Dickens and Thackeray. But when you have ruled that out, what remains is pure delight. Isn't it nice to find a man who knows history almost entirely by tradition? History to Scott means *the stories remembered in the old families*, or sometimes the stories remembered by sects or villages. I should say he was almost the last person in modern Europe who did know it that way; and that, don't you think, is at the back of all his best work? Claverhouse, say, was to Scott, not a character out of Macaulay but the man about whom old Lady so-and-so tells one story and about whom some antediluvian local minister's father told another. Printed and documented history probably kills a lot of this traditional local history and what is left over is put in guide books (when nothing else can be said about an old Church you can always say that Cromwell stabled his horses in it).

Scott was only just in time to catch it still living. This (so historians tell me) has had one unforeseen result, that Scotch history has ever since been more neglected than that of any other civilized country; the tradition, once stamped by Scott's imagination, has so satisfied curiosity that science has hardly ventured to show its head. It's a pity that no one similarly caught the tradition in England—tho' probably there was less to catch.

I suppose the Scotch were a people unusually tenacious of old memories, as for example Mr. Oldbuck. I am not sure that *The Antiquary* is not the best. . . . Nothing militates so much against Scott as his popularity in Scotland. . . . The Scotch have a curious way of rendering wearisome to the outside world whatever they admire; I daresay Burns is quite a good poet—really; if only he could ever escape from the stench of that unmerciful haggis and the lugubrious jollities of Auld Lang Syne. . . . I have just seen what is the trouble about all this Scotchness. When you want to be typically English you pretend to be very hospitable and honest, and hearty. When you want to be typically Irish you try to be very witty and dashing and fanciful. . . . But the typically Scotch attitude consists not in being loud or quiet, or merry or sad, but just in being *Scotch*. . . .

TO HIS FATHER.

(Undated: postmarked 19 May 1929)

I have re-read Pickwick. . . . It won't do. I like the Wellers, father and son, and I like the trial; but Eatanswill and Mrs. Leo Hunter and Bill Stumps, his Mark, seem to me laboured and artificial, and I can't forgive him for showing us poor Jingle in prison and repentance. The whole spirit in which we enjoy a comic rogue depends on leaving out any consideration of the consequences which his character would have in real life; bring that in, and every such character (say Falstaff) become tragic. To invite us to treat Jingle as a comic character and then spring the tragic side on us, is a mere act of bad faith. No doubt that is how Jingle would end in real life. But in real life it would have been our fault if we had originally treated him as a comic character. In the book you are forced to do so and are therefore unjustly punished when the tragedy comes. . . .

TO HIS FATHER.

(Undated: postmarked 17 July 1929)

This week a curious thing has happened. I have had a letter from Malvern stating that 'Malvern College Ltd.' has been wound up and the school has now been put under a Board of Governors, and asking me to allow my name to be put up for election as one of them. As they are to number over a hundred the honour is not so overwhelming as at first appears. In my first heat I composed a very fine letter declining on the ground of my 'limited knowledge of Public School life, and, still more, my imperfect sympathy with the aims and ideals of Public Schools'. This I enjoyed doing; but then alas 'the native hue of resolution was sickled o'er with the pale cast of thought'. I reflected that this would get about and that the great junta of Old Boys and masters of various schools would pass from one to another the word, 'If you have a boy going to Oxford, I shouldn't recommend Magdalen. Lot of queer fish there now. Cranks etc., etc.' So I funked it, tore it up, and wrote an acceptance. I hope I should have been able to hold out against the purely prudential considerations ('funk' is the simpler word) if I had not been supported by the feeling, as soon as I had cooled, that membership of such a huge board would be purely nominal, except for the ring of 'insiders', and that therefore if I refused I should only be making a storm in a teacup. But won't Warnie be tickled? If I remember you and I discussed this situation, purely as a joke, when I was last at home....

TO HIS BROTHER.

29 August 1929

I have just finished the formidable task of reading the whole of the work of Rabelais.... Would I advise you to do the same? I hardly know. He is very long, very incoherent, and very very stercoraceous. But you must base no opinion of him on what you hear from uneducated people who had never read any other comic book written before the reign of Queen Victoria and are therefore so blinded by a few familiar words when they first see them in print that they never go on seeing the drift of a page, much less of a chapter, as a whole. The first surprise is that about a quarter of the book is perfectly serious propaganda in favour of humanist education.... Some of the satire—tho' satire tends always to bore me—is very 'sly', to use a good old word which we moderns have dropped or degraded without finding a better to fill its place....

TO HIS BROTHER.

30 August 1929

Do you know that Macaulay developed his full manner as a schoolboy and wrote letters home from school which read exactly like pages out of the *Essays*? He was talking about the nature of government, the principles of human prosperity, the force of the domestic affections and all that junk at the age of fourteen. He cd. not at that age have *known* anything about them; least of all could he have known enough for the flowing generalizations which he makes. One can see quite clearly that having so early acquired the *talk* he found he could go on quite comfortably for the rest of his life without bothering to notice the things. He was clever enough from the first to produce a readable and convincing slab of claptrap on any subject whether he understood it or not, and hence he never to his dying day discovered that there was such a thing as understanding....

TO OWEN BARFIELD: *written during the last illness of Jack's father.*

9 September 1929

Many thanks for your letter. I am not sure that the distinction between 'intimacy' and 'familiarity' is really very profound. It seems to be largely a matter of accident that you know so little of my previous history. I know more of yours because we met in England: if we had met in Ireland the position would be reversed. Again, we do not much narrate our past lives, but this is because we have so much else to talk about. Any day might have started a topic to which such narrative would have been relevant, and out it would have come. Consider how many bores whose history you know well after a short acquaintance, not because familiarity has in their case replaced intimacy but because they had nothing to say and would not be silent.

I am not saying that there is nothing in the distinction. When the parties are of different sexes it may be more important. I suppose a good Greek was familiar with his wife and intimate with his ἑταίρα. But between men I suspect that intimacy includes familiarity potentially. Now with a woman, of course, no degree of intimacy includes any familiarity at all: for that there must be στόργη or ἔρως or both.

The test really is this. When you have talked to a man about his soul, you will be able, whenever the necessity arises, say, to assist him in using a catheter or nurse him through an attack of dysentery, or help him (if it should so happen) in a domestic problem. This is not so in the case of a woman....

My father and I are physical counterparts: and during these days more than ever I notice his resemblance to me. If I were nursing you I should look forward to your possible death as a loss lifelong and irremediable: but I don't think I should shrink from the knife with the sub-rational sym-pathy (in the etymological sense) that I feel at present.

Having said all this, I must proceed to correct the exaggeration which seems to be inherent in the mere act of writing. Who was it said that disease has its own pleasures of which health knows nothing? I have my good moments to which I look forward, and perhaps, though the whole tone of the picture is lowered, there is as much chiaroscuro as ever. When my patient is settled up for the night I go out and walk in the garden. I enjoy enormously the cool air after the atmosphere of the sickroom. I also enjoy the frogs in the field at the bottom of the garden, and the mountains and the moon. I often get an afternoon walk when things are going well, and my friend Arthur Greeves—the "friend" of It, you know, who mentioned the beech tree in his letter—sees me every day, and often twice a day. Some of my consolations are very childish and may seem brutal. When Arthur and I talk late into the night there is, even now, a magical feeling of successful conspiracy: it is such a breach, not of course of the formal rules but of the immemorial custom of a house where I have hardly ever known freedom. There is pleasure of the same kind in sitting with open windows in rooms where I have suffocated ever since childhood: and in substituting a few biscuits and fruit for the Gargantuan mid-day meal which was hitherto compulsory. I hope this is not so uncharitable as it sounds. I do not suppose I look after him the worse for it.

At any rate, I have never been able to resist the retrogressive influence of this house, which always plunges me back into the pleasures and pains of a boy. That, by the bye, is one of the worst things about my present life. Every room is soaked with the bogeys of childhood—the awful 'rows' with my father, the awful returnings to school; and also with the old pleasures of an unusually ignoble adolescence.

By the way, that is just the point about intimacy *containing* familiarity. If it ever became really relevant to some truth that we were exploring in common, I could and would expand the last sentence into detail; on the other hand, I have not the slightest inclination to do so—i.e., what would be an *end* for familiars is only an instrument for intimates.

TO HIS BROTHER, *after his father's death.*

27 October 1929

What you say in your letter is very much what I am finding myself. I always before condemned as sentimentalists or hypocrites the people whose view of the dead was so different from the view they held of the same people living. Now one finds out that it is a natural process. Of course, on the spot, one's feelings were in some ways different. I think the mere pity for the poor old chap and for the life he had led really surmounted everything else. It was also (in the midst of home surroundings) almost impossible to believe. A dozen times while I was making the funeral arrangements I found myself mentally jotting down some episode or other to tell him; and what simply got me between wind and water was going into Robinson & Cleavers to get a black tie and suddenly realizing, 'You can never put anything down to his account again'.

By the way, a great deal of his jollity and jokes remained until the end. One of the best things he ever said was the day before I left—four days before his death. As I came in, the day nurse said, 'I've just been telling Mr. Lewis that he's exactly like my father'. Papy: 'And how am I like your father?' Nurse, 'Why he's a pessimist'. Papy (after a pause): 'I suppose he has several daughters'.

As time goes on, the thing that emerges is that, whatever else he was, he was a terrific *personality*. You remember 'Johnson is dead. Let us go to the next. There is none. No man can be said to put you in mind of Johnson'. How he filled a room. How hard it was to realize that physically he was not a big man. Our whole world is either direct or indirect testimony to the same fact. . . . The way we enjoyed going to Little Lea, and the way we hated it, and the way we enjoyed hating it; as you say, one can't grasp that *that* is over. And now you could do anything on earth you cared to in the study at midday on a Sunday, and it is beastly. . . .

TO HIS BROTHER.

21 December 1929

One of the pities of the present state of affairs seems to be that it is impossible for either of us to write the other a real letter. I will try to break the spell by giving you some account of my adventures since you last heard from me before the great divide. The chief adventure is the quite new light thrown on Papy by a closer knowledge of his two brothers. One of his failings—his fussily directing manner, 'Have you got your keys?' etc.—takes on a new air when one discovers that in his generation the brothers all habitually treated one another in exactly the same way. On the morning of the funeral Uncle Dick arrived before breakfast and came to Uncle Bill, who was sleeping in the spare room. I drifted in. After a few greetings, it was with a mild shock that I heard Uncle Bill suddenly cut short a remark of Uncle Dick's with the words, 'Now Dick, you'd better go and take off your collar, huh (gesture) and wash yourself and that sort of thing, eh, and have a bit of a shave'. To which his brother, with perfect seriousness, replied, 'Now how had we better handle the thing, eh Jacks?' 'You'd better go to the bathroom first and I'll go downstairs and get a cup of tea. Bill, you'd better lie down (gesture) and cover yourself up and I'll come and tell you. . . .' Uncle Bill (cutting in), 'Well Dick, get along downstairs, huh, and Jacks you go along to the bathroom, wha', and Dick you wait downstairs and Jacks will go and tell you, wouldn't that be best, eh?' . . .

Another light came to me during the visit to the undertakers; the whole scene had such an insane air of diabolical farce that I cannot help recording it. After a man with a dusty face had approached me with the assurance that he had buried my grandfather, my mother, and my uncle, a superior person led us into an inner room and enquired if we wanted a 'suite of coffins'. Before I had recovered from this—and it sounded like the offer of some scaly booking clerk at an hotel in Hell—the brute suddenly jerked out of the wall a series of enormous vertical doors, each one of which when lowered revealed on its inner side a specimen coffin. . . . Clapping one of them like a drum, he remarked, 'That's a coffin I'm always very fond of'—and it was then that the light came. Uncle Bill—and even he came as a relief in such an atmosphere—put an end to this vulgarity by saying in his deepest bass, 'What's been used before, huh? There must be some tradition about the thing. What has the custom been in the family, eh?' And then I suddenly saw what I'd never seen before, that to them family traditions—the square sheet, the two thirty dinner, the gigantic overcoat—were what school and college traditions are, I don't say to me, but to most of our generation. How could it be otherwise in those large Victorian families with the intense vitality, when they had not been to Public Schools and when the family was actually the solidest tradition they experienced? It puts a great many things in a more sympathetic light than I ever saw them in before.

But apart from this, what I carried away from these few days was the feeling that all the other members of the family were only fragments of our own father. . . . In Uncle Bill of course you see simply all the bad points and none of the good; with the additional property of being an outrageous bore, which is the one thing our father never was at any time. His idea of conversation is almost unbelievable. On the evening of the day of his arrival, after dinner, having been supplied with whiskey, he drew up the little wooden-seated study chair to the fire . . . and proceeded to enunciate the following propositions. 'I usually leave town (Glasgow) about quarter to six, huh, and then I get out to Helensburgh about quarter past and walk up to m'house, eh, and then I go upstairs, huh, and wash m'hands and face and that sort of thing (Jacks, I'll have another drop of that whiskey) and put on an old coat, huh, then I come down and have something to drink and a bit of a chat with your Aunt Minnie, huh, and then . . .' Without any exaggeration he kept me up till 1.30 with this drivel. . . .

TO OWEN BARFIELD.

10 June 1930

I have just finished *The Angel in the House*. Amazing poet! How all of a piece it is—how the rivetted metre both exposes and illustrates his almost fanatical love of incarnation. What particularly impressed me was his taking—what one expects to find mentioned only in anti-feminists—the Lilithian desire to be admired, and making it his chief point: the lover as primarily the mechanism by which the woman's beauty apprehends itself. I . . . have at last brought into consciousness the important truth: Venus is a female deity, *not* "because men invented the mythology", but because she *is*. The idea of female beauty is the erotic stimulus for women as well as men . . . i.e., a lascivious man thinks about women's bodies, a lascivious woman thinks about her own. *What* a world we live in! . . .

TO OWEN BARFIELD, *with one of the first clear indications of Jack's impending re-conversion to Christianity.*

(Undated: 1930)

Terrible things are happening to me. The "Spirit" or "Real I" is showing an alarming tendency to become much more personal and is taking the offensive, and behaving just like God. You'd better come on Monday at the latest or I may have entered a monastery.

TO A PUPIL. (*This is the earliest survivor of the innumerable painstaking and courteous letters which Jack wrote constantly to a multitude of pupils and ex-pupils.*)

18 June 1931

Now as to work. If you are staying up over the week-end and could call on me on Saturday morning we could discuss this. If this is impossible, my present advice is this:—

Doing Chaucer and Shakespeare in the same term seems to me a hazardous experiment, unless there is some special reason which I don't know yet. Our usual plan here is to spend a term on Chaucer and his contemporaries. As regards reading for the Vac., my general view is that the Vac. should be given chiefly to reading the actual literary texts, without much attention to problems, getting thoroughly familiar with stories, situation, and style, and so having all the data for *aesthetic* judgement ready; then the term can be kept for more scholarly reading. Thus, if you were doing Chaucer and contemporaries next term, I shd. advise you to read Chaucer himself, Langland (if you can get Skeat's edtn., the selection is not much good), Gower (again Macaulay's big edtn. if possible, not so that you may read every word of the *Confessio* but so that you may select yourself—not forgetting the end which is one of the best bits), Gawain (Tolkien and Gordon's edtn.), Sisam's XIV century prose and verse (all the pieces of any literary significance). If you can borrow Ritson's *Metrical Romance* so much the better.

But perhaps you have read all these before. If so, and if there are other special circumstances, we must try to meet. If Saturday is impossible, ring me up on Friday and I will squeeze in a time somehow or other.

TO HIS BROTHER.

24 October 1931

I hasten to tell you of a stroke of good luck for us both—I now have the 15-volume Jeremy Taylor, in *perfect* condition. . . . My old pupil Griffiths spent the night with me last Monday and told me that Saunders, the bookseller, who is a friend of his, had a copy. . . . On the same visit Griffiths presented me with a poorly bound but otherwise delightful copy (1742) of Law's *An Appeal/To all that doubt, or disbelieve/The Truths of the Gospel/ Whether they be Deists, Arians/Socinians or Nominal Christians.* It bears the bookplate of Lord Rivers. I like it much better than the 'Serious Call', and indeed like it as well as any religious work I have ever read. The *prose* of the *Serious Call* has here been all melted away and the book is saturated with delight and the sense of wonder; one of those rare works which make you say of Christianity, 'Here is the very thing you like in poetry and the romances, but this time it's true'. . . .

I'm glad you liked Browne as far as you had got when your letter was written. Your query, 'Was there anything he didn't love?' hits the nail on the head. It seems to me that his peculiar strength lies in liking everything, *both* in the serious sense (Christian charity and so forth) *and* in the Lambian sense of natural gusto; he is at once sane and whimsical, and sweet and pungent in the same sentence—as indeed Lamb often is. I imagine that I get a sort of double pleasure out of Thomas Browne, one from the author himself and one reflected from Lamb. I always feel Lamb, as it were, reading the book over my shoulder. . . .

Yes, indeed; how many essays have I heard read to me on Descartes' proofs of the existence of God (there are more than one). It was a remark of Harwood's first suggested to me that God might be defined as 'a being who spends His time in having his existence proved and disproved'. The particular one you quote ('I have the idea of a perfect being') seems to me to be valid or invalid according to the meaning you give the words, 'have an idea of'. I used to work it out by the analogy of a machine. If I have the idea of a machine which I, being unmechanical, couldn't have invented on my own, does this prove that I had received the idea from some really mechanical source? e.g. a talk with the real inventor? To which I answer, 'Yes, if you mean a really detailed idea'; but of course there is the other sense in which e.g. a lady novelist 'has an idea' of a new airship invented by her hero—in the sense that she attaches *some* vague meaning to her words which proves nothing of the sort. So that if anyone asks me whether the idea of God in human minds proves His existence, I can only ask, '*What* idea?' Mr. ——'s for instance, clearly not, for it contains nothing whereof his own fear, pride, and malevolence could not easily provide the materials. On the other hand it is arguable that the 'idea of God' in *some* minds, does contain, not a mere abstract definition, but a real imaginative perception of goodness and beauty beyond their own resources; and this not only in minds which already believe in God. It certainly seems to me that the 'vague something' which has been suggested to one's mind as desirable, all one's life, in experiences of nature, music, and poetry, even in such ostensibly irreligious forms as 'The land east of the Sun and West of the Moon' in Morris, and which rouses desires that no finite object even pretends to satisfy, can be argued *not* to be any product of our own minds. Of course I am not suggesting that these vague ideas of something we want and haven't got, which occur in the Pagan period of individuals and of races (hence mythology), are any more than the first and most rudimentary form of 'the idea of God'. . . .

TO HIS BROTHER.

22 November 1931

I am sorry I have not been able to write for some weeks. During the week it is out of the question. My ordinary day is as follows. Called (with tea) 7.15. After bath and shave I usually have time for a dozen paces or so in Addison's Walk (at this time of year my stroll exactly hits the sunrise) before Chapel at 8. 'Dean's Prayers'—which I have before described to you, lasts about a quarter of an hour. I then breakfast in Common Room with the Dean's Prayer party. . . . I have usually left the room at about 8.25, and then saunter, answer notes etc. till 9. From 9 till 1 is all pupils—an unconscionable time for a man to act the gramophone in. At one, Maureen is waiting for me with the car and I am carried home.

Almost every afternoon as I set out hillwards with my spade, this place gives me all the thrill of novelty. The scurry of the waterfowl as you pass the pond, and the rich smell of autumnal litter as you leave the drive and strike into the little path, are always just as good as new. At 4.45 I am usually driven into College again, to be a gramophone for two more hours, 5 till 7. At 7.15 comes dinner. On Tuesday, which is my really shocking day, pupils come to me to read Beowulf at 8.30 and usually stay till about 11, so that when they have gone and when I have glanced round the empty glasses and coffee cups and the chairs in the wrong places, I am glad enough to crawl to bed. . . .

The only exception to this programme (except of course Saturday when I have no pupils after tea) is Monday, when I have no pupils at all. . . . It has become a regular custom that Tolkien should drop in on me of a Monday morning and drink a glass. This is one of the pleasantest spots in the week. Sometimes we talk English School politics; sometimes we criticize one another's poems; other days we drift into theology or 'the state of the nation'; rarely we fly no higher than bawdy or puns. . . .

The weekend before last I went to spend a night at Reading with a man called Hugo Dyson—now that I come to think of it, you heard all about him before you left. . . . You would enjoy Dyson very much, for his special period is the late 17th century; he was much intrigued by your library when he was last in our room. He is a most fastidious bookman . . . but as far from being a dilettante as anyone can be; a burly man, both in mind and body, with the stamp of the war on him, which begins to be a pleasing rarity, at any rate in civilian life. Lest anything should be lacking, he is a Christian and a lover of cats. The Dyson cat is called Mirralls, and is a Viscount. . . .

Tutorial necessities have spurred me into reading another Carlyle, *Past and Present*, which I recommend; specially the central part about Abbot Sampson. Like all Carlyle it gets a little wearisome before the end—as all listening to these *shouting* authors does. But the pungency and humour and frequent sublimity is tip-top. . . . I get rather tired of the endless talk about books 'living by their style'. Jeremy Taylor 'lives by his style in spite of his obsolete theology'; Thomas Browne does the same, in spite of 'the obsolete cast of his mind'; Ruskin and Carlyle do the same in spite of their 'obsolete social and political philosophy'. To read histories of literature, one would suppose that the great authors of the past were a sort of chorus of melodious idiots who said, in beautifully cadenced language, that black was white and that two and two made five. When one turns to the books themselves—well I, at any rate, find nothing obsolete. The silly things the great men say were as silly then as they are now; the wise ones are as wise now as they were then....

I had to set a paper the other day for School Certificate on... Cowper.... How delicious Cowper is—the letters even more than the poetry. Under every disadvantage—presented to me as raw material for a paper, and filling with a job an evening I had hoped to have free—even so he charmed me. He is the very essence of what Arthur calls 'the homely', which is Arthur's favourite genre. All these cucumbers, books, parcels, tea-parties, parish affairs. It is wonderful what he makes of them....

TO HIS BROTHER.

25 December 1931

I also heard at the same party a very interesting piece of literary history from an unexceptionable source—that the hackneyed 'A German officer crossed the Rhine' was being sung at undergraduate blinds in 1912. What do you make of that? Can it date from the Franco-Prussian War? Or is it a German student song made in anticipation of *Der Tag* about 1910? The latter would be an interesting fact for the historian. I never heard the ballad as a whole, but think it is poor—in fact nasty. Bawdy ought to be outrageous and extravagant... must have nothing cruel about it... must not approach anywhere near the pornographic. ... Within these limits I think it is a good and wholesome *genre*; though I can't help feeling sorry that it should be the *only* living folk-art left to us. If our English party had been held in a mediaeval university we should have had, mixed with the bawdy songs, tragical and even devotional pieces, equally authorless and handed on from mouth to mouth in the same way, with the same individual variations....

F. K. really surpassed himself the other day when he said that he objected to the early chapters of St. Luke (the Annunciation particularly) on the ground that they were—*indelicate*. This leaves one gasping. One goes on re-acting against the conventional modern re-action against nineteenth century prudery and then suddenly one is held up by a thing like this. If you turn up the passage in St. Luke the thing becomes even more grotesque. The Middle Ages had a different way with these things. Did I tell you that in one of the Miracle Plays, Joseph is introduced as the typical comic jealous husband, and enters saying, 'This is what comes of marrying a young woman'....

TO HIS BROTHER.

17 January 1932

It is one of the mysteries of history that all languages progress from being very particular to being very general. In the first stage they are bursting with meaning, but very cryptic because they are not general enough to show the common element in different things; e.g. you can talk (and therefore think) about all the different kinds of trees, but not about *trees*.... In their final stage they are admirably clear but one is so far away from real things that they really say nothing.... Compare 'Our Father which art in Heaven' with 'The supreme being transcends space and time'. The first goes to pieces if you begin to apply the literal meaning to it.... The second falls into no such traps. On the other hand the first really *means* something, really represents a concrete experience in the minds of those who use it; the second is mere dexterous playing with counters, and once a man has learnt the rule he can go on that way for two volumes without really using the words to refer to any concrete fact at all....

Most of my recent reading before term has been of a rather simple and boyish kind. I re-read *The People of the Mist*—a tip-top yarn of the sort. If someone would start re-issuing all Rider Haggard at 1/- a volume, I would get them all, as a permanent fall-back for purely recreational reading. Then I read *The Wood beyond the World*—with some regret that this leaves me no more W. Morris prose romances to read.... I wish he had written a hundred of them. I should like to have the knowledge of a new romance always waiting for me the next time I am sick or sorry and want a real treat. . . .

On my long, slow, solitary journey to Cambridge and back, through fields white with frost, I read Pater's *Marius the Epicurean*. This is the best specimen extant of the Epicurean-aesthetic business; which one wrongs by reading it in its inferior practitioners such as George Moore and Oscar Wilde . . . but Pater's position, in the long run, is all nonsense. But it is a very beautiful book. . . . Gad! How it would have bowled one over at eighteen. One would be only just beginning to recover now.

If your idea of reading Descartes holds, begin with the 'Discourse on Method'. . . . But I'm not at all sure that a man so steeped in the 17th century as you would not find his natural starting point in Boethius—I suppose 'Boece' is as common in France at that time as he was in England? . . . How one's range of interest grows. Do you find a sort of double process going on with relation to books—that while the number of subjects one wants to read is increasing, the number of books on each which you find worth reading steadily decreases. Already in your own corner of French history you have reached the point at which you know that most of the books published will be merely rehashes, but in revenge you are reading Vaughan and thinking of reading Taylor. Ten years ago you would have read eight books on your period (getting only what the *one* book behind those eight would have given you) and left Vaughan and Taylor out of account. . . .

TO HIS BROTHER, *who was then in Shanghai, and possibly in danger by reason of the Japanese attack on the Chinese part of that city.*

21 February 1932

I have had your cheering letter of Jan. 14th—'cheering' for giving one some conversation with you, though of course it does not bear at all on the source of anxiety. I must confess . . . to a shudder when I read your proposals about walks in Ulster etc. In fact I have two unpleasantly contrasted pictures in my mind. One features the two of us with packs and sticks, de-training into the sudden stillness of the moors at Parkmore; the other is of you progressing along the Bund to Gt. Western Rd. with an eye cocked skyward just in the old French manner, curse it, and ducking at the old Wh-o-o-o-p Bang! Like Boswell on that perilous crossing in the Hebrides 'I at last took refuge in piety; but was much embarrassed by the various objections which have been raised against the doctrine of special providences'. Unfortunately I have not at hand the work of Dr. Ogden in which Boswell found the difficulty solved.

I suppose the solution lies in pointing out that the efficacy of prayer is, at any rate, no *more* of a problem than the efficacy of *all* human acts. i.e., if you say 'It is useless to pray because Providence already knows what is best and will certainly do it', then why is it not equally useless (and for the same reason) to try to alter the course of events in any way whatever? . . .

TO HIS BROTHER.

20 March 1932

Next to the good news from China, the best thing that has happened to me lately is to have assisted at such a scene in the Magdalen smoking room as rarely falls one's way. That perfectly ape-faced man whom I have probably pointed out to you was seated on the padded fender with his back to the fire, bending down to read a paper, and thus leaving a tunnel-shaped aperture between his collar and the nape of his neck. A few yards in front of him stood M. Let M. now light a cigarette and wave the match to and fro in the air to extinguish it. And let the match be either not wholly extinguished or so recently extinguished that no fall in the temperature of the wood has occurred. Let M. then fling the match towards the fire in such a way that it enters the aperture between ape-face's neck and his collar with the most unerring accuracy. For a space of time which must have been infinitesimal but which seemed long to us as we watched in the perfect silence which this very interesting experiment so naturally demanded, ape-face, alone ignorant of his fate, continued absorbed in the football results. His body then rose in a vertical line from the fender, without apparent muscular effort, as though propelled by a powerful spring under his bottom. Re-alighting on his feet, he betook himself to a rapid movement of the hands with the apparent intention of applying them to every part of his back and buttocks in the quickest possible succession; accompanying the exercise with a distention of the cheeks and a blowing noise. After which exclaiming (to me) in a heightened voice, 'It isn't so bloody funny', he darted from the room. The learned Dr. Hope . . . who alone had watched the experiment with perfect gravity, at this stage remarked placidly to the company in general, 'Well, well, the match will have gone out by now', and returned to his periodical. . . . But the luck of it! How many shots would a man have taken before he succeeded in throwing a match into that tiny aperture if he had been trying?

You asked Mrs. Moore in a recent letter about this Crashaw man. . . . I had to go for a walk with him. . . . It seemed good to him to take a bus to the station and start our walk along a sort of scrubby path between a factory and a greasy strip of water. . . . He is a ladylike little man of about fifty, and is to a T that 'sensible, well-informed man' with whom Lamb dreaded to be left alone. . . . I blundered at once by referring to the water as a canal. 'Oh, could it be possible that I didn't know it was the Thames? Perhaps I was not a walker?' I foolishly said that I was. He gave me an account of his favourite walks, with a liberal use of the word 'picturesque'. He then called my attention to the fact that the river was unusually low . . . and would like to know how I explained that? I scored a complete Plough, and was told how *he* explained it. By this time we were out on Port Meadow, and a wide prospect opened before him. A number of hills and Church spires required to be identified, together with their 'picturesque', mineral, or chronological details. A good many problems arose, and again I did very badly. As his map, though constantly brought out, was a geological one, it did not help us much. A conversation on weather followed, and seemed to offer an escape from unmitigated fact. The escape however was quite illusory and my claim to be rather fond of all sorts of weather was received with the stunning information that psychologists detected the same trait in children and lunatics. Anxious to turn my attention from this unpleasing fact, he begged my opinion of various changes which had recently been made in the river;

indeed every single lock, bridge, and style has apparently been radically altered in the last few months. As I had never seen *any* of the places before ('But I thought you said you were a walker . . ?') this bowled me middle stump again. The removal of a weir gave us particular trouble. He could not conceive how it had been done. What did I think? And then, just as I was recovering from this fresh disgrace and hoping that the infernal weir was done with, I found that the problem of *how* it had been removed was being raised only as the preliminary to the still more intricate problem of *why* it had been removed. . . . For a mile or so after the weir we got along famously, for Crashaw began, 'I was once passing this very spot—or, no let me see—perhaps it was a little further on—no. It was exactly here—I remember that very tree—when a very remarkable experience, really remarkable in a small way, happened to me'. The experience, remarkable in a small way, with the aid of a judicious question or two on my part, was bidding fair to last out the length of the walk, when we had the horrible misfortune of passing a paper-mill. . . . Not only a paper-mill, but *the* paper-mill of the Clarendon Press. 'Of course I had been over it? No? Really etc.' (The great attraction was that you could get an electric shock).

But I must stop my account of this deplorable walk somewhere. It was the same all through—sheer information. Time after time I attempted to get away from the torrent of isolated, particular facts; but anything tending to opinion, a discussion, to fancy, to ideas, even to putting some of his infernal facts together and making something out of them—anything of that sort was received in blank silence. Once, while he was telling me the legendary foundation of a church, I had a faint hope that we might get into history; but it turned out that his knowledge was derived from an Edwardian Oxford *pageant*. . . .

TO HIS BROTHER.

8 April 1932

I wonder can you imagine how reassuring your bit about Spenser is to me who spend my time trying to get unwilling hobble-de-hoys to read poetry at all? One begins to wonder whether literature is not, after all, a failure. Then comes your account of the *Faerie Queene* on your office table, and one remembers that all the professed 'students of literature' don't matter a rap, and that the whole thing goes on, unconcerned by the fluctuations of the kind of 'taste' that gets itself printed, living from generation to generation in the minds of the few disinterested people who sit down alone and read what they like and find that it turns out to be just the things that everyone has liked since they were written. I agree with all you say about it, except about the distinctions of character. The next time I dip into it I shall keep my weather eye on them. . . .

By the way I most fully agree with you about 'the lips being invited to share the banquet' in poetry, and always 'mouth' it while I read. . . . I look upon this 'mouthing' as an infallible mark of the man who really likes poetry. Depend upon it, the man who reads verses in any other way is after 'noble thoughts' or 'philosophy' (in the revolting sense given to that word by Browning societies and Aunt Lily), or social history or something of the kind, not poetry.

To go back to Spenser—the battles *are* a bore. . . .

The whole puzzle about Christianity in non-European countries is very difficult. . . . Sometimes, relying on Christ's remark, 'other sheep have I that are not of this fold' I have played with the idea that Christianity was never intended for Asia—even that Buddha is the form in which Christ appears to the Eastern mind. But I don't think this will really work. When I have ruled out all my prejudices I still can't help thinking that the Christian world is (partially) saved in a sense in which the East is not. We may be hypocrites, but there is a sort of unashamed and *reigning* iniquity of temple prostitution and infanticide and torture and political corruption and obscene imagination in the East, which really does suggest that they are off the rails—that some necessary part of the human machine, restored to us, is still missing with them. . . . For some reason which we cannot find out, they are still living in the B.C. period and it is apparently not intended that they should yet emerge from it. . . .

TO HIS BROTHER. (*'Bultitude' is a bear.*)

14 June 1932

I have just read your letter of May 15th, but not as you suppose, in College. 'Schools' has arrived and I am invigilating and although your letter arrived before lunch I deliberately brought it here unopened so that the reading of it might occupy at least part of the arid waste of talkless, smoke-less, exercise-less time between 2 p.m. and 5 p.m. Theoretically, of course, there ought to be no greater blessing than three hours absolutely safe from interruption and free for reading; but somehow or other—everyone has made the same discovery—reading is quite impossible in the Schools. There is a sort of atmosphere at once restless and soporific which always ends in that stage which (for me) is a signal to stop reading—the stage I mean at which you blink and ask yourself, 'Now what *was* the last page about?' . . .

I have read, or rather re-read one novel, *Pendennis*. How pleased our father would have been—why hadn't I the grace to read it a few years ago? Why I re-read it now I don't quite know—I suppose some vague idea that it was time I gave Thackeray another trial. The experiment, on the whole, has been a failure. I can just see, mind you, why they use words like 'great' and 'genius' in talking of him which we don't use of Trollope. There are indications or breakings in, all the time, of something beyond Trollope's range. The scenery for one thing (though to be sure there is only one scene in Thackeray—always summer-evening, English-garden, rooks-cawing) has a sort of depth (I mean in the painting sense) wh. Trollope hasn't got. Still more, there are sudden 'depths' in a very different sense in Thackeray. There is one v. subordinate scene in *Pendennis* where you meet the Marquis of Steyne and a few of his led captains and pimps in a box at a theatre. It only lasts for a page or so—but the sort of rank, salt, urinous stench from the nether pit nearly knocks you down and clearly has a kind of power that is quite out of Trollope's range. I don't think these bits really improve Thackeray's books; they do, I suppose, indicate whatever we mean by 'genius'. And if you are the kind of reader who values genius you rate Thackeray highly.

My own secret is—let rude ears be absent—that to tell you the truth, brother, *I don't like genius.* I like enormously some *things* that only genius can do; such as *Paradise Lost* and *The Divine Comedy*. But it is the results I like. What I don't care twopence about is the sense (apparently dear to so many) of being in the hands of 'a great man'—you know, his dazzling personality, his lightening energy, the strange force of his mind—and all that. So that I quite definitely prefer Trollope—or rather this re-reading of *Pen.* confirms my long-standing preference. No doubt Thackeray was a genius; but Trollope wrote the better books. All the old things I objected to in Thackeray I object to still. Do you remember saying in one of your letters of Thomas Browne, 'Was there anything he didn't love?' One can ask just the opposite of Thackeray. He is wrongly accused of making his virtuous women too virtuous; the truth is that he does not make them virtuous enough. If he makes a character what he calls 'good' he always gets his own back by making her (it's always a female character) a bigot and a blockhead. Do you think, Sir, pray, that there are many slum parishes which could not produce half a dozen women quite as chaste and affectionate as Helen Pendennis, and ten times more charitable and sensible? . . . Still, the Major deserves his place in our memory. So does Foker—surely the most *balanced* picture of the kindly, vulgar young fop that there is. I'm not sure about Costigan. There's a good deal too much of Thackeray's habit of laughing at things like poverty and mispronunciation in the Costigan parts. Then of course there is the 'style'. Who the deuce wd. begin talking about the style in a novel till all else was given up?

I have had another visit to Whipsnade. . . . Bultitude was still in his old place. . . . Wallaby Wood, owing to the different season, was improved by masses of bluebells; the graceful, fawn-like creatures hopping out of one pool of sunshine into another over English wildflowers—and so much tamer now than when you saw them that it is really no difficulty to stroke them—and

English wildbirds singing deafeningly all round, came nearer to one's idea of the world before the Fall than anything I ever hoped to see. . . .

TO OWEN BARFIELD.

(Undated: 1933)

Since I have begun to pray, I find my extreme view of personality changing. My own empirical self is becoming more important, and this is exactly the opposite of self-love. You don't teach a seed how to die into treehood by throwing it into the fire: and it has to become a good seed before it's worth burying . . .

TO SISTER MADELEVA, C.S.C., *of Notre Dame, Indiana.* (*This letter reveals something of the lines of thinking and research that led to the Oxford* Prolegomena *lectures and ultimately to* The Discarded Image.)

7 June 1934

In answer to your first question, there are probably such printed bibliographies as you mention, but I have no knowledge of them.

The history of my lecture is this. After having worked for some years on my own subject (wh. is the medieval allegory) I found that I had accumulated a certain amount of general in-information which, tho' far from being very recondite, was more than the ordinary student in the school could gather for himself. I then conceived the idea of my 'prolegomena'. There were however several gaps in the general knowledge which I had accidentally got. To fill these up I adopted the simple method of going through Skeat's notes on Chaucer and Langland, and other similar things, and following these up to their sources when they touched on matters which seemed to me important. This led me sometimes to books I already knew, often to new ones. This process explains why I inevitably appear more learned than I am, e.g. my quotations from Vincent of Beauvais don't mean I turned from a long reading of Vincent to illustrate Chaucer, but that I turned from Chaucer to find explanations in Vincent. In fine, the process is inductive for the most part of my lecture: tho' on allegory, courtly love, and (sometimes) on philosophy, it is deductive—i.e. I *start* from the authors I quote. I elaborate this point because, if you are thinking of doing the same kind of thing (i.e. telling people what they ought to know as the *prius* of a study of medieval vernacular poetry) I think you would be wise to work in the same way—starting *from* the texts you want to explain. You will soon find of course that you are working the other way at the same time, that you can correct current explanations, or see things to explain where the ordinary editors see nothing. I suppose I need not remind you to cultivate the wisdom of the serpent; there will be misquotations and misunderstood quotations in the best books, and you must always hunt up all quotations for yourself and find what they are really like *in situ*.

But, of course, I do not know what it is your purpose to do. I have therefore mentioned all the more imporant 'sources' in my notebook without any attempt at selection. You will see at once that this is the bibliography of a man who was following a particular subject (the Love-allegory) and this doubtless renders the list much less useful to you, who are hardly likely to be after the same quarry. In the second part, texts, I have been more selective, and have omitted a certain amount of low or lowish Latin love poetry which is useful only for my own special purpose. You will observe that I begin with classical authors. This is a point I would press on anyone dealing with the Middle Ages, that the first essential is to read the relevant classics over and over: the key to everything—allegory, courtly love, etc.—is there. After that the two things to know really well are the *Divine Comedy* and the *Romance of the Rose*. The student who has really digested these (I don't claim to be such a person myself!) with good commentaries, and who also knows the Classics and the Bible (including the *apocryphal* New Testament) has the game in his hands and can defeat over and over again those who have simply burrowed in obscure parts of the actual middle ages.

Of scholastic philosophy and theology you probably know much more than I do. If by any chance you don't, stick to Gilson as a guide and beware of the people who are at present running what they call 'neo-scholasticism' as a fad. Of periodicals you will find *Romania*, *Speculum*, and *Medium Aevum* useful. Remember (this has been all-important to me) that what you want to know about the Middle Ages will often not be in a book on the Middle Ages, but in the early chapters of some history of general philosophy or science. The accounts of your period in such books will, of course, usually be patronizing and ill-informed, but it will mention dates and authors whom you can follow up and thus put you in the way of writing a *true* account for yourself.

If there is any way in which I can assist you, or if you would care to call and discuss anything with me, do not hesitate to let me know.

P.S. I shd. warn you that I am very bad at German and this has doubtless influenced my choice of reading.

I suppose you will have access to a complete Aristotle wherever you are working? He is often useful.

TO MRS. JOAN BENNETT (*of Cambridge*).

13 January 1937

A foul copy of an essay (which now that I re-read it doesn't seem as good as I had hoped) is a poor return for the delightful, the champagny holiday you gave me. But you asked for it and here it is.

What splendid talk goes on in your house!—and what a wonderful thing . . . your English Faculty is. If only we and you could combine into a single teaching body (leaving out your freaks and our nonentities) we could make 'English' into an education that would not have to fear any rivalries. In the meantime we have lots to exchange. I am *sure* you practise more 'judgement'; I suspect we have more 'blood'. What we want is to be well commingled.

The Lucas book proves disappointing as you go on. His

attack on Richards for splitting up poetic effects which we receive as a unity, is silly; that is what analysis *means* and R. never suggested that the products of analysis were the same as the living unity. Again, he doesn't seem to see that Richards is on his side in bringing poetry to an ethical test in the long run; and his own ethical standard is so half-hearted—he's so afraid of being thought a moralist that he tries to blunt it by gas about 'health' and 'survival'. As if survival can have any value apart from the prior value of what survives. To me especially it is an annoying book; he attacks *my* enemies in the wrong way . . . and a good deal of mere 'superiority' too. . . .

TO A FORMER PUPIL.

8 March 1937

I haven't yet got Grierson's new book, *Milton and Wordsworth*, but I'm going to; it ought to kill two of your birds with one stone. Have you read F. L. Lucas' *Decline and Fall of the Romantic Ideal*? Hideously over-written in parts, but well worth reading; he has grasped what seems a hard idea to modern minds, that a certain degree of a thing might be good and a further degree of the same thing bad. Elementary you will say—yet a realization of it would have forbidden the writing of many books. These are new. A few years old—but you may have read it—is E. K. Chambers' *Sir Thomas Wyatt and other studies*. Some of the essays are medieval, but most of it is 16th century. I can't think of anything much on 'general tendencies of the 17th century', since one you almost certainly read when you were up, Grierson's *Cross currents of XVIIth c. Litt*, very good indeed. By the bye a *festschrift* to Grierson shortly appearing (Tillyard, Nichol Smith, Joan Bennett, and myself are among the contributors) might contain something of what you want. The book on the 17th century by Willey (I have forgotten the title) is more on the thought background than the poets, rather doing for that century what my Prolegomena tried to do for the middle ages. I don't know of anything general on the 18th century. Sherburn's *Early Life of Pope*, tho' good, is hardly what you want. . . .

TO OWEN BARFIELD.

2 September 1937

"Curiously comfortless stuff in the background" is the criticism of a sensible man just emerging from the popular errors about Morris. Not so curiously, nor quite in the background—that particular *discomfort* is the main theme of all his best work, the thing he was born to say. The formula is: "Retiring to what seems an ideal world, to find yourself all the more face to face with greavest reality, without ever drawing a pessimistic conclusion, but fully maintaining that heroic action in—or amelioration of—a temporal life is an absolute duty, though the disease of temporality is incurable".

Not quite what you expected, but just what the essential Morris is. "Defeat and victory are the same, in the sense that victory will open your eyes only to a deeper defeat: so fight on." In fact, he is the final statement of *good* Paganism: a faithful account of what things are and always must be to the *natural* man. Cf. what are in comparison the ravings of Hardy on the one hand and optimistic Communists on t'other. . . .

TO MRS. JOAN BENNETT.

(Undated)

I also have been having 'flu or you should have heard from me sooner. I enclose the article; pray make whatever use you please of it. . . . It is a question (for your sake and that of the *Festschrift*, not mine) whether a general pro-Donne paper called *Donne and his critics*—a glance at Dryden and Johnson and then some contemporaries including me—wouldn't be better than a direct answer. C. S. L. as professional controversialist and itinerant prize-fighter is, I suspect, becoming already rather a bore to our small public, and might in that way infect you. Also, if you really refute me, you raise for the editor the awkward question, 'Then why print the other article?' However, do just as you like . . . and good luck with it whatever you do.

I've had a grand week in bed—*Northanger Abbey*, *The*

Moonstone, *The Vision of Judgement*, *Modern Painters* (Vol. 3), *Our Mutual Friend*, and *The Egoist*. Of the latter I decided this time that it's a rare instance of the conception being so good that even the fantastic faults can't kill it. There's a good deal of the ass about Meredith—that dreadful first chapter—Carlyle in icing sugar. And isn't the supposedly witty conversation much poorer than much we have heard in real life? Mrs. Mountstuart is a greater bore than Miss Bates—only he didn't mean her to be. The Byron was not so good as I remembered; the Ruskin, despite much nonsense, glorious.

TO A LADY.

(Undated)

Of course Shaw is not a scientist and the attack is not on science as such. But there is a sort of creed which might be called 'scientific humanism', tho' many of its votaries know very little science (just as some people go to Church who know very little theology), and which *is* shared by people so different as Haldane, Shaw, Wells, and Olaf Stapleton. . . . cf. Shaw's Lilith's 'Beyond' with Haldane p. 309. 'It is possible that under the conditions of life on the outer planets the human brain may alter in such a way as to open up possibilities inconceivable to our own minds'. (On p. 303 one of these alterations, the elimination of pity, had already occurred.) All tarred with the same brush in fact. . . .

TO OWEN BARFIELD.

10 June 1938

Think not the doom of man reversed for thee. Apropos of Johnson, isn't this good, from the *Rambler*, from a man who decided not to marry a blue-stocking on finding her an atheist and a determinist. "It was not difficult to discover the danger of committing myself forever to one who might at any time mistake the dictates of passion, or the calls of appetite, for the decree of fate; or consider cuckoldom as necessary to the general system, as a link in the everlasting chain of successive causes."

And, in another way, isn't this splendid—"Whenever, after the shortest relaxation of vigilance, reason and caution return to their charge, they find hope again in possession."

They keep sheep in Magdalen grove now, and I hear the fleecy care bleating all day long: I am shocked to find that none of my pupils, though they are all acquainted with pastoral poetry, regards them as anything but a nuisance: and one of my colleagues has been heard to ask why sheep have their wool cut off. (Fact.)

It frightens me, almost. And so it did the other night, when I heard two undergrads. giving a list of pleasures which were (a) Nazi, (b) leading to homosexuality. They were: feeling the wind in your hair, walking with bare feet on the grass, and bathing in the rain. Think it over: it gets worse the longer you look at it.

More cheering is the true report from Cambridge of a conversation: A.: "What is this *Ablaut* that X keeps talking about in his lectures?" B.: "Oh, don't you know, he was in love with Eloise."

TO OWEN BARFIELD, *at the time of Munich.*

12 September 1938

What awful quantities of this sort of thing seem necessary to break us in, or, more correctly, to break us off. One thinks one has made some progress towards detachment, some *μελετὴ θανάτου*, and begun to realise, and to acquiesce in, the rightly precarious hold we have on all our natural loves, interests, and comforts: then when they are really shaken, at the very first breath of that wind, it turns out to have been all a sham, a field-day, blank cartridges.

This is how I was thinking last night about the war danger. I had so often told myself that my friends and books and even brains were not given me to keep: that I must teach myself at bottom to care for something else more (and also of course to care for them more, but in a different way), and I was horrified to find how *cold* the idea of really losing them struck.

An awful symptom is that part of oneself still regards troubles as "interruptions"—as if (ludicrous idea) the happy bustle of our personal interests was our real ἔργον, instead of the opposite. I did in the end see (I dare not say 'feel') that since nothing but these forcible shakings will cure us of our worldliness, we might have at bottom reason to be thankful for them. We *force* God to surgical treatment: we won't (mentally) diet. . . .

Of course, our whole joint world may be blown up before the end of the week. I can't feel in my bones that it will, but my bones know damn-all about it. If we are separated, God bless you, and thanks for a hundred good things I owe to you, more than I can count or weigh. In some ways we've had a corking time these twenty years.

Be thankful you have nothing to reproach yourself about in your relations with your father (I had lots) and that it is not some worse disease. The horror of a stroke must be felt almost entirely by the spectators. . . .

TO OWEN BARFIELD, *who was proposing a visit.*

8 February 1939

You will be able to hear Tillyard and me finishing our controversy *viva voce*. . . . No doubt I shall be defeated. . . .

I don't know if Plato *did* write the *Phaedo*: the canon of these ancient writers, under the surface, is still quite chaotic. It is also a very corrupt text. Bring it along by all means, but don't pitch your hopes too high. We are both getting so rusty that we shall make very little of it—and my distrust of all lexicons and translations is increasing. Also of Plato—and of the human mind.

I suppose for the sake of the others we must do something about arranging a walk. These maps are so unreliable by now that it is rather a farce—but still "Try, lad, try! no harm in trying". Of course hardly any districts in England are unspoiled enough to make walking worth while: and with two new members—I have very little doubt it will be a ghastly failure.

I haven't seen Charles Williams' play: it is not likely to be at all good. As for *Orpheus*—again, it's no harm trying. If you can't write it, console yourself by reflecting that if you did you would have been very unlikely to get a publisher. I am more and more convinced that there is no future for poetry.

Nearly everybody has been ill here: I try to prevent them all croaking and grumbling, but it is hard being the only optimist.

Let me know which week-end: whichever you choose, something will doubtless prevent it. I hear the income-tax is going up again. The weather is bad and looks like getting worse. I suppose war is certain now. . . .

P.S. Even my braces are in a frightful condition. "Damn braces", said Blake.

TO OWEN BARFIELD.

(Undated)

You could hardly expect the man in the *T.L.S.* to know the esoteric doctrine of myths.

By the bye, we now need a new word for the "science of the nature of myths", since "mythology" has been appropriated for the myths themselves. Would "mythonomy" do? I am quite serious. If your views are not a complete error, this subject will become more important; and it's worth while trying to get a good word before they invent a beastly one. "Mytho-lógic" (noun) wouldn't be bad, but people would read it as an adjective. I have also thought of "mythopoeics" (cf. "metaphysics"), but that leads to "a mythopoeician", which is frightful; whereas "a mythonomer" (better still "The Mythonomer Royal") is nice. Or shall we just invent a new word—like "gas". (Nay, sir, I meant nothing.)

I am writing a great new poem—also a mnemonic rime on English sound changes in octosyllabic verse:

> (Thus Æ to Ē they soon were fetchin',
> Cf. such forms as ÞÆC and ÞECCEAN.)

which will be about as long as the *Cursor Mundi*, and great fun.

P.S. Would "Mythologics" do?

TO MRS. JOAN BENNETT.

5 April 1939

I'm sorry about the Athanasian Creed—the passage illustrates how important it is in writing to say what you mean and not to say anything you don't mean. As the context suggests, I was thinking purely of the Trinitarian doctrine and had quite forgotten the damnatory clauses. There are however several palliatives. Residence in Limbo I am told is compatible with 'perishing everlastingly' and you'll find it quite jolly, for whereas Heaven is an acquired taste, Limbo is a place of 'perfect *natural* happiness'. In fact you may be able to realize your wish 'of attending with one's whole mind to the history of the human spirit'. There are grand libraries in Limbo, endless discussions, and no colds. There will be a faint melancholy because you'll all know that you have missed the bus, but that will provide a subject for poetry. The scenery is pleasant though tame. The climate endless autumn.

Seriously, I don't pretend to have any information on the fate of the virtuous unbeliever. I don't suppose this question provided the solitary exception to the principle that actions on a false hypothesis lead to some less satisfactory result than actions on a true. That's as far as I would go—beyond feeling that the believer is playing for higher stakes and incurring danger of something really nasty. . . .

TO DOM BEDE GRIFFITHS, O.S.B. (*an ex-pupil*).

8 May 1939

It was nice to hear from you again. I think I said before that I have no contribution to make about re-union. It was never more needed. A united Christendom should be the answer to the new Paganism. But how reconciliation of the Churches as opposed to conversions of individuals from one church to another is to come about, I confess I cannot see. I am inclined to think that the immediate task is vigorous co-operation on the basis of what even now is common—combined of course with full admission of the differences. An *experienced* unity on some things might then prove the prelude to a confessional unity on all things. Nothing would give such strong support to the Papal claims as the spectacle of a Pope actually functioning as the head of Christendom. But it is not, I feel sure, my vocation to discuss reunion.

Yes, I like George Eliot. *Romola* is a most purgative work on the *facilis descensus* because the final state of the character is so different from his original state and yet all the transitions are so dreadfully natural. Mind you, I think George Eliot *labours* her morality a bit; it has something of the ungraceful ponderousness of all heathen ethics. (I recently read all Seneca's epistles and think I like the Stoics better than George Eliot.) The best of all her books as far as I have read is *Middlemarch*. It shows such an extraordinary understanding of different kinds of life—different classes, ages, and sexes. Her humour is nearly always admirable. I thought we had talked of Patmore. I think him really great within his own limited sphere. To be sure he pushes the parallel between Divine and human love as far as it can sanely or decently go, and at times perhaps a little further. One can imagine his work being most pernicious to a devout person who read it at the wrong age. But a superb poet. Do you remember the comparison of the naturally virtuous person who receives grace at Conversion to a man walking along and suddenly hearing a band playing and then, 'his step unchanged, he steps in time'? Or on the poignancy of spring, 'With it the blackbird breaks the young day's heart'. Or the lightening during a storm at sea which reveals 'The deeps standing about in stony heaps'. That is sheer genius. And the *tightness* (if you know what I mean) of all his work. The prose one (*Rod, Root and Flower*) contains much you might like.

No. I haven't joined the Territorials, I am too old. It wd. be hypocrisy to say that I regret this. My memories of the last war haunted my dreams for years. Military service, to be plain, includes the threat of every *temporal* evil; pain and death which is what we fear from sickness; isolation from those we love which is what we fear from exile: toil under arbitary masters, injustice, humiliation, which is what we fear from slavery: hunger, thirst and exposure wh. is what we fear from poverty. I'm not a pacifist. If it's got to be it's got to be. But the flesh is weak and selfish and I think death would be much better than to live through another war. Thank God he has not allowed my *faith* to be greatly tempted by the present horrors. I do not doubt that whatever misery He permits will be for our ultimate good unless by rebellious will we convert it to evil. But I get no further than Gethsemane: and am daily thankful that that scene of all others in Our Lord's life did not go unrecorded. But what state of affairs in this world can we view with satisfaction? If we are unhappy, then we are unhappy. If we are happy, then we remember that the crown is not promised without the Cross and tremble. In fact one comes to realize what one always admitted theoretically, that there is nothing here that will do us good: the sooner we are safely out of this world the better. But 'would it were evening, Hal, and all was well'. I have even (I'm afraid) caught myself wishing that I had never been born, wh. is sinful. Also meaningless if you think it out.

The process of living seems to consist in coming to realize truths so ancient and simple that, if stated, they sound like barren platitudes. They cannot sound otherwise to those who have not had the relevant experience: that is why there is no real teaching of such truths possible and every generation starts from scratch....

TO A LADY.

9 July 1939

The letter [at the end of *Out of The Silent Planet*] is pure fiction and the 'circumstances which put the book out of date' are merely the way of preparing for a sequel. But the danger of

'Westonism' I meant to be real. What set me about writing the book was the discovery that a pupil of mine took all that dream of interplanetary colonization quite seriously, and the realization that thousands of people in one way and another depend on some hope of perpetuating and improving the human race for the whole meaning of the universe—that a 'scientific' hope of defeating death is a real rival to Christianity. . . .

You will be both grieved and amused to hear that out of about 60 reviews only 2 showed any knowledge that my idea of the fall of the Bent One was anything but an invention of my own. But if there only was someone with a richer talent and more leisure I think that this great ignorance might be a help to the evangelisation of England; any amount of theology can now be smuggled into people's minds under cover of romance without their knowing it.

I have given your *God Persists* a first reading with great pleasure. I value it particularly for its frank emphasis on those elements in the faith which too many modern apologists try to keep out of sight for fear they will be called mythical. . . . I like very much your treatment of heathenism. . . . On p. 43 'God sat again for His portrait' is a most successful audacity. I think your task of finding suitable fiction for the convalescents must be interesting. Do you know George Macdonald's fantasies for grown-ups (his tales for children you possibly know already): *Phantastes* and *Lilith* I found endlessly attractive and full of what I felt to be holyness before I really knew what it was. . . . One of his novels, *Sir Gibbie* (Everyman), though like all his novels often amateurish, is worth reading. And do you know the works of Charles Williams? Rather wild, but full of love and excelling in the creation of convincing *good* characters. (The reason that these are so rare in fiction is that to imagine a man worse than yourself you've only got to stop doing something, whilst to imagine one better you've got to do something). . . . Though I'm forty years old I'm only about twelve as a Christian, so it wd. be a maternal act if you found time sometimes to mention me in your prayers.

TO HIS BROTHER, *who had been recalled to service on the outbreak of war.*

10 September 1939

One of the most reminiscent features of the last war has already reappeared, i.e. the information which always comes too late to prevent you doing an unnecessary job. We have just been informed that New Building will not be used by Govt. and that Fellows' rooms in particular will be inviolable; also that we *are* going to have a Term and quite a lot of undergraduates up. So you see—I had pictured myself either never seeing those books again or else, with you, and in great joy, unearthing them after the war. Tomorrow I suppose I must start on the never-envisaged task of bringing them up singlehanded during a war. . . . In the Litany this morning we had some extra petitions one of which was 'Prosper Oh Lord, our righteous cause'. Assuming that it was the Bishop or someone higher up, when I met the Vicar in the porch I ventured to protest against the audacity of informing God that our cause was righteous—a point on which he may have His own view (I hope it is quite like ours of course: but you never know with Him). But it turned out to be the Vicar's own. However, he took the criticism very well.

Along with these not very pleasant indirect results of the war, there is one pure gift—the London branch of the University Press has moved to Oxford, so that Charles Williams is living here. . . . Life at the Kilns is going on at least as well as I expected. . . . The main trouble of life at present is the blacking out which is done (as you may imagine) with a most complicated Arthur Rackham system of odd rags—quite effectively, but at the cost of much labour. Luckily I do most of the rooms myself, so it doesn't take nearly as long as if I were assisted. . . .

TO HIS BROTHER. (*The children referred to are the household's 'evacuees'.*)

18 September 1939

I have said that the children are 'nice', and so they are. But modern children are poor creatures. They keep on coming to Maureen and asking, 'What shall we do now?' She tells them to play tennis, or mend their stockings, or write home; and when that is done, they come and ask again. Shades of our childhood. . . ! One unexpected feature of life at present is that it is quite hard to get a seat in church—every local family apparently taking the view that whether they go or not, at any rate their evacuees *shall*. But I don't like to be surrounded by a writhing mass of bored urchins who obviously have no idea what's going on, or why. . . .

I quite agree that one of the worst features of this war is the spectral feeling of all having happened before. As Dyson said, 'When you read the headlines (French advance—British steamship sunk) you feel as if you'd had a delightful dream during the last war and woken up to find it still going on'. . . . More and more sleep seems to be the best thing—short of waking up and finding yourself safely dead and not quite damned. . . .

TO HIS BROTHER.

5 November 1939

I had a pleasant evening on Thursday with Williams, Tolkien and Wrenn, during which Wrenn expressed *almost* seriously a strong wish to burn Williams, or at least maintained that conversation with Williams enabled him to understand how inquisitors had felt it right to burn people. . . . The occasion was a discussion of the most distressing text in the Bible ('Narrow is the way, and few they be that find it'), and whether one could really believe in a universe where the majority were damned and also in the goodness of God. Wrenn, of course, took the view that it mattered precisely nothing whether it conformed to our ideas of goodness or not, and it was at this stage that the combustible possibilities of Williams revealed themselves to him in an attractive light. The general sense of the meeting was in favour of a view taken in *Pastor Pastorum*—that Our Lord's replies are never straight answers and never gratify curiosity, and whatever this one meant, its purpose was certainly not statistical. . . .

TO SISTER PENELOPE, C.S.M.V.

8 November 1939

The Tableland [in *Pilgrim's Regress*] represents *all* high and dry states of mind, of which High Anglicanism then seemed to me to be one—most of the representatives of it whom I had then met being v. harsh people who called themselves scholastics and appeared to be inspired more by hatred of their fathers' religion than anything else. I would modify that view now; but I'm still not what you would call High. To me the real distinction is not between high and low, but between religion with a real supernaturalism and salvationism on the one hand, and all watered-down and modernist versions on the other. I think St. Paul has really told us what to do about the divisions in the Ch. of England; i.e. I don't myself care twopence what I eat on Fridays but when I am at table with High Anglicans I abstain in order not 'to offend my weak brother'. . . .

TO HIS BROTHER. (*For the Inklings, see Introduction, p.* 13.)

11 November 1939

On Thursday we had a meeting of the Inklings—you and Coghill both absent unfortunately. We dined at the Eastgate. I have never in my life seen Dyson so exuberant—'A roaring cataract of nonsense'. The bill of fare afterwards, consisted of a section of the new Hobbit book from Tolkien, a nativity play from Ch. Williams (unusually intelligible for him, and approved by all), and a chapter out of the book on the Problem of Pain from me. . . . I wished very much that we cd. have had you with us. . . .

Yes, I too enjoyed our short time together in College enormously, until the shadow of the end began to fall over it; not that one had lost the art of dealing with such shadows (our boyhood was well trained in it) but that one *resents* having to start putting it into practice again after so many years. Pox on the whole business.

TO HIS BROTHER, *serving at a base depot in France.*

24 November 1939

There is a curious irony about your present job, because thirty years ago bustling about between trains and ships would have seemed to you the ideal occupation. . . . No, I hadn't thought of its being a crime to keep an engine waiting, though it's fairly obvious when you come to think of it. . . .

A few hours ago outside Magdalen I saw a sight I bet you've never seen—an undergraduate approaching with what I took to be a dead pheasant in his hand, but which turned out to be a live falcon on his wrist. It was hooded with a little leather hood and is quite a gaily coloured bird, provided on the lower leg with natural spats of a kind of yellow varnish. Blessings on the man who while waiting to be called up for a first class European war is exclusively intent on restoring the ancient sport of hawking. . . .

In the French library where the exam was held I picked up Balzac's *Curé de Tours* and was immediately enchanted—just as I was by *Père Goriot* in 1917. It is so very *unlike* most French things—the Curé and the whole cathedral surroundings in Tours are almost Trollopian; so provincial, so lovable, prosaic, unobtrusive. . . .

Today is wet—an outside world of dripping branches and hens in the mud and cold, which I am glad to have shut out. . . . How nasty the sugar cottage in *Hansel and Gretel* must have been in wet weather. I gave your greetings to those of the Inklings who were present on Thursday, which were received with gratification.

TO HIS BROTHER.

3 December 1939

On Sunday I had the odd experience of leaving home for College at about 6, as H. [a schoolmaster] had announced his intention of coming for a night. . . . He has been evacuated to Minehead. . . . His son John is not with them, but billeted in the neighbourhood—with the local M.F.H. (!) and already has acquired a new language and says that his father ought to get his hair cut. I hardly know which to pity more—a father like H. who watches his son being 'translated' or a son in process of such translation who has the embarrassment of a father like H. I think, the son; for as some author whom I've forgotten says, the anxiety that parents have about their children 'being a credit to them' is a mere milk and water affair beside the anxiety of the children that their parents should not be an absolute disgrace. Certainly it would not be pleasant to have to explain to an M.F.H. that one's father was an anthroposophist—except that the only impression left on the M.F.H.'s mind wd. probably be that your father was some sort of chemist. (If the M.F.H. was like *our* father it might of course lead to almost anything—'Sort of fellow who comes to the door offering to feel your bumps'). . . .

Talking of books, I have been looking rapidly through St. François de Sales . . . and have derived much 'social pleasure' from your pencillings; as I have experienced before, to read a book marked by you, in your absence, is almost the nearest thing to a conversation. When I read that hares turn white in winter because they eat nothing but snow (used as an argument for frequent Communion) and see your mark, it is almost as if one of us were pointing the passage out to the other in the study. . . .

The usual Thursday party did not meet . . . so I went up to Tolkien's. We had a very pleasant evening drinking gin and lime-juice and reading our recent chapters to each other—his from the new Hobbit and mine from *The Problem of Pain*. (N.B. If you are writing a book about pain and then get some actual pain, as I did in my ribs, it does *not* either, as the cynic would expect, blow the doctrine to bits, nor, as a Christian wd. hope, turn it into practice, but remains quite unconnected and irrelevant, just as any other bit of actual life does when you are reading or writing. . . .)

TO HIS BROTHER.

18 December 1939

Yes, I know well what you mean by the *materialistic* gains of being a Christian. It more often presents itself to me the other way round—how on earth did we manage to enjoy all these books so much as we did in the days when we had really no conception of what was at the centre of them? . . . And I quite agree about Johnson. If one had not experienced it, it wd. be hard to understand how a dead man out of a book can be almost a member of one's family circle—still harder to realize, even now, that you and I have a chance of some day really meeting him. . . .

We had a very pleasant 'cave' in Balliol last Wednesday. . . . During the evening Ridley read us a Swinburne ballad and, immediately after it, that ballad of Kipling's which ends up, 'You've finished with the flesh, my lord' . . . it just *killed* the Swinburne as a real thing kills a sham. I then made him read *Iron, cold Iron* with the same result, and later he drifted into *McAndrews' Hymn*. Surely Kipling must come back? When people have had time to forget *If* and the inferior Barrack Room Ballads, all this other stuff must come into its own. I know hardly any poet who can deliver such a *hammer-stroke*. . . .

TO HIS BROTHER.

1 January 1940

I went to see ——, a professor of London, the same morning. Here is a man of my own age, who knew Barfield when he was up; of my own profession, who has written on Spenser. You'd have thought that there were all the materials for a good conversation. But no . . . every single time I tried to turn it to books, or life, or friends (as such) I was completely frustrated, i.e. about friends, he'd talk of their jobs, marriages, houses, incomes, arrangements, but not about them. Books—oh yes, editions, prices, suitability for exams—not their contents. In fact hardly since the old days have I had to endure so much irredeemably 'grown up' conversation. Unless I misjudge him he is one of those dreadful fellows who never refer to literature except during the hours they are paid to talk about it. . . . How small a nucleus there is in each liberal profession of people who care about the thing they are supposed to be doing; yet I suppose the percentage of garage-hands and motor touts who are really interested in motoring is about 95. . . .

TO HIS BROTHER.

9 January 1940

It seems almost brutal to describe a January walk taken without you in a letter to you. . . . When I reached Taunton it was definitely a warm evening. God send us to be soon together again, for here came that moment in a holiday which you would have so appreciated and wh. cannot be fully enjoyed alone—the moment when, at the last of the *big* stations, you find, far from other traffic, in a remote, silent bay, the little, dark, non-corridor train of two coaches—usually for some reason exuding steam from all the compartments—which is going to jerk and bump you to your real destination. And then those stops at unheard-of halts with wooden platforms, and the gleam of an oil lantern in a porter's hand. . . .

Next morning to H's billet and collected him. His children are now so numerous that one ceases to notice them individually any more than a scuffle of piglets in a field or a waddle of ducks. A few platoons of them accompanied us for about the first mile, but returned, like tugs, when we were out of harbour. . . . Tea in one of those slippery, oil clothy, frosty best parlours with a small colony of *reference* works. One that specially intrigued us was 'Every man his own lawyer—*Illustrated*'. We looked in vain however for a portrait of a tort or a south aspect of Habeas Corpus—the pictures consisting entirely of court-houses and famous judges. Can you imagine anything more infuriating than, on turning to such a book to try to extricate yourself from an Income Tax muddle or an injudicious betrothal (and for what other purpose wd. you ever open it?) to be met with the bland features of Lord Darling? . . .

TO DOM BEDE GRIFFITHS, O.S.B.

17 January 1940

Thanks for letter and article. I believe I found myself in agreement with every point you made in the latter. The Platonic and neo-Platonic stuff has no doubt been reinforced (*a*) by the fact that people not very morally sensitive or instructed but trying to do their best recognise temptations of appetite as temptations but easily mistake all the spiritual (and worse) sins for harmless or even virtuous states of mind; hence the illusion that 'the bad part' of one is one's body. (*b*) By a misunderstanding of the Pauline use of σάρξ which in reality cannot mean the body (since envy, witchcraft, and other spiritual sins are attributed to it) but I suppose means the unregenerate manhood as a whole (You have no doubt noticed that σῶμα is nearly always used by St. Paul in a good sense). (*c*) By equating 'matter' in the ordinary sense with *materia* in the scholastic sense and the Aristotelian, i.e. equating the concrete corporality of flesh, grass, earth or water with 'pure potentiality'. The latter, being nearest to not-being, and furthest from the Prime Reality can, I suppose, be called the 'least good' of things. But I fear Plato thought the concrete flesh and grass bad, and have no doubt he was wrong. (Besides these two senses of 'matter' there is a third—the thing studies in physics. But who would dare to vilify such a miracle of unceasing energy as that? it's more like pure form than pure potentiality.)

Yes, I've read *The Scale of Perfection* with much admiration. I think of sending the anonymous translator a list of passages that he might reconsider for the next edition. I've also read the work of R. W. Chambers[1] which you mention. It is first class as an essay on the continuity of the devotional tradition, but not, what it professes, the continuity of prose style. At least I think some of the passages he quotes as similar in style are really similar only in matter. I doubt if he recognises that More's style is greatly inferior to Milton's. But Chambers is a very good man. If you have his *Man's Unconquerable Mind* read the essay on *Measure for Measure*. He simply treats it as an ordinary Christian story and all the old stuff about 'Shakespeare's dark period' vanishes into thin air. I see what you mean by calling George Eliot's Dorothea a

[1] *The Continuity of English Prose.*

saint *manqué*; nothing is more pathetic than the potential holiness in the quality of devotion which actually wrecks itself on Casaubon. If you like such leisurely novels let me recommend John Galt: specially *The Entail.*

About active service—I think my account was true in what it said, but false in what it excluded. I quite agree that obedience and comradeship are very good things: and I have no sympathy with the modern view that killing or being killed is a great evil. But perhaps these truths are rather odious on the lips of a civilian, unless some pastoral or civil office absolutely obliged him to utter them. Fascism and Communism, like all other evils, are potent because of the good they contain or imitate. . . . And of course their occasion is the failure of those who left humanity starved of that particular good. This does not for me alter the conviction that they are very bad indeed. One of the things we must guard against is the penetration of both into Christianity—availing themselves of that very truth you have suggested and I have admitted. Mark my words: you will presently see both a Leftist and a Rightist pseudo-theology developing—the abomination will stand where it ought not. . . .

TO HIS BROTHER: *the Inklings again.*

3 February 1940

We had the usual pleasant party on Thursday evening in College, with the welcome addition of Havard (our doctor) who has been bidden all along but has hitherto been prevented from attending for various reasons. He read us a short paper on his clinical experience of the effects of pain, wh. he had written in order that I might use all or part of it as an appendix to my book. We had an evening almost equally compounded of merriment, piety, and literature. Rum this time again. The Inklings is now really very well provided, with Adam Fox as chaplain, you as army, Barfield as lawyer, Havard as doctor—almost all the estates—except of course anyone who could actually produce a single necessity of life—a loaf, a boot, or a hut. . . .

TO HIS BROTHER

11 February 1940

On Monday Charles Williams lectured, nominally on *Comus* but really on Chastity. Simply as criticism it was superb—because here was a man who really cared with every fibre of his being about 'The sage and serious doctrine of virginity' which it would never occur to the ordinary modern critic to take seriously. But it was more important still as a sermon. It was a beautiful sight to see a whole roomful of modern young men and women sitting in that absolute silence which can *not* be faked, very puzzled, but spell-bound. . . . What a wonderful power is in the direct appeal which disregards the temporary climate—I wonder is it the case that the man who has the audacity to get up in any corrupt society and squarely preach justice or valour or the like *always* wins? . . .

TO HIS BROTHER.

18 February 1940

The world as it is is becoming, and has partly now become, simply *too much* for people of the old square-rigged type like you and me. I don't understand its politics, or its economics or any dam' thing about it. Even its theology. . . . Did you fondly believe—I did—that where you got among Christians, there at least you would escape from the horrible ferocity and grimness of modern thought? Not a bit of it. I blundered into it all, imagining that I was the upholder of the old, stern doctrines against modern quasi-Christian slush; only to find that *my* sternness was *their* slush. . . . They all talk like Covenanters or Old Testament prophets. They don't think human reason or human conscience of any value at all; they maintain, as stoutly as Calvin, that there's no reason why God's dealings should appear just (let alone merciful) to us. . . . One may bewail for a moment, happier days—the old world when Politics meant Tariff Reform, and war was war with Zulus, and even religion meant (beautiful word) Piety—'The *decent* church that crowns the neighbouring hill'—Sir Roger at Church—'Mr. Arabin sent the farmers home to their baked mutton very well satisfied'. . . .

TO HIS BROTHER.

25 February 1940

The vicar preached a very good sermon on Joseph. . . . Reflection on the story raised in my mind a problem I never happen to have thought of before; why was Joseph imprisoned, and not killed by Potiphar? Surely it seems extraordinarily mild treatment for attempted rape of a great lady by a slave? Or must one assume that Potiphar, tho' ignorant of the lady's intention to make him a cuckold, was aware in general that her stories about the servants were to be taken with a grain of salt—that his real view was 'I don't suppose for a moment that Joseph did anything of the sort, but I foresee there'll be no peace till I get him out of the house'? One is tempted to begin to imagine the whole life of the Potiphar family, e.g. how often had he heard similar stories from her before? . . .

TO HIS BROTHER.

3 March 1940

A visit from Dyson on Thursday produced a meeting of all the Inklings except yourself and Barfield. Adam Fox read us his latest 'Paradisal' on Blenheim park in winter. The only line I can quote (wh. seems to me very good) is 'Beeches have figures: oaks anatomies'. It was in the Troilus stanza and full of his own 'cool, mellow flavour' as the tobacconists say. Dyson . . . was in his usual form and on being told of Williams' Milton lectures on 'the sage and serious doctrine of virginity', replied, 'The fellow's becoming a common *chastitute*'. . . .

TO HIS BROTHER.

22 March 1940

Why should quiet ruminants like you and I have been born in such a ghastly age? Let me palliate the apparent selfishness of this complaint by asserting that there *are* people who, while not of course liking actual suffering when it falls to their own share, *do* really like the 'stir', the 'sense of great issues'. Lord! how I loathe great issues. How I wish they were all adjourned *sine die*. 'Dynamic' I think is one of the words invented by this age which sums up what it likes and I abominate. Could one start a Stagnation Party—which at General Elections would boast that during its term of office *no* event of the least importance had taken place? . . .

TO A LADY.

26 March 1940

(1) About obedience. Nearly everyone will find himself in the course of his life in positions where he ought to command and in positions where he ought to obey. . . . Now each of them requires a certain training or habituation if it is to be done well; and indeed the habit of command or of obedience may often be more necessary than the most enlightened views on the ultimate moral grounds for doing either. You can't begin training a child to command until it has reason and age enough to command someone or something without absurdity. You can at once begin training it to obey; that is teaching it the art of obedience *as such*—without prejudice to the views it will hold later on as to who should obey whom, or when, or how much . . . since it is perfectly obvious that every human being is going to spend a great deal of his life in obeying.

(2) Psychoanalysis. In talking to me you must beware, because I am conscious of a partly pathological hostility to what is fashionable. I may therefore have been betrayed into statements on this subject which I am not prepared to defend. No doubt,

like every young science, it is full of errors, but so long as it remains a science and doesn't set up to be a philosophy, I have no quarrel with it, i.e. as long as people judge what it reveals by the best human logic and scheme of values they've got and do not try to derive logic and values from it. In practice no doubt, as you say, the patient is always influenced by the analyst's own values. And further, in so far as it attempts to *heal*, i.e. to make better, every treatment involves a value-judgement. This could be avoided if the analyst said, 'Tell me what sort of a chap you want to be and I'll see how near that I can make you'; but of course he really has his own idea of what goodness and happiness consist in and works to that. And his idea is derived, not from his science (it couldn't) but from his age, sex, class, culture, religion and heredity, and is just as much in need of criticism as the patient's....

Another way in which *any* therapeutic art may have bad philosophical results is this. It must, for the sake of method, take perfection as the norm and treat every departure from it as disease; hence there is always a danger that those who practise it may come to treat a perfectly ideal perfection as 'normal' in the popular sense and consequently waste their lives in crying for the moon....

I see no reason why a Christian shd. not be an analyst. Psychoanalysis after all merely defines what was always admitted, that the moral choices of the human soul operate inside a complex non-moral situation.... The Christian view would be that every psychological situation, just like every degree of wealth or poverty, had its own peculiar temptations and peculiar advantages; that the worst could always be turned to a good use and the best could always be abused, to one's spiritual ruin.... This doesn't mean that it wd. be wrong to try to cure a complex any more than a stiff leg; but it does mean that if you can't, then so far from the game being up, life with a complex or a stiff leg, is precisely the game you have been set.... We must play the parts we find ourselves given.... Once make the medical norm our ideal of the 'normal' and we shall never lack an excuse for throwing up the sponge. But these are all illegitimate abuses of analysis.

(3) Christianity. My own experience in reading the Gospels was at one stage even more depressing than yours. Everyone told

me that there I should find a figure whom I couldn't help loving. Well, I could. They told me I would find moral perfection—but one sees so very little of Him in ordinary situations that I couldn't make much of that either. Indeed some of His behaviour seemed to me open to criticism e.g. accepting an invitation to dine with a Pharisee and then loading him with torrents of abuse. Now the truth is, I think, that the sweetly-attractive-human-Jesus is a product of 19th century scepticism, produced by people who were ceasing to believe in His divinity but wanted to keep as much Christianity as they could. It is not what an unbeliever coming to the records with an open mind will (at first) find there. The first thing you find is that we are simply not *invited* to speak, to pass any moral judgement on Him, however favourable; it is only too clear that He is going to do whatever judging there is; it is *we* who are *being* judged, sometimes tenderly, sometimes with stunning severity, but always *de haut en bas*. (Have you ever noticed that your imagination can hardly be forced to picture Him as shorter than yourself?) The first real work of the Gospels on a fresh reader is, and ought to be, to raise very acutely the question, 'Who or What is this?' For there is a good deal in the character which, unless He really is what He says he is, is not lovable or even tolerable. If He *is*, then of course it is another matter; nor will it then be surprising if much remains puzzling to the end. For if there is anything in Christianity, we are now approaching something which will never be fully comprehensible. On this whole aspect of the subject I should go on . . . to Chesterton's *Everlasting Man*. You might also find Mauriac's *Vie de Jesus* useful. . . . If childish associations are too intrusive, in reading the New Testament it's a good idea to try it in some other language, or Moffatt's translation.

As for theology proper; a good many misunderstandings are cleared away by Edwyn Bevan's *Symbolism and Belief*. A book of composite authorship and of varying merit, but on the whole good, is *Essays Catholic and Critical* ed. E. G. Selwyn, S.P.C.K. Gore's *The Philosophy of the Good Life* (Everyman) is rather wordy, but taught me a lot. If you can stand serious faults of style (and if you can get them, they are long out of print) Geo. Macdonald's 3 vols. of *Unspoken Sermons* go to the very heart of the matter. I think you would also find it most illuminating to re-read now many things you once read in 'Eng. Lit' without knowing their real importance—Herbert, Traherne, *Religio Medici*.

As for a person 'with whom to discuss', choice is more ticklish. L. W. Grensted is very interested in psychoanalysis and wrote a book on its relations to Christianity; would that be an advantage or the reverse? O. S. Quick whom I know and like. Milford, the present rector of St. Mary's, some like and some don't. Let me know what, or what sort you want, and I'll see what can be done.

Come and see me when you're better and bring the gudeman.

TO DOM BEDE GRIFFITHS, O.S.B.

16 April 1940

Congratulations (if that is the right word) on becoming a Priest, and thanks for the pleasing woodcut. Yes, Melchisedech is a figure who might have been intended (nay, *was* intended, since God provides not for an abstraction called Man but for individual souls) for people who were being led to the truth by the peculiar route that you and I know.

I do most thoroughly agree with what you say about Art and Literature. To my mind they can only be healthy when they are either (a) admittedly aiming at nothing but innocent recreation or (b) definitely the handmaids of religious or at least moral truth. Dante is alright and Pickwick is alright. But the great *serious irreligious* art—art for art's sake—is all balderdash; and incidentally never exists when art is really flourishing. In fact one can say of Art as an author I recently read said of love (sexual love I mean), 'It ceases to be a devil when it ceases to be a god'. Isn't that well put? So many things—nay every real *thing*—is good if only it will be humble and ordinate. One thing we want to do is to kill the word 'spiritual' in the sense in which it is used by writers like Arnold and Croce. Last term I had to make the following remark to a room full of Christian undergraduates—'A man who is eating or lying with his wife or preparing to go to sleep in humility, thankfulness, and temperance, is, by Christian standards, in an infinitely *higher* state than one who is listening to Bach or reading Plato in a state of pride'—obvious to you, but I could see that it was a quite new light to them.

I don't know what to think about the present state of the world. The sins on the side of the democracies are very great. I suppose they differ from those on the other side by being less deliberately blasphemous, fulfilling less the conditions of a perfectly *mortal* sin. Anyway the question 'Who is righteous?' (in a given quarrel) is quite distinct from the question 'Who is in the right?'—for the worse of two disputants may always be in the right on one particular issue. It is therefore *not* self-righteous to claim that we are in the right now. But I am chary of doing what my emotions prompt me to do every hour; i.e. identifying the enemy with the forces of evil. Surely one of the things we learn from history is that God never allows a human conflict to become unambiguously one between simple good and simple evil?

The practical problem about charity (in one's prayer) is very hard work, isn't it? When you pray for Hitler and Stalin how do you actually teach yourself to make the prayer real? The two things that help me are (*a*) A continual grasp of the idea that one is only joining one's feeble little voice to the perpetual intercession of Christ who died for these very men. (*b*) A recollection, as firm as I can make it, of all one's own cruelty; wh. might have blossomed under different conditions into something terrible. You and I are not at bottom so different from these ghastly creatures.

I have been reading Lady Julian of Norwich. What do you make of her? A dangerous book clearly and I'm glad I didn't read it much earlier. . . . One thing in it pleased me immensely. *Contemptus mundi* is dangerous and may lead to Manicheeism. Love of the creature is also dangerous. How the good of each is won and the danger rejected in her vision of 'all that is made' as a little thing like a hazel nut 'so small I thought it could hardly endure'. Not bad you see; just very very small. I enclose a book in which you might like the last essay. I've been busy this winter on a book called *The Problem of Pain* wh. I was asked to write for a thing called the Christian Challenge series. I have hopes you may like it. . . .

TO A LADY.

18 April 1940

On the marriage service. . . . The modern tradition is that the proper reason for marrying is the state described as 'being in love' . . . wh. seems to me to be simply moonshine. . . . Is it not usually transitory? . . . Frankly, it would be undesirable, even if it were possible, for people to be 'in love' all their lives. . . .

The Prayer Book therefore begins with something universal and solid—the biological aspect. . . . In this regard marriages are the fountains of *history*. Surely to put the mere emotional aspect first would be sheer sentimentalism? Then the second reason. . . . In this second reason the Prayer Book is saying, 'If you can't be chaste (and most of you can't) the alternative is marriage'. This may be brutal sense, but to a man it is *sense* and that's that. The third reason gives the thing that matters far more than 'being in love' and will last and increase between good people long after 'love' in the popular sense is only as a memory of childhood—the partnership, the loyalty to 'the firm', the composite creature. . . .

Now the second reason involves the whole Christian view of sex. It is all contained in Christ's saying, that two shall be 'one flesh'. He says nothing about two who 'married for love'; the mere fact of marriage *at all*—however it came about—sets up the 'one flesh'. There is a terrible comment on this in I. Cor. VI. 16: 'he that is joined to an harlot is one flesh'. You see? Apparently if Christianity is true, the mere fact of sexual intercourse sets up between human beings a relation which has, so to speak, transcendental repercussions. . . .

Regarding the *Headship* of the man. You see of course that if marriage is a permanent relation, intended to produce a kind of new organism (the 'one flesh') there must be a Head. It is only so long as you make it a temporary arrangement, dependant on 'being in love' and changeable by frequent divorce, that it can be strictly democratic. . . . That being so, do you really *want* the Head to be a woman? In a particular instance no doubt you may. But do you really want a matriarchal world? Do you really like women in authority? When you seek authority yourself, do you naturally seek it in a woman? Your phrase about the 'slave-wife' is mere rhetoric, because it assumes servile submission to be the only kind of subordination. Aristotle could have taught you better. . . . My own feeling is that the Headship of the house is necessary to protect the outer world against the family. . . . What do nine women out of ten care about justice to the outer world when the health, or career, or happiness of their own children is at stake? That is why I want the 'foreign policy' of the family, so to speak, to be determined by the man; I expect more mercy from him. . . . P.S. The Marriage Service is *not* a place for celebrating the flesh but for making a solemn *agreement* in the presence of God and society—an agreement which involves a good many other things besides the flesh. Distinguish the Church from the bedroom, and don't be silly. . . . 'Sober and godly matrons' may be a stickler if you haven't read the English School; but *you* ought to know that all the associations you are putting into it are modern and accidental. It *means* 'Married women (matrons) who are religious (godly) and have something better and happier to think about than jazz and lipstick (sober)'.

TO HIS BROTHER.

21 April 1940

I never told you a curious thing wh. provides a new instance of the malignity of the Little People. I was going into town one day and had got as far as the gate when I realized that I had odd shoes on, one of them clean, the other dirty. There was no time to go back. As it was impossible to clean the dirty one, I decided that the only way of making myself look less ridiculous was to *dirty* the clean one. Now wd. you have believed that this is an impossible operation? You can of course get some mud on it—but it remains obviously a clean shoe that has had an accident and won't look in the least like a shoe that you have been for a walk in. One discovers new snags and catches in life every day. . . .

TO OWEN BARFIELD.

2 June 1940

Mr Moore told me yesterday about your loss of your mother. I cannot imagine myself, in similar circumstances, not feeling very strongly *felix opportunitate mortis*, but I daresay, when it comes to the point, that is very far from being the predominant emotion; I have always remembered what you told me of the dream in which you were condemned to death and of the part your mother played in it. I am very sorry you should have had this particular desolation added to the general one in which we all are. It is like the first act of *Prometheus*: "Peace is in the grave, the grave hides all things beautiful and good". He was near, however, to his release when he said that, and I accept the omen—that you and I and our friends will soon be past the worst, if not in one way, then in the other. For I am very thankful to say that while my *θρεπτική* often plays tricks I am ashamed of, I retain my faith, as I have no doubt you do yours. "All shall be well, and all shall be well, and all manner of thing shall be well"—this is from Lady Julian of Norwich, whom I have been reading lately and who seems, in the fifteenth century, to have rivalled Thomas Aquinas' reconciliation of Aristotle and Christianity by nearly reconciling Christianity with Kant.

The real difficulty is—isn't it?—to adapt one's steady beliefs about tribulation to this *particular* tribulation: for the particular, when it arrives, always seems so peculiarly intolerable. I find it helpful to keep it very particular—to stop thinking about the ruin of the world, etc., for no-one is going to experience *that*, and to see it as each individual's personal sufferings, which never can be more than those of one man, or more than one man (if he were very unlucky) might have suffered in peacetime.

Do you get sudden lucid intervals—islands of profound peace? I do; and although they don't last, I think one brings something away from them. . . .

And oddly enough, I notice that since things got really bad, everyone I meet is less dismayed. Macdonald observes somewhere that "the approach of any fate is usually also the preparation for it". I begin to hope he is right. Even at this present moment I don't feel nearly so bad as I should have done if anyone had prophesied it to me eighteen months ago. . . .

TO HIS BROTHER, *after Dunkirk.*

12 July 1940

Before my illness was over I read your copy of Southey's letters with great enjoyment; a bad poet but a delightful man. I also found things in it that were very consoling; as (a) The daily fear of invasion, (b) The haunting fear of traitors on the home front (c) The repeated statement that 'even now' we might pull through if only we had a decent government. (d) The settled conviction that 'even if' we defeated Buonaparte we should still have to face revolution at home. . . .

Other impressions were (a) How much *nicer people*, tho' worse writers, the Tory Romantics were than the other crew—the Shelleys and L. Hunts and even Keats. (b) What a happy life Southey had on the whole, and yet what a grim business even a happy human life is when you read it rapidly through to the inevitable end. . . .

TO DOM BEDE GRIFFITHS, O.S.B.

16 July 1940

A lot of work and an illness have kept me from answering your letter, but I have been intending ever since I got it to let you know that I think your criticisms on my Aristotelian idea of leisure are largely right. I wouldn't write that essay now. In fact I have recently come to the conclusion that a besetting sin of mine all my life has been one which I never suspected—laziness—and that a good deal of the high-sounding doctrine of leisure is only a defence of *that*. The Greek error was a punishment for their sin in owning slaves and their consequent contempt for labour. There was a good element in it—the recognition, badly needed by modern commercialism, that the economic activities are not the *end* of man: beyond that they were probably wrong. If I still wanted to defend my old view I shd. ask you why *toil* appears in Genesis not as one of the things God originally created and pronounced 'very good' but as a punishment for sin, like death. I suppose one cd. point out in reply that Adam was a gardener before he was a sinner, and that we must distinguish two degrees and kinds of work—the one wholly good and necessary to the animal side of the *animal rationale*, the other a punitive deterioration of the former due to the Fall.

My enjoyment of the Psalms has been greatly increased lately. The point has been made before, but let me make it again: what an admirable thing it is in the divine economy that the sacred literature of the world shd. have been entrusted to a people whose poetry, depending largely on parallelism, shd. remain poetry in any language you translate it into. . . .

TO HIS BROTHER: *the conception of* Screwtape.

20 July 1940

After the service was over—one could wish these things came more seasonably—I was struck by an idea for a book which I think might be both useful and entertaining. It would be called 'As one Devil to another' and would consist of letters from an elderly retired devil to a young devil who has just started work on his first 'patient'. The idea would be to give all the psychology of temptation from the other point of view. For example. . . .

TO HIS BROTHER.

11 August 1940

I have commenced my Home Guard duties with the 1.30 a.m. patrol on what they call Saturday morning and mortals call Friday night. . . . I set out for my rendezvous at Lake St., eating my sandwiches on the way as I didn't feel that I could provide sandwiches for the whole party and hadn't the face to eat mine in their presence. I was with two men much younger than myself, both very nice and intelligent and neither too talkative nor too silent. One is allowed to smoke and I was pleased to find that our tour of duty included quite a long loaf on the verandah of a college pavilion—a pleasant spot, looking out over broad playing fields on a mild but windy night. Unfortunately our watch was not so well arranged as Dogberry's ('All sit in the church porch till two, and then every man to bed'). Still, the three hours passed surprisingly quickly, and if it hadn't been for the bother of lugging a rifle about all the time, I should have said that pleasure distinctly predominated. I had quite forgotten the weight of a rifle. We broke off at 4.30 and after a really beautiful walk back through an empty and twilit Oxford I was in bed by 5. . . .

TO OWEN BARFIELD.

(Undated)

As regards our argument about Gethsemane, I quite see that it sounds odd to attribute to perfect man a fear which imperfect men have often overcome. But one must beware of interpreting "perfect man" in a sense which would nullify the temptation in the wilderness: a sense on which, at first, one would be tempted to comment (a) —as regards the stones and bread—"Imperfect men have voluntarily starved", (b) —as regards Satan's demand for worship—"Most men have never sunk so low as to feel this temptation at all".

If we are to accept the Gospels, however, we must interpret Christ's perfection in a sense which admits of his feeling *both* the commonest and most animal temptations (hunger and the fear of death) *and* those temptations which usually occur only to the worst of men (devil-worship for the sake of power). I am assuming that the stones and bread represent hunger: but if you prefer to regard it as primarily a temptation to *thaumaturgy* ("If thou be the Son of God, command these stones") then it falls into my second class.

The consideration of this second class at once raises the question "Are there not temptations proper to the very best and the very worst, which the middle sort of men do not feel?": or again, "Do not common temptations attack most fiercely the best and the worst?" I should answer Yes, and say that the fear of death was one of these: and in respect of that fear I would divide men into three classes.

A. The very bad to whom death represents the final defeat of the systematic self-regarding caution and egoism which has been the sole occupation of life. (False freedom defeated.)

B. The virtuous. These in fact do not conquer fear of death without the support of any or all of the following:

(i) Pride. . . .
(ii) Fear. (Charge, charge, 'tis too late to retreat!)
(iii) Taedium vitae. (My baby at my breast, that sucks the nurse asleep.)
(iv) Abandonment of the exhausting attempt at real freedom which makes the Necessary appear as a relief. (The ship glides under the green arch of peace.)

C. The Perfect. He cannot resort to any of the aids which class B have, for they all depend on defect. His position is thus closely parallel to class A; death for Him also is the final defeat, but this time of *real* Freedom. (I am taking it for granted that the spiritual essence of death is "the opposite of freedom": hence the most mortal images are rigidity, suffocation, etc.)

No doubt, He also knows the answer—that voluntary death (really voluntary, not the anodynes and dutch courages) makes unfreedom itself the assertion of freedom. But voluntary submission does not mean that there is nothing to submit to.

What is it to an ordinary man to die, if once he can set his teeth to bear the merely animal fear? To give in—he has been doing that nine times out of ten all his life. To see the lower in him conquer the higher, his animal body turning into lower animals and these finally into the mineral—he has been letting this happen since he was born. To relinquish control—easy for him as slipping on a well-worn shoe. But in Gethsemane it is essential Freedom that is asked to be bound, unwearied control to throw up the sponge, Life itself to die. Ordinary men have not been so much in love with life as is usually supposed: small as their share of it is, they have found it too much to bear without reducing a large portion of it as nearly to non-life as they can: we love drugs, sleep, irresponsibility, amusement, are more than half in love with easeful death—if only we could be sure it wouldn't hurt! Only He who really lived a human life (and I presume that only one did) can fully taste the horror of death. I am sure that if the thing were presented to you in a myth you would be the first to cry out upon the prosaic critic who complained that the Sun was discredited because it fled from the wolves.

Your idea of Christ as *suffering* from the mere fact of being in the body, and therefore tempted—if at all—to hasten rather than postpone his death, seems to imply that he was not (as the Christian mystery runs) "perfect God and perfect man" but a kind of composite being, a δαίμων or archangel imprisoned in a vehicle unsuitable to it (like Ariel in the oak) and in constant revolt against that vehicle. This is mythological in the bad sense. The Son was certainly not incarnated in such a sense as not also to remain God (if He had been, the universe would have disappeared). I don't pretend to have an explanation: but I take it that the precise *differentia* of the Christian doctrine is that "Something which eternally *is* in the Noumenal world (and is impassible, blessed, omniscient, omnipotent, etc.) nevertheless once *was* in the phenomenal world (and was suffering, etc.)". You can't regard the earthly life of Jesus as an episode in the eternal life of the Son: as the slavery to Admetus was an episode in the immortal life of Apollo.

I need not say that, on my view, the doctrine (do you hold it?) that what was incarnated was "One of the hierarchies" (or "one of" the "anythings") appears to me quite incompatible with the position given to Christ by his own words by his followers. (*Aut deus aut malus angelus* is as true as the old *aut deus aut malus homo*.)

TO A LADY.

4 January 1941

Congratulations . . . on your own decision. I don't think this decision comes either too late or too soon. One can't go on thinking it over for ever; and one can begin to try to be a disciple before one is a professed theologian. In fact they tell us, don't they, that in these matters to act on the light one has is almost the only way to more light. Don't be worried about feeling flat, or about feeling at all. As to what to *do*, I suppose the normal next step, after self-examination, repentance and restitution, is to make your Communion; and then to continue as well as you can, praying as well as you can . . . and fulfilling your daily duties as well as you can. And remember always that religious *emotion* is only a servant. . . . This, I say, would be the obvious course. If you want anything more e.g. Confession and Absolution which our church enjoins on no-one but leaves free to all—let me know and I'll find you a *directeur*. If you choose this way, remember it's not the psychoanalyst over again; the confessor is the representative of Our Lord and declares His forgiveness—his advice or 'understanding' tho' of real, is of secondary importance.

For daily reading I suggest (in small doses) Thomas à Kempis' *Imitation of Christ* and the *Theologia Germanica* (Golden Treasury series, Macmillan) and of course the Psalms and N.T. Don't worry if your heart won't respond; do the best you can. You are certainly under the guidance of the Holy Ghost, or you wouldn't have come where you now are; and the love that matters is His for you—yours for Him may at present exist only in the form of obedience. He will see to the rest.

This has been great news for me I need hardly say. You have all my prayers (not that mine are worth much).

TO THE SAME.

29 January 1941

Thanks very much for your kind letter. My own progress is so very slow (indeed sometimes I seem to be going backwards) that the encouragement of having in any degree helped some one else is just what I wanted. *Of course* the idea of not relying on emotion carries no implication of not rejoicing in it when it comes; you may remember Donne's *Litanie*—'that our affections kill us not—nor die'. One of the minor rewards of conversion is to be able to last to see the real point of all the old literature which we were brought up to read with the point left out. . . .

TO SISTER PENELOPE, C.S.M.V.

10 April 1941

Yes, I will come and address your Junior Sisters next Easter unless 'wife and oxen' have by that time taken the form of incarceration in a German concentration camp, an English Labour Company, or (to pitch on a brighter idea) some sort of Borstal institution on the lower foot-hills of the mountains of Purgatory. But (if one may, *salva reverentia*, say so) what very odd tasks God sets us: if anyone had told me ten years ago that I should be lecturing in a convent——! Thanks for the offer of hospitality in the Gate House, which I accept gratefully, though the Protestant in me had just a little suspicion of an oubliette or a chained skeleton . . . the doors do open outwards as well, I trust?

Thank you very much for the book. It has given me real help. What I particularly enjoy in all your work, specially this, is the avoidance of that curious drabness which characterises so many 'little books on religion'. Partly it is due to your Hebraic background, which I envy you; partly, no doubt, to deeper causes. . . . There are in fact a good many Gifford Lectures and other such weighty tomes out of which I've got less meat (and indeed less efficient cookery). . . .

TO SISTER PENELOPE, C.S.M.V.

15 May 1941

We ought to meet about BBC talks if nothing else, as I'm giving four in August. Mine are *praeparatio evangelica* rather than evangelism, an attempt to convince people that there is a moral law, that we disobey it, and that the existence of a Lawgiver is at least very probable and also (*unless* you add the Christian doctrine of the Atonement) that this imports despair rather than comfort. You will come after to heal any wounds I succeed in making. So each of us ought to know what the other is saying. I've given talks to the RAF at Abingdon already, and so far as I can judge they were a complete failure. . . . Yes, jobs one dare neither refuse or perform. One must take comfort in remembering that

God used an *ass* to convert the prophet; perhaps if we do our poor best we shall be allowed a stall near it in the celestial stable—rather like this. [The remainder of the sheet is filled with an amusing drawing of the ass, flanked by a nun and a figure in a mortarboard, seated outside a stable in the radiance of the heavenly city.]

TO SISTER PENELOPE, C.S.M.V.

9 October 1941

I am ashamed of having grumbled. And your act was not that of a brute—in operation it was more like that of an angel, for (as I said) you started me on a quite new realization of what is meant by 'being in Christ', and immediately after that 'the power which erring men call chance' put into my hands Mascall's two books in the 'Signpost' series wh. continued the process. So I lived for a week (at Aberystwyth) in one of those delightful *vernal* periods when doctrines which have hitherto been only buried seeds begin actually to come up—like snowdrops or crocuses. I won't deny they've met a touch of frost since (if only things would last or rather if only *we* would). But I'm still very much and gladly in your debt. The only real evil of having read your scripts when I was tired is that it was hardly fair to them and not v. useful to you. I have had to refuse a request from Sister Janet. Will you tell her that 'the wives and oxen' are quite real ones.

I enclose the MS of *Screwtape*. If it is not a trouble I shd. like you to keep it safe until the book is printed (in case the one the publishers have has got blitzed)—after which it can be made into spills or used to stuff dolls or anything. Thank you very much for the photo of the Shroud. It raises a whole question on which I shall have to straighten my thoughts one of these days.

TO SISTER PENELOPE, C.S.M.V. (*The book referred to is* Perelandra.)

9 November 1941

I've got Ransom to Venus and through his first conversation with the 'Eve' of that world; a difficult chapter. I hadn't realized till I came to write it all the *Ave-Eva* business. I may have embarked on the impossible. This woman has got to combine characteristics which the Fall has put poles apart—she's got to be in some ways like a Pagan goddesss and in other ways like the Blessed Virgin. But, if one can get even a fraction of it into words, it is worth doing.

Have you room for an extra prayer? Pray for Mrs. Moore if you have. She is the old lady I call my mother and live with (she is really the mother of a friend)—an unbeliever, ill, old, frightened, full of charity in the sense of alms, but full of uncharity in several other senses. And I can do so little for her.

TO SISTER PENELOPE, C.S.M.V.

19 November 1941

It is a curious fact that the advice one can give to others we cannot give to ourselves, and truth is more effective through any lips rather than our own. Chas. Williams in *Taliessin* is good on this. 'No one can live in his own house. My house for my neighbour, his for me'. I think what really worries me is the feeling (often on waking in the morning) that there is really nothing I *dislike* so much as religion—that it's all against the grain, and I wonder if I can really stand it. Have you ever had this? Does one outgrow it? Of course there is no intellectual difficulty. If our faith is true, then this is just what it ought to feel like until the new man is fullgrown. But it's a considerable bore. What you say about 'disappointed with oneself' is very true—and a tendency to mistake mere disappointment (in which there is much wounded pride and much of a mere sportsman's irritation at breaking a record) for true repentance. I ought to have devoted a *Screwtape* letter to this. . . .

TO A LADY.

8 December 1941

When I said it was 'no good' trying to regard Jesus as a human teacher I only meant that it was logically untenable—as you might say, 'It's no good trying to maintain that the earth is flat'. I was saying nothing in that sermon about the destiny of the 'virtuous unbeliever'. The parable of the sheep and the goats suggests that they have a very pleasant surprise coming to them. But in the main, we are not told God's plans about them in any detail. If the Church is Christ's body—the thing He works through—then the more worried one is about the people outside, the more reason to get *inside* oneself, where we can help. You are giving Him, as it were, a new finger. I assumed last night that I was talking to those who already believed. If I'd been speaking to those who didn't, of course everything I'd said would have been different.

Fear isn't repentance—but it's alright as a *beginning*—much better at that stage than *not* being afraid.

TO DOM BEDE GRIFFITHS, O.S.B.

21 December 1941

I'm extremely glad that you have got on to my friend Chas. Williams, tho' to one of his worst books. He is living in Oxford during the war and we made him lecture to the Faculty on Milton; and (wd. you believe it, remembering the English lectures of your period) we actually heard a lecture on *Comus* wh. put the importance where Milton put it. In fact the lecture was a panegyric of chastity. Just imagine the incredulity with which (at first) an audience of undergraduates listened to something so unheard of. But he beat them in the end.

He is an ugly man with rather a cockney voice. But no one ever thinks of this for 5 minutes after he has begun speaking. His face becomes almost angelic. Both in public and in private he is of nearly all the men I have met, the one whose address most overflows with *love*. It is simply irresistible. These young men and women were lapping up what he said about Chastity before the end of the hour. It's a big thing to have done. I have seen his impress on the Milton papers when I examined. Fancy an Oxford student, and a girl, writing about Mammon's speech in Book II: 'Mammon proposes an ordered state of sin with such majesty of pride that but for the words 'live to ourselves' which startle our consciences we shd. hardly recognize it as sin, so natural it is to man'. (Compare that with the sort of bilge you and I were proud to write in Schools).

Williams, Dyson of Reading and my brother (Anglicans) and Tolkien and Havard (our doctor), your Church, are the 'Inklings' to whom my *Problem of Pain* was dedicated. We meet on Friday evenings in my rooms; theoretically to talk about literature, but in fact nearly always to talk about something better. What I owe to them all is incalculable. Dyson and Tolkien were the immediate human causes of my conversion. Is any pleasure on earth as great as a circle of Christian friends by a good fire? His stories (I mean Williams') are his best work. *Descent into Hell* and *The Place of the Lion* are the best. I quite agree with you about what you call his 'affectations'—not that they are affectations, but honest defects of taste. He is largely a self-educated man, labouring under an almost oriental richness of imagination ('Clotted glory from Charles' as Dyson called it) which could be saved from turning silly or even vulgar in print only by a severe early discipline which he never had. But he is a lovely creature. I'm proud of being among his friends.

Now about the scripts. (a) The claim to forgive sins *is* in S. Mark and all the Synoptics. (b) Yes—I think I gave the impression of going further than I intended in saying that all theories of the Atonement were 'to be rejected if we don't find them helpful'. What I meant was 'need not be used—'a v. different thing. Is there, on your view, a real difference here: that the Divinity of Our Lord *has to be believed* whether you find it a help or a 'scandal' (otherwise you are not a Xtian at all) but the Anselmic theory of Atonement is *not* in that position. Would you admit that a man was a Xtian (and could be a member of your Church) who said 'I believe that Christ's death redeemed man from sin, but I can make nothing of the theories as to *how*!' You see, what I wanted to do in these talks was simply to give what is common to us all, and I've been trying to get a *nihil obstat* from friends in various communions. (The other dissentient besides you is a Methodist who says I have said nothing about justification by faith.) It therefore doesn't much matter what you think of my *own* theory, because it is advanced only as my own. But I'd like to be able to meet you on the other point—how far any theory is *de fide*. The Council of Trent 'made satisfaction' seems to be the real hitch. What was the context? What error was it directed against? Still, don't bother, for I fear I shall have to give up my original hope. I think I cd. get something that you and your friends would pass, but not without making the talk longer or shorter: but I'm on the Procrustes' bed of neither less nor more than 15 minutes. You can imagine the difficulty.

What did you think of *In Memoriam* on re-reading it? I re-read it (with Barfield) some months ago and thought (1) that the last quarter is a falling off—and can hardly help being since a poem represents a sorrow neither being transmuted nor ending in tragedy, but just a petering out. (2) That the mere difficulty of *construing* some stanzas is v. great. (3) That a great deal of the poetry is overwhelmingly good.

About the Son being subject to the Father (as God—of course obviously subject as Man in the Incarnation)—yes, that's what I think: but was contradicted by a theologian. Can you back me up? What is the correct interpretation of 'equal to His Father as touching His Godhead' in the Athanasian Creed?

The talks will be on at 4.40 p.m. on January 11th, 4.45 Jan. 18th, 4.40 Feby. 8th, 4.45 Feby. 15th.

You look positively fat in the photo—you abbey lubber!

TO OWEN BARFIELD.

(Undated)

Have you read *Esmond* lately? What a detestable woman is Lady Castlewood: and yet I believe Thackeray means us to like her, on the ground that all her actions spring from "love". This love is, in his language, "pure"—i.e., it is not promiscuous or sensual. It is none the less a wholly uncorrected natural passion, idolatrous and insatiable. Was that the great 19th century heresy

—that "pure" or "noble" passions didn't need to be crucified and re-born, but could of themselves lead to happiness? Yet one sees it makes Lady C. disastrous both as a wife and a mother, and is a source of misery to herself and all whom she meets. . . .

TO A LADY.

20 January 1942

Sorry you're in a trough. I'm just emerging (at least I hope I am) from a long one myself. As for the difficulty of believing it is a trough, one wants to be careful about the word 'believing'. We too often mean by it 'having confidence or assurance as a psychological state'—as we have about the existence of furniture. But that comes and goes and by no means always accompanies intellectual assent, e.g. in learning to swim you believe, and even know intellectually, that water will support you, long before you feel any real confidence in the fact. I suppose a perfection of faith would make this confidence invariably proportionate to the assent. In the meantime, as one has learnt to swim only by acting on the assent in the teeth of all instinctive conviction, so we shall proceed to faith only by acting as if we had it. Adapting a passage in the *Imitation* one can say 'What would I do now if I had a full assurance that this was only a temporary trough', and having got the answer, go and do it. I am a man, therefore lazy; you a woman, therefore probably a fidget. So it may be good advice to you (though it wd. be bad to me) not even to try to do in the trough all you can do on the peak.

I know all about the despair of overcoming chronic temptations. It is not serious, provided self-offended petulance, annoyance at breaking records, impatience etc. don't get the upper hand. *No amount* of falls will really undo us if we keep on picking ourselves up each time. We shall of course be v. muddy and tattered children by the time we reach home. But the bathrooms are all ready, the towels put out, and the clean clothes in the airing cupboard. The only fatal thing is to lose one's temper and give it up. It is when we notice the dirt that God is most present in us; it is the v. sign of His presence. . . .

TO SISTER PENELOPE, C.S.M.V. (Perelandra *is dedicated "To some Ladies at Wantage". The other allusion is to the 1942 British Academy lecture*, Hamlet: The Prince or the Poem?)

11 May 1942

Commend me to all whom I met at Wantage. I shall look back on the visit with quite a new sort of pleasure—it was not like anything else that has happened to me so far. . . .

The Venus book is now finished except that I find the first two chapters need re-writing. I will send you a typed MS as soon as it is typed, and you can report on it to Revd. Mother for her consent to the dedication.

The British Academy made a v. stupid audience compared with your young ladies. They were all the sort of people whom one sees so often getting out of taxis and then going into some big doorway, and wonders who on earth they are—all those beards and double chins and fur collars and lorgnettes. Now I know.

TO SISTER PENELOPE, C.S.M.V., *who was engaged upon a translation of St. Athanasius'* De Incarnatione.

29 July 1942

After having to abandon S. Athanasius for examining, I have now returned to the *De Incarnatione* and have just finished the long section on the Jewish prophecies. If that is the bit you are omitting I expect you are right. Though it crosses my mind that modern apologetics may have given up too completely the old 'proof from prophecy'. Each individual passage can be explained away as really meaning something else, or accidental; but could it still be argued to apply this to the whole lot involves stretching the arm of coincidence rather far? . . .

About 'became Man' versus 'a man'. There is, you will admit, a very obvious sense in which He 'became a man'—a man of a particular height and weight, the Son of a particular Mother, who was in one place and time and *not* (in that mode) elsewhere. The Fathers, writing in a language with no definite article, didn't have to plump for one or the other. Are you correct in saying 'the Person, the Ego of the incarnate lord is God'? I had thought that there was a human *soul* involved (when one speaks of His humanity we don't mean simply His body), and that the human and divine natures together made one Person. Your way of putting it suggests that there was simply a human body with God *substituted for* the human soul one would ordinarily have expected. Is this right? I thought not, but I don't know. . . .

TO MARTYN SKINNER.

(Undated)

I hope you got through Sanders some time ago my great enjoyment of your 'Letters to Malaya'. A really good poem. Not in the least a pastiche as the silly people will say, but a real proof that the Popian manner is a real *lingua franca* wh. anyone who has anything to say can use for original work. In fact it is already *less* 'archaic' than the manner of Georgian poetry. The pother about 'originality' all comes from the people who have nothing to say; if they had, they'd be original without noticing it. . . .

TO DOM BEDE GRIFFITHS, O.S.B.

13 October 1942

I shouldn't have written as I did if I had thought that there was a consensus of theologians in favour of the Anselmic theory. I believed that it was not to be found either in the N.T. or most of the Fathers. If I'm wrong in this, it is a matter of plain historical ignorance.

War and Peace is in my opinion *the* best novel—the only one which makes a novel really comparable to epic. I have read it about 3 times. What we lose (I'm told) in our translation is the *humour* which is an important merit in the real book.

You wouldn't be surprised at the space I give to Dualism

if you knew how attractive it is to some simple minds. As for retiring into 'private life' I don't see how one can, while feeling very strongly the evil of publicity. I don't *look* for engagements. . . .

TO SISTER PENELOPE, C.S.M.V.

22 December 1942

How does one feel thankful? I am thinking of the improvement in the war news, and I don't mean (rhetorically) 'How can we be thankful enough?' but just what I say. It seems to be something that disappears or becomes a mere word the moment one recognizes that one *ought* to be feeling it. I always tell people not to bother about 'feelings' in their prayers, and above all never to *try* to feel, but I'm a bit puzzled about gratitude; for if it is not a feeling, what is it? A funny thing how merely formulating a question awakes the conscience. I hadn't a notion at the bottom of the last sheet, but now I know exactly what you are going to say—'*Act* your gratitude and let feelings look after themselves'. Thank you. (Do all theoretical problems conceal shirkings by the will?)

TO A LADY.

31 January 1943

I'm the worst person in the world to write to someone who is feeling weak and listless . . . because I don't myself *dislike* it nearly as much as most people. To lie in bed—to find one's eyes filling with facile tears at the least hint of pathos in one's book—to let the book drop from one's hand as one sinks deeper and deeper into reverie—to forget what you were thinking about a moment ago and *not to mind*—and then be roused by the unexpected discovery that it is already tea-time—all this I do *not* find disagreeable.

Yes, it is funny what horrid young men one meets in Dickens and Thackeray. Of course the *descent* of David Copperfield is partly due to the fact that no later chapters *could* come up to the early ones. Have you noticed that nearly all writers describe childhood (when it is in the first person) well? *Jane Eyre* is also best at the beginning; and almost every biography. But is it also due to the convention whereby Victorian novelists are not allowed to attribute their hero's peccadilloes in respect of chastity? Hence the 'scrapes' of youth all have to be represented by other less probable and (to me) more repellent sins. You notice that Tom Jones does not similarly lose our regard as he grows up. . . .

No. Bears seem to be very modest. No one seems to know anything about their love passages. Perhaps they neither marry nor are given in marriage, but gather their young from the flowers as Virgil thought the bees did. It would explain why the bear's whelp has to be 'licked into shape'.

I've re-read *The Ring and the Book* in trains lately with great enjoyment; but don't recommend it to you in your present state. . . . Jane Austen, Scott, and Trollope are my favourite authors when ill. . . .

TO SISTER PENELOPE, C.S.M.V.

20 February 1943

'Creation' as applied to human authorship seems to me to be an entirely misleading term. We re-arrange elements He has provided. There is not a vestige of real creativity *de novo* in us. Try to imagine a new primary colour, a third sex, a fourth dimension, or even a monster which does not consist of bits of existing animals stuck together. Nothing happens. And that surely is why our works (as you said) never mean to others quite what we intended; because we are re-combining elements made by Him and already containing *His* meanings. Because of those divine meanings in our materials it is impossible that we shd. ever know the whole meaning of our own works, and the meaning we never intended may be the best and truest one. Writing a book is much less like creation than it is like planting a garden or begetting a child; in all three cases we are only entering as *one* cause into a causal stream which works, so to speak, in its own way. I would not wish it to be otherwise. If one could *really* create in the strict sense, would not one find that one had created a sort of Hell?

TO SISTER PENELOPE, C.S.M.V.

10 August 1943

I *should* like a few days at Wantage, but things are so bad at home that I'm cancelling several of my RAF engagements. Pray for me, sister, and for poor Mrs. Moore. . . . There is never any time when *all* three women are in a good temper. When A is in B is out; and when C has just got over her resentment at B's last rage and is ready to forgive, B is just ripe for her next and so on. But out of evil comes good. From praying anxiously for a little of God's peace to communicate to *them*, I have been given more of it myself than I ever had before . . .

TO THE SOCIETY FOR THE PREVENTION OF PROGRESS, OF WALNUT CREEK, CALIFORNIA: *in reply to an offer of membership.*

(Undated: May 1944)

While feeling that I was *born* a member of your Society, I am nevertheless honoured to receive the outward seal of membership. I shall hope by continued orthodoxy and the unremitting practice of Reaction, Obstruction, and Stagnation to give you no reason for repenting your favour.

I humbly submit that in my Riddell Lectures entitled *The Abolition of Man* you will find another work not all unworthy of consideration for admission to the canon.

TO AN AMERICAN SCHOLAR, CHARLES A. BRADY, *who had made a study of his works and their sources.*

29 October 1944

Obviously one ought never to thank a critic for praise; but perhaps one can congratulate a fellow scholar on the thoroughness of his work. . . .

Morris and Macdonald were more or less given to you (Morris is more important than you suggest, I think) I admit, but you are the first to stress them properly. On the Tir-na'an Og element you hit the bull and might even have deduced much reading of the early Yeats (worth twenty of the reconditioned 1920 model) and of James Stevens. Space and Time fiction, yes; but oddly enough not Rice-Burroughs. . . . The real father of my planet books is David Lindsay's *Voyage to Arcturus*, which you will also revel in if you don't know it. I had grown up on Wells's stories of that kind; it was Lindsay who first gave me the idea that the 'scientifiction' appeal could be combined with the 'supernatural' appeal. . . . R. H. Benson is wrong; at least I think *The Dawn of All* never meant much to me. Chesterton of course; but more I think on thought than on imagination. Rackham, yes; but having mentioned him you just missed tapping my whole Norse complex—Old Icelandic, Wagner's *Ring* and (again) Morris. The Wagner is important; you will see if you look, how *operatic* the whole building up of the climax is in *Perelandra*. Milton I think you possibly over-rate. . . .

The only place where, as it seems to me, your work contains a *warning* for us all is the bit based on the portrait. The whole thing depends upon the portrait's being a good one. In fact it was drawn from a photo by a man who had never seen me and I'm told is only just recognizable. . . . Let us both remember this next time we are writing about an Elizabethan or a 17th century author. . . . I have now had an orgy of talking about myself. But let me congratulate you again on your thorough and perceptive piece of work. . . .

TO OWEN BARFIELD, *on the death of Charles Williams.*

18 May 1945

It has been a very *odd* experience. This, the first really severe loss I have suffered, has (a) given a corroboration to my belief in immortality such as I never dreamed of—it is almost tangible now; (b) swept away all my old feelings of mere horror and disgust at funerals, coffins, graves, etc.—if need had been I think I could have handled *that* corpse with hardly any unpleasant sensations; (c) greatly reduced my feeling about ghosts. I think (but who knows?) that I should be, though afraid, more pleased than afraid if his turned up. . . . To put it in a nutshell: what the idea of death has done to him is nothing to what he has done to the idea of death. Hit it for six: yet it used to rank as a fast bowler! . . .

TO A LADY.

20 May 1945

I also have become much acquainted with grief now through the death of my great friend Charles Williams, my friend of friends, the comforter of all our little set, the most angelic man. The odd thing is that his death has made my faith stronger than it was a week ago. And I find that all that talk about 'feeling that he is closer to us than before' isn't just talk. It's just what it does feel like—I can't put it into words. One seems at moments to be living in a new world. Lots, lots of pain, but not a particle of depression or resentment. . . .

TO SISTER PENELOPE, C.S.M.V.

28 May 1945

I was intensely interested in your story of the healing of the little dog. I don't see why one shouldn't. Perhaps indeed those to whom God allows a gift in this way should confirm their own faith in it by practising on beasts, for in one way they may be easier to heal than men. Although they cannot have faith in Him (I suppose) they certainly have faith in us, which is faith in Him at one remove; and there is no sin in them to impede or resist. I am glad it happened....

Mrs. Moore is up and down; very liable I'm afraid to fits of bad jealousy—she can't bear to see other people doing the work. Pray for her, dear Sister.

TO I. O. EVANS.

26 September 1945

I'm glad you recognized the N.I.C.E. as not being quite the fantastic absurdity some people think. I hadn't myself thought that any of the people in contemporary rackets were *really* dabbling in magic; I had supposed that to be a romantic addition of my own. But there you are. The trouble about writing satire is that the real world always anticipates you, and what were meant for exaggerations turn out to be nothing of the sort.

About Merlin: I don't know much more than you do. Apart from Malory . . . you will get something more in Geoffrey of Monmouth . . . and Layamon. . . . For Arthur in general, see *Arthur of Britain* by E. K. Chambers, Collingwood in Vol. I of *Oxford History of England*, and Vinaver's *Malory*. But the blessing about Merlin (for you and me) is that 'very little is known'—so you have a free hand.

TO MISS DOROTHY SAYERS.

10 December 1945

Although you have so little time to write letters you are one of the great English letter writers. (Awful vision for you—'It is often forgotten that Miss Sayers was known in her own day as an Author. We who have been familiar from childhood with the *Letters* can hardly realize! . . .) But I'm not. No, Hopkins is not contributing to the volume [*Essays presented to Charles Williams*]. A dear creature, though. I'm all for little books on other subjects with their Xtianity latent. I propounded this in the S.C.R. at Campion Hall and was told that it was 'Jesuitical'. The Hall Porter at the Bull, Fairford, likes *The Man born to be King* (and of such is the kingdom). I've got to have a long talk with you about the Socratic Club soon.

TO A FRIEND, *who was troubled about a younger woman's unsuitable devotion.*

(Undated)

'Frown not!' . . . ? We frown when we see a child too near a puddle: do we *frown* when we see it on the edge of a precipice (skeletons white on the rocks a thousand feet below)? . . .

I suppose it *is* all right, is it? I wish Charles Williams were alive: this was just his pigeon. His solution was, in a peculiar way, to teach 'em the *ars honesta amandi* and then bestow them on other (younger) men. *Sic vos non vobis*. He was not only a lover himself but the cause that love was in other men.

But it's a ticklish game. Perhaps I'm taking it all too seriously—but the world is growing chilly and I just couldn't stand any serious miscarriage in your life. ("Save yourself for my sake, Pickwick!" said Mr Tupman.) I burn to explain to this young woman that a good many people have a concern in your happiness and Gad! she'd better mind what she's about. . . .

TO SISTER PENELOPE, C.S.M.V.

31 January 1946

The rush of pupils returning from the forces makes Terms quite different from what they were in war time. By the way, the returning men are *nice*; far nicer than my generation was when we came out of the army—and a much higher percentage of Christians. . . . *That Hideous Strength* has been unanimously damned by all reviewers.

About Holst's *Planets*. I heard Mars and Jupiter long ago and greatly admired them . . . but his characters are rather different from mine I think. Wasn't his Mars brutal and ferocious? —in mine I tried to get the *good* element in the martial spirit, the discipline and freedom from anxiety. On Jupiter I am closer to him; but I think he is more 'jovial' in the *modern* sense of the word. The folk tune on which he bases it is not regal enough for my conception. But of course there is a general similarity because we're both following the mediaeval astrologers. His is anyway a rich and marvellous work. . . .

TO MISS DOROTHY SAYERS.

2 August 1946

I don't think the difference between us comes where you think. Of course one mustn't do *dishonest* work. But you seem to take as the criterion of honest work the sensible *desire* to write, the itch. That seems to me precious like making 'being in love' the only reason for going on with a marriage. In my experience the *desire* has no constant ratio to the value of the work done. My own frequent uneasiness comes from another source—the fact that apologetic work is so dangerous to one's own faith. A doctrine never seems dimmer to me than when I have just successfully defended it. Anyway, thanks for an intensely interesting letter.

TO SISTER PENELOPE, C.S.M.V.: *in reference to early rumours of actual travel in space.*

21 October 1946

Yes, it is only too true. I begin to be afraid that the villains will really contaminate the moon.

TO MRS. FRANK L. JONES.

(Undated: 1947)

(1) The doctrine that Our Lord was God and man does *not* mean that He was a human body which had God instead of the normal human soul. It means that a real man (human body *and* human soul) was in Him so united with the 2nd Person of the Trinity as to make one Person: just as in you and me a complete anthropoid animal (animal body *and* animal "soul", i.e. instincts, sensations, etc.) is so united with an immortal rational soul as to be one person. In other words, if the Divine Son had been removed from Jesus what would have been left would have been not a corpse but a living man.

(2) This human soul in Him was unswervingly united to the God in Him in that which makes a personality one, namely, Will. But it had the *feelings* of any normal man: hence could be tempted, could fear etc. Because of these feelings it could pray 'If it be possible, let this cup pass from me': because of its perfect union with His Divine Nature it unwaveringly answered 'Nevertheless, not as I will but as thou wilt'. The Matthew passage (M. 26. 39) and the John passage (John 18. 11) both make clear this unity of will. The Matthew one gives in addition the human feelings.

(3) God could, had He pleased, have been incarnate in a man of iron nerves, the Stoic sort who lets no sigh escape him. Of His great humility He chose to be incarnate in a man of delicate sensibilities who wept at the grave of Lazarus and sweated blood in Gethsemane. Otherwise we should have missed the great lesson that it is by his *will* alone that a man is good or bad, and that *feelings* are not, in themselves, of any importance.

We should also have missed the all-important help of knowing that He has faced all that the weakest of us face, has shared not only the strength of our nature but every weakness of it except sin. If He had been incarnate in a man of immense natural courage, that would have been for many of us almost the same as His not being incarnate at all.

(4) The prayer recorded in Matthew is much too short to be long enough for the disciples to go to sleep! They record the bit they heard before they fell asleep.

(5) It is probable that all the gospels are based on acts and sayings which the disciples deliberately learned by heart: a much surer method even now than transmission by writing; still more so among people whose memories were uninfected by too many books and whose books were only MSS. With all good wishes.

Keep clear of psychiatrists unless you know that they are also Christians. Otherwise they start with the assumption that your religion is an illusion and try to "cure" it: and this assumption they make not as professional psychologists but as amateur philosophers. Often they have never given the question any serious thought.

TO MARTYN SKINNER.

15 October 1947

I have just finished your admirable 'Letters V'. . . . I think it is the best yet, and full of plums. . . . A beautiful book and terrible too for one who shares (as I do) your apprehensions. It wd. be less terrible if one cd. really attribute the murder of beauty to any particular set of evil men; the trouble is that from man's first and wholly legitimate attempt to win safety and ease from Nature it seems, step by step, to lead on quite logically to universal suburbia. . . .

TO OWEN BARFIELD.

16 December 1947

You must bear with me. Things were never worse at The Kilns. W(arren) is away, so correspondence was never heavier in College. "Sleep hath forsook and giv'n me o'er." . . .

P.S. Of course the real trouble is within. All things would be bearable if I were delivered from this internal storm (*buffera infernal*) of self-pity, rage, envy, terror, horror, and general bilge!

TO OWEN BARFIELD.

22 December 1947

(This absurd notepaper is a present from an American.)

I already regret my last letter except in so far as it produced such a valuable one from you. It was two-thirds temper and melodrama. Thus, "Sleep hath forsook and giv'n me o'er" meant "I have had one or two bad nights lately" *plus* "Isn't *Samson Agonistes* fine?"

There is no problem about vocation. Quite obviously one can't leave an old semi-paralyzed lady in a house alone for days or even hours: and the duty of looking after one's people rests on us all and is common form.

The rage comes from *impatientia* in the strict theological sense: because one treats as an interruption of one's (self-chosen) vocation, the vocation actually imposed on one—regards the exam. paper actually set as a distraction from the one you would like to be doing. . . .

Don't imagine I didn't pitch into Charles Williams for his obscurity for all I was worth.

TO EDWARD A. ALLEN, OF WESTFIELD, MASS.: *a letter typical of many.*

29 January 1948

I just don't know what to say in answer to your letter of 23rd January. One, two, perhaps even three parcels can be inadequately, but not entirely unsuitably acknowledged, but what is one to say when bombarded with a non-stop stream of kindnesses? Nothing has in my time made such a profound impression in this country as the amazing outburst of individual American generosity which has followed on the disclosure of our economic situation. (I say nothing of government action because naturally this strikes the 'man in the street' much less obviously.) The length of time which a parcel takes to cross the Atlantic is a significant indication of the volume of food which must be pouring into England.

As regards the 'tuxedo'—'dinner jacket' here, 'le smoking' in Paris—if it doesn't fit me, it will certainly fit one of my friends, and will save some grateful man a year's clothing coupons; and at least £25 in cash.

As regards things to send . . . a packet or two of envelopes are almost always welcome; a small thing, but the constant shortage of them becomes very irritating to a busy man after a time. . . .

TO MISS VERA MATHEWS, *another American benefactor.*

7 February 1948

How lovely! Bacon, tea, shortening, what not—and again. A thousand thanks. Typing expert is away, as you see, and me hardly able to write legibly. But (if you *can* make it out) believe me our hearts are very warm and we enjoy the kindness and friendship as well as its tangible (and chew-able) results. I really hardly know how to say what I feel; thank you again and again.

TO EDWARD A. ALLEN.

29 May 1948

So once more I have to send you my sincere, but very inadequate thanks. . . . The extent to which your folk have come to our rescue is amazing and moving. I knew in a general way of course that very large quantities of gift food, clothing, etc. were coming into Britain, but I was none the less surprised to read in a recent debate in the House of Lords that every household in the kingdom benefits by American aid to the tune of £1. 0. 0. a week, and has done so for the past *two years*. . . .

'Just what a Don does?' Like a woman, his work is never done. Taking 'tutorials' occupies the best part of his day, i.e. pupils come in pairs, read essays to him, then follows criticism, discussion etc.; then he gives public lectures on his own subject; takes his share in the business of managing the College; prepares his lectures and writes books; and in his spare time stands in queues. . . .

TO JOHN WAIN. (*"D.C." is Lord David Cecil.*)

6 November 1948

I am wondering whether you have thought of applying for the tutorial fellowship in English at New College? I understand (this is of course strictly confidential) that they have a strong candidate who is an old New College man but are not *settled* to elect him, i.e. if a definitely stronger candidate puts in they will elect that candidate. I know you are well thought of by D.C., it is therefore possible that you might be the stronger candidate if you applied. If you were out of a job of course it wd. be obvious that you shd. try for this. As things are, I don't know if you will wish to or not. I shall never be satisfied myself until you are at Oxford; and this job wd. no doubt be better paid than your present one. On the other hand it wd. probably mean more work and of course, house-hunting. I don't know that I cd. add anything by writing at greater length. Think it over for 24 hours and let me know.

TO OWEN BARFIELD.

10 November 1948

I wonder whether what you say about depressions does not really mark an advance in self-criticism and objectivity—i.e., that the very same experiences which would once have led you to say "How nasty everyone (or the weather, or the political situation) is at present" now leads you to say "*I* am depressed". A Copernican revolution, revealing as motion in the self what in one's more naïf period was mistaken for motion in the cosmos....

TO DR. FIROR OF MARYLAND, *who had sent a number of hams.*

(Undated: January 1949)

Only yesterday I said to myself that I should like to see America if only one could see the quiet places and not the cities—things which in every country interest me only if I want to hear an opera or buy a book. And you anticipated me. But it's all impossible. An old invalid ties me to home. Absence in the afternoon, even for one day, has to be carefully planned ahead. A visit to another continent is as impossible to me as one to the Moon. Oh what a pity. To think that I might as your guest have seen bears, beavers, Indians, mountains. How did you know what I wanted? Meanwhile the only chance of a meeting is that you shd. visit this island prison. To all my set you are by now an almost mythical figure—Firor-of-the-Hams, a sort of Fertility god.

TO A GODCHILD.

3 April 1949

I think of myself as having to be two people to you. (1) the real, serious, Christian godfather. (2) The fairy godfather. As regards (2) I enclose a bit of the only kind of magic (a very dull kind) which I can work. Your mother will know how to deal with the spell. I think it will mean one or two, or even five pounds for you *now* to get the things you want, and the rest in the Bank for future use. As I say, it is a dull kind of magic and a really good godfather would do something much more interesting; but it is the best an old bachelor can do, and it is with my love.

As for No. 1, the serious Christian godfather, I feel very unfit for the work—just as you I dare say feel very unfit for being confirmed and for receiving the Holy Communion. But then an angel would not really be fit, and we must all do the best we can. So I suppose I must try to give you advice. And the bit of advice that comes into my head is this; don't expect (I mean don't *count on* and don't *demand*) that when you are confirmed, or when you make your first communion, you will have all the *feelings* you would like to have. You may of course; but also you may not. But don't worry if you don't get them. They aren't what matter. The things that are happening to you are quite real things whether you feel as you wd. wish or not. . . . Our Lord will give us right feelings if He wishes—and then we must say, Thank you. If he doesn't, then we must say to ourselves (and Him) that He knows best. This, by the way, is one of the very few subjects on which I feel I do know something. For years after I became a regular communicant I can't tell you how dull my feelings were, and how my attention wandered at the most important moments. It is only in the last year or two that things have begun to come right—which just shows how important it is to keep on doing what you are told.

Oh—I'd nearly forgotten—I have *one* other piece of advice. Remember that there are only three kinds of things anyone need ever do. (1) Things we *ought* to do. (2) Things we've *got* to do. (3) Things we *like* doing. I say this because some people seem to spend so much of their time doing things for none of these reasons, things like reading books they don't like because other people read them. Things you ought to do are things like doing one's work in school, or being nice to other people. Things one has got to do are things like dressing and undressing, or household shopping. Things one likes doing—but of course I don't know what *you* like. Perhaps you'll write and tell me one day. Of course I shall always mention you in my prayers and will most especially on Saturday. Do the same for me.

TO OWEN BARFIELD: *with allusion to some very unpleasant characters in* That Hideous Strength.

4 April 1949

Did I ever mention that Weston, Devine, Frost, Wither, Curry, and Miss Hardcastle were all portraits of you? (If I didn't, that may have been because it isn't true. By gum, though, wait until I write another story.)

Plus aux bois? We will, Oscar, we will.

Henry 7th had some mastiffs hanged for fighting a lion: said they were rebelling against their natural sovereign. That's the stuff. Also, had his own hawk decapitated for fighting an eagle.

Talking of beasts and birds, have you ever noticed this contrast: that when you read a scientific account of any animal's life you get an impression of laborious, incessant, almost rational economic activity (as if all animals were Germans), but when you study any animal you know, what at once strikes you is their cheerful fatuity, the pointlessness of nearly all they do. Say what you like, Barfield, the world is sillier and better fun than they make out. . . .

TO A LADY.

1 August 1949

Don't bother about the idea that God 'has known for millions of years exactly what you are about to pray'. That isn't what it's like. God is hearing you *now*, just as simply as a mother hears a child. The difference His timelessness makes is that this *now* (which slips away from you even as you say the word *now*) is for Him infinite. If you must think of His timelessness at all, don't think of Him *having* looked forward to this moment for millions of years; think that to Him you are always praying this prayer. But there's really no need to bring it in. You have gone into the Temple ('one day in Thy courts is better than a thousand') and found Him, as always, there. That is all you need to bother about.

There is *no* relation of any importance between the Fall and Evolution. The doctrine of Evolution is that organisms have changed, sometimes for what we call (biologically) the better . . . quite often for what we call (biologically) the worse. . . . The doctrine of the Fall is that at one particular point one species, Man, tumbled down a moral cliff. There is neither opposition nor support between the two doctrines. . . . Evolution is not only not a doctrine of *moral* improvement, it is not even a doctrine of biological improvement, but of biological changes, some improvements, some deteriorations. . . .

TO MRS. EDWARD A. ALLEN.

16 August 1949

I shd. think I *do* like salt water and in all its forms; from a walk on the beach in winter when there is not a soul in sight, or seen washing past (rather like beaten copper) from the deck of a ship, or knocking one head over heels in great green ginger-beer-coloured waves. I grew up close to it, but there's no chance of getting there now. On the other hand I have discovered the joys of shallow river bathing. . . . It is like bathing in *light* rather than in water; and having walked for miles, you can *drink* it at the same time. . . . We also are in a drought and heat wave. . . .
PS. C is for CLIVE—no connection with the iniquitous Anglo-Indian of that name.

TO MRS. L., *whose husband had taken a mistress.*

2 September 1949

Apparently I was mistaken in thinking that to condone the infidelity and submit to the arrangement your husband suggests would be *wrong*. My adviser of course says that it is impossible to him to 'give a fair ruling without knowing more of the parties'. But with that reservation he suggests (1) Mrs. A. shd. refuse to have intercourse with her husband, otherwise carry on, completely ignoring the existence of the mistress. (2) Mr. A. must never mention the mistress in his house nor when he has seen her, nor shd: he let Mrs A. or anyone else have any suspicion when or where he meets the mistress. I can't myself quite see the point of No. 2, and I take it that anyway it is impracticable. . . .

On the actual practical arrangements I don't feel that I—an elderly bachelor and the most amateurish of theologians—can be useful. Where I *might* help, on the internal and spiritual problems for yourself, you obviously do not need my help. All the things I would have said to most women in your position (about charity, submission to God's will, and the poisonous nature of indulged jealousy, however just the cause) you clearly know already. I don't think it can do you any harm to know that you have these graces, provided you know that they are *Graces*, gifts from the Holy Spirit, and not your own merits. God, who foresaw your tribulation, has specially armed you to go through it, not without pain but without stain; not a case of 'tempering the wind to the shorn lamb' but of giving the lamb a coat proportional to the wind. On all *that* side you have only to go on as you are doing. And you certainly needn't worry at all about there being any material for psychotherapy in you. . . .

One point in your story looms large in my mind—the fatal consequences of your husband's lack of faith in you when he did not get those letters. For this is just how *we* also might desert God. If nothing, or nothing we recognize comes through, we imagine He has let us down and reject Him, perhaps at the very moment when help was on its way. No doubt your husband may have been readier to desert you because a quite different temptation had already begun. But then that applies to the God-Man situation also. . . .

TO THE SAME MRS. L.

6 September 1949

Telling these things to someone you approach as a consultant is no more disloyalty than revealing one's body to a doctor is indecent exposure. With a trained confessor this, as it were, *disinfectant* situation would be even more so.

I don't think the arrangement the old man suggested is 'dishonest'. I think his advice turns on the fine but important distinction between *enduring* a situation which is some one else's fault and *sanctioning* it in a way wh. makes one an accessory. After all, your husband has no right to have it both ways and you have no duty (or right) to make him feel as if he had. It wd. do him no harm to realize that this affair is *just as much* adultery as if it were 'furtive visits to a prostitute'. . . .

TO THE SAME MRS. L.

(Undated)

I don't think your objection to 'setting yourself up as a judge' is cowardly. It may spring from the fact that you are the injured party and have a v. proper conviction that the plaintiff cannot also be on the Bench. I also quite realized that he didn't feel the sin as a Christian wd.; but he must, as a man, feel the dishonour of breaking a promise. After all constancy in love thunders at him from every love-song in the world, quite apart from our mystical conception of marriage. . . .

As you say, the thing is to rely *only* on God. The time will come when you will regard all this misery as a small price to pay for having been brought to that dependence. Meanwhile (don't I know) the trouble is that relying on God has to begin all over again every day as if nothing had yet been done. . . .

The reason why I am saddled with many people's troubles is, I think, that I have no natural curiosity about private lives and am therefore a good subject. To anyone who (in *that* sense) enjoyed it, it wd. be a dangerous poison.

TO THE SAME MRS. L.

22 September 1949

The intellectual problem (why some children lose one or both parents in this way and other ways) is no harder than the problem why some women lose their husbands. In each case, no doubt what we regard as a mere hideous interruption and curtailment of life is really the *data*, the concrete situation on which life is to be built. . . . When the *data* are of the kind we naturally like (wealth, health, good fathers or husbands) of course we tend not to notice that they are data or limitations at all. But we're told that they are; and what seem to us the easiest conditions may really be the hardest ('How hardly shall they that have riches' etc.). . . .

TO THE SAME MRS. L.

27 September 1949

Yes, yes, I know. The moment one asks oneself 'Do I believe?' all belief seems to go. I think this is because one is trying to turn round and look *at* something which is there to be used and work *from*—trying to take out one's eyes instead of keeping them in the right place and seeing *with* them. I find that it happens about other matters as well as faith. In my experience only v. robust pleasures will stand the question, 'Am I really enjoying this?' Or attention—the moment I begin thinking about my attention (to a book or a lecture) I have *ipso facto* ceased attending. St. Paul speaks of 'Faith actualized in Love'. And 'the heart is deceitful'; you know better than I how very unreliable introspection is. I shd. be much more alarmed about your progress if you wrote claiming to be overflowing with Faith, Hope and Charity.

TO I. O. EVANS.

(Undated: 1949)

I'm with you on the main issue—that art can teach (and much great art deliberately sets out to do so) without at all ceasing to be art. On the particular case of Wells I would agree with Burke, because in Wells it seems to me that one has *first*-class pure fantasy (*Time Machine*, *First Men in the Moon*) and *third*-class didacticism; i.e. I object to his novels with a purpose not because they have a purpose but because I think them bad. Just as I object to the preaching passages in Thackeray not because I dislike sermons but because I dislike bad sermons. To me therefore Wells and Thackeray are instances that obscure the issue. It must be fought on books where the doctrine is as good on its own merits as the art—e.g. Bunyan, Chesterton (as you agree), Tolstoi, Charles Williams, Virgil.

TO A CHILD.

9 January 1950

I just must tell you what I saw in a field—one young pig cross the field with a great big bundle of hay in its mouth and deliberately lay it down at the feet of an old pig. I could hardly believe my eyes. I'm sorry to say that the old pig didn't take the slightest notice. Perhaps *it* couldn't believe *its* eyes either.

TO SISTER PENELOPE, C.S.M.V.

12 January 1950

All good wishes for St. Bernard. My book with Tolkien—any book in collaboration with that great, but dilatory and unmethodical man—is dated I fear to appear on the Greek Calends. . . . Pray for me; I am suffering incessant temptations to uncharitable thoughts at present; one of those black moods in which nearly all one's friends seem to be selfish or even false. And how terrible that there shd. be even a kind of *pleasure* in thinking evil. . . .

TO SISTER MARY ROSE (A ROMAN CATHOLIC NUN).

(Undated: January 1950)

I am sorry if I misunderstood your letter; and I think that you misunderstood mine. What I meant was that if I replied to your original question (why I am not a member of the Roman Church) I shd. have to write a v. long letter. It would of course be answerable; and your answer would be answerable by me . . . and so on. The resulting correspondence would certainly not, of course, be in excess of the importance of the subject; but haven't you and I both probably more pressing duties? For a real correspondence on such a subject wd. be nearly a wholetime job. I thought we cd. both discuss the matter more usefully with people nearer at hand. Even the two letters which we have exchanged have already revealed the pitfalls of argument by letter. With all good wishes.

TO A LADY.

28 November 1950

I avoided the word 'Grace' because I thought it didn't carry much clear meaning to the uninstructed readers I had in view. I think the *thing* is dealt with in a rough and ready way in *Case for Christianity* and *Beyond Personality*. Any advanced or technical theology of Grace was quite beyond my scope. Naturally that does not mean that I thought the subject unimportant.

The other question, about the limits of faith and superstition, is also important. But my own mind is v. far from clear on it. I think you must seek counsel (if it is a practical problem for you) from a real theologian, not from an amateur like me. I am sorry to disappoint you; but it is better to refuse than to mislead.

TO A LADY.

7 December 1950

(1) To the best of my knowledge the Episcopalian Church in America is exactly the same as the Anglican Church.

(2) The only rite which we know to have been instituted by Our Lord Himself is the Holy Communion ('Do this in remembrance of me'. 'If ye do not eat the flesh of the Son of Man and drink His blood, ye have no life in you'). This is an order and must be obeyed. The other services are, I take it, traditional and might lawfully be altered. But the New Testament does not envisage solitary religion; some kind of regular assembly for worship and instruction is everywhere taken for granted in the Epistles. So we must be regular practising members of the Church. Of course we differ in temperament. Some (like you—and me) find it more natural to approach God in solitude; but we must go to Church as well. For the Church is not a human society of people united by their natural affinities but the Body of Christ, in which all members, however different, (and He rejoices in their differences and by no means wishes to iron them out) must share the common life, complementing and helping one another precisely by their differences. (Re-read 1st Corinthians Chap. 12 and meditate on it. The word translated *members* wd. perhaps be better translated *organs*.) If people like you and me find much that we don't naturally like in the public and corporate side of Christianity all the better for us; it will teach us humility and charity towards simple low-brow people who may be better Christians than ourselves. I naturally *loathe* nearly all hymns; the face and life of the charwoman in the next pew who revels in them, teach me that good taste in poetry or music are *not* necessary to salvation.

(3) I am not clear *what* question you are asking me about spiritual healing. That this gift was promised to the Church is certain from Scripture. Whether any instance of it is a real instance, or chance, or even (as might happen in this wicked world) fraud, is a question only to be decided by the evidence in that particular case. And unless one is a doctor one is not likely to be able to judge the evidence. V. often I expect, one is not called upon to do so. Anything like a sudden *furore* about it in one district, especially if accompanied by a publicity campaign on

modern commercial lines, would be to me suspect; but even there I might be wrong. On the whole my attitude wd. be that any claim *may* be true, and that it is not my duty to decide if it is.

(4) 'Regular but cool' in Church attendance is no bad symptom. Obedience is the key to all doors; *feelings* come (or don't come) and go as God pleases. We can't produce them at will, and mustn't try

TO MRS. EDWARD A. ALLEN.

(Undated)

In term time I have my meals in College, including a free dinner, which has from time immemorial been part of the stipend of a Tutor. My brother takes a snack in town in the middle of the day—usually something he has bought on the way in—and has the rest of his meals out at the house; he keeps a very sharp eye on my, or perhaps I should say *your* parcels and abstracts anything likely to be useful for his lunches, justifying his peculations by quoting that 'the labourer is worthy of his hire'....

The whole question of the atomic bomb is a very difficult one; the Sunday after the news of the dropping of the first one came through, our minister asked us to join in prayer for forgiveness for the great crime of using it. But *if* what we have since heard is true, i.e. that the first item on the Japanese anti-invasion programme was the killing of every European in Japan, the answer did not to me seem so simple as all that....

TO MISS RUTH PITTER.

(Undated: January 1951)

What is the point in keeping in touch with the contemporary scene? Why shd. one read authors one doesn't like because they happen to be alive at the same time as oneself? One might as well read everyone who had the same job or the same coloured hair or the same income or the same chest measurement, as far as I can see. I whistle and plunge into the tunnel of term.

TO A LADY.

(Undated)

Whether any individual Christian who attempts Faith Healing is prompted by genuine faith and charity or by spiritual pride is I take it a question we cannot decide. That is between God and him. Whether the cure occurs in any given case is clearly a question for the doctors. I am speaking now of healing by some *act* such as anointing or laying on of hands. *Praying* for the sick, i.e. praying simply, without any overt act, is unquestionably right and indeed we are commanded to pray for all men. And *of course* your prayers can do real good. Needless to say they don't do it either as a medicine does or as magic is supposed to do, i.e. automatically. Prayer is a request. . . . One cannot establish the efficacy of prayer by statistics. . . . It remains a matter of faith and of God's personal action; it could become a matter of demonstration only if it were impersonal or mechanical. When I say 'personal' I do not mean private or individual. All our prayers are united with Christ's perpetual prayer and are part of the Church's prayer. (In praying for people one dislikes I find it helpful to remember that one is joining in *His* prayer for them.)

TO THE SAME.

7 February 1951

If 'planning' is taken in the literal sense of thinking before one acts and acting on what one has thought out to the best of one's ability, then of course planning is simply the traditional virtue of Prudence and not only compatible with, but demanded by, Christian ethics. But if the word is used (as I think you use it) to mean some particular politico-social programme, then one cd. only say after examining that programme in detail. . . . Where benevolent planning, armed with political or economic power, becomes wicked is when it tramples on people's *rights* for the sake of their *good*. . . .

TO THE MRS. L. *with whom he had corresponded in the autumn of 1949 (see pp.* 218–221). *The book referred to is* The Lion, the Witch and the Wardrobe.

5 March 1951

How right you are: the great thing is to stop thinking about happiness. Indeed the best thing about happiness itself is that it liberates you from thinking about happiness—as the greatest pleasure that money can give us is to make it unnecessary to think about money. And one sees why we have to be taught the 'not thinking' when we lack as well as when we have. And I am sure that, as you say, you will 'get through somehow in the end'. Here is one of the fruits of unhappiness; that it forces us to think of life as something to go *through*. And out at the other end. If only we could steadfastly do that while we are happy, I suppose we shd. need no misfortunes. It is hard on God really. To how few of us He *dare* send happiness because He knows we will forget Him if He gives us any sort of nice things for the moment. . . .

I *do* get that sudden feeling that the whole thing is hocus-pocus, and it now worries me hardly at all. Surely the mechanism is quite simple? Sceptical, incredulous, materialistic *ruts* have been deeply engraved in our thought, perhaps even in our physical brains, by all of our earlier lives. At the slightest jerk our thought will flow down those old ruts. And notice when the jerks come. Usually at the precise moment when we might receive Grace. And if you were a devil would you not give the jerk just at these moments? I think that all Christians have found that he is v. active near the altar or on the eve of conversion; worldly anxieties, physical discomforts, lascivious fancies, doubt, are often poured in at such junctures. . . . But the Grace is not frustrated. One gets *more* by pressing steadily on through these interruptions than on occasions when all goes smoothly. . . .

I am glad you all liked *The Lion*. A number of mothers, and still more, schoolmistresses, have decided that it is likely to frighten children, so it is not selling very well. But the real children like it, and I am astonished how some *very* young ones seem to understand it. I think it frightens some adults, but v. few children. . . .

TO DOM BEDE GRIFFITHS, O.S.B.

23 April 1951

A succession of illnesses and a holiday in Ireland have so far prevented me from tackling Lubac. *The Prelude* has accompanied me through all the stages of my pilgrimage: it and the *Aeneid* (which I never feel you value sufficiently) are the two long poems to which I most often return. The tension which you speak of (if it *is* a tension) between doing full and generous justice to the Natural while also paying humble and unconditional obedience to the Supernatural is to me an absolute key position. I have no use for mere *either-or* people (except of course in that last resort when the choice, the plucking out the right eye, is upon us: as it is in some mode every day. But even then a man needn't abuse and blackguard his right eye. It was a good creature: it is my fault, not its, that I have got myself into a state which necessitates jettisoning it).

The reason I doubt whether it is, in principle, even a tension is that, as it seems to me, the subordination of Nature is demanded if only in the interests of Nature herself. All the beauty withers when we try to make it an absolute. Put first things first and we get second things thrown in: put second things first and we lose *both* first and second things. We never get, say, even the sensual pleasure of food at its best when we are being greedy.

As to Man being 'in evolution' I agree, tho' I shd. rather say 'in process of being created'. I am no nearer to your Church than I was, but don't feel v. inclined to re-open the discussion. I think it only widens and sharpens differences. Also, I've had enough of it on the opposite flank lately, having fallen among—a new type to me—bigoted and proselytising Quakers. I really think that in our days it is the 'undogmatic' and 'liberal' people who call themselves Christians that are the most arrogant and intolerant. I expect justice and even courtesy from many Atheists and, much more, from your people: from Modernists I have to take bitterness and rancour as a matter of course. . . .

TO FATHER PETER MILWARD.

23 May 1951

I saw nothing rude in your manner, tho' I thought that you were misunderstanding me. I, you see, come to the matter from fighting on another front, against Atheists who say (I have seen it in print) 'Christians believe in a God who committed adultery with a carpenter's wife'. You use language which cd. have been interpreted as an agreement with *them*. Naturally there is no disagreement between us on that point. And I wd. agree that the supernatural begetting of Our Lord is the archtype and human marriage the ectype: not the *perversion* (that wd. seem to me Manichaean). All these agreements are perfectly consistent with a disagreement between us on the Immaculate Conception of Mary and your general Marian theology. Of course when one has decided that A is the archtype and B the ectype one has not said that A equals B, i.e. whichever way you work it, it remains true that Mary was not the Bride of the Holy Ghost *in the same sense* in which the words are used in ordinary marriages; whereas she was the mother of Jesus in exactly the same sense in wh. my mother was my mother—as Gervase Mathew said.

TO A LADY.

(Undated)

The question for me (naturally) is not 'Why should I not be a Roman Catholic' but 'Why should I?' But I don't like discussing such matters, because it emphasises differences and endangers charity. By the time I had really explained my objection to certain doctrines which differentiate you from us (and also in my opinion from the Apostolic and even the Medieval Church), you would like me less.

TO MISS VERA MATHEWS.

27 March 1951

I have just got your letters of the 22nd containing the sad news of your father's death. But, dear lady, I hope you and your mother are not really trying to pretend it didn't happen. It does happen, happens to all of us, and I have no patience with the high-minded people who make out that it 'doesn't matter'. It matters a great deal, and very solemnly. And for those who are left, the pain is not the whole thing. I feel v. strongly (and I am not alone in this) that some great good comes from the dead to the living in the months or weeks after the death. I think I was much helped by my own father after his death; as if Our Lord welcomed the newly dead with the gift of some power to bless those they have left behind.... Certainly they often seem just at that time to be very near us....

TO A LADY.

19 April 1951

I think that if God forgives us we must forgive ourselves. Otherwise it is almost like setting up ourselves as a higher tribunal than Him.

Many religious people, I'm told, have physical symptoms like the 'prickles' in the shoulder. But the best mystics set no value on that sort of thing, and do not set much on visions either. What they seek and get is, I believe, a kind of direct experience of God, immediate as a taste or colour. There is no *reasoning* in it, but many would say that it is an experience of the intellect—the reason resting in its enjoyment of its object. . . .

TO A LADY.

(Undated)

About loving one's country, you raise two different questions. . . . About there seeming to be (now) no reason for loving it, I'm not at all bothered. As Macdonald says, 'No one loves because he sees reason, but because he loves'—Surely, where we love, the very faults and blemishes of the object are a spur to love more? Or say there are two kinds of love; we love wise and kind and beautiful people because we need them, but we love (or try to love) stupid and disagreeable people because they need us. This second kind is the more divine because that is how God loves us; not because we are loveable but because He is love, not because he needs to receive but because He delights to give.

But the other question (*what* one is loving in loving a country) I do find v. difficult. What I feel sure of is that the personifications used by journalists and politicians have v. little reality. A treaty between the govts. of two countries is not like a friendship between two people; more like a transaction between two people's lawyers. I think love for one's country means chiefly love for people who have a good deal in common with oneself (language, clothes, institutions) and in that is very like love of one's family or school; or like love (in a strange place) for anyone who once lived in one's home town. The familiar is in itself ground for affection. And it is good; because any *natural* help towards our spiritual duty of loving is good and God seems to build our higher loves round our merely natural impulses—

sex, maternity, kinship, old acquaintances etc. And in a less degree there are similar grounds for loving other nations—historical links and debts for literature, etc. . . . But I would distinguish that from the talk in the papers. . . .

TO SISTER PENELOPE, C.S.M.V.

5 June 1951

My love for G. Macdonald has not extended to most of his poetry, though I have naturally made several attempts to like it. Except for *The Diary of an Old Soul* it won't (so far as I am concerned) do. . . . As for me I specially need your prayers because I am (like the pilgrim in Bunyan) travelling across 'a plain called Ease'. Everything without, and many things within, are marvellously well at present. Indeed (I do not know whether to be more ashamed or joyful in confessing it) I realize that until about a month ago I never really believed (tho' I thought I did) in God's forgiveness. What an ass I have been both for not knowing and for thinking I knew. I now feel that one must never say one believes or understands anything; any morning a doctrine I thought I already possessed may blossom into this new reality. . . .

TO A LADY.

13 June 1951

(1) I think you are confusing the Immaculate Conception with the Virgin Birth. The former is a doctrine peculiar to the Roman Catholics and asserts that the mother of Jesus was born free of original sin. It does not concern us at all.

(2) The Virgin birth is a doctrine plainly stated in the Apostle's Creed that Jesus had no physical father, and was not conceived as a result of sexual intercourse. It is not a doctrine on which there is any dispute between Presbyterians as such and Episcopalians as such. A few individual Modernists in both these

churches have abandoned it; but Presbyterianism or Episcopalianism in general and in actual historical instances through the centuries both affirm it. The exact details of such a miracle—an exact point at which a supernatural enters this world (whether by the creation of a new spermatozoon, or the fertilization of an ovum without a spermatozoon or the development of a foetus without an ovum) are not part of the doctrine. These are matters in which no one is obliged and everyone is free, to speculate. *Your* starting point about this doctrine will not, I think, be to collect the opinions of individual clergymen, but to read Matthew and Luke I and II.

(3) Similarly, your question about the resurrection is answered in Luke XXIV. This makes it clear beyond any doubt that what is claimed is *physical* resurrection. (All Jews except Sadducees already believed in spiritual revival—there would have been nothing novel or exciting in that.)

(4) Thus the questions that you raise are not questions at issue between real P. and real Ep. at all for both these claim to agree with scripture. Neither church by the way seems to be very intelligently represented by the people you have gone to for advice, which is bad luck. I find it very hard to advise in your choice. At any rate the programme, *until* you can make up your mind, is to read your New Testament (preferably a modern translation) intelligently. Pray for guidance, obey your conscience in small as well as in great matters, as strictly as you can.

(5) Don't bother much about your feelings. When they are humble, loving, brave, give thanks for them; when they are conceited, selfish, cowardly, ask to have them altered. In neither case are they *you*, but only a thing that happens to you. What matters is your intentions and your behaviour. (I hope all of this is not very dull and disappointing. Write freely again if I can be of any use to you.)

P.S. Of course God does not consider you hopeless. If He did he would not be moving you to seek Him (and He obviously is). What is going on in you at present is simply the beginning of the *treatment*. Continue seeking Him with seriousness. Unless He wanted you, you would not be wanting Him.

TO A LADY.

12 September 1951

I have not a word to say against the doctrine that Our Lord suffers in all the suffering of His people (see Acts IX. 6) or that when we willingly accept what we suffer for others and offer it to God on their behalf, then it may be united with His sufferings and, in Him, may help to their redemption or even that of others whom we do not dream of. So that it is not in vain; tho' of course we must not count on seeing it work out exactly as we, in our present ignorance, might think best. The key text for this view is Colossians I. 24. Is it not, after all, one more application of the truth that we are all 'members one of another'? I wish I had known more when I wrote *Problem of Pain*. . . .

TO MISS VERA MATHEWS.

(Undated)

Since then I have been in really quiet and unearthly spots in my native Ireland. I stayed for a fortnight in a bungalow which none of the peasants will approach at night because the desolate coast on which it stands is haunted by 'the good people'. There is also a ghost but (and this is interesting) they don't seem to mind *him*; the faeries are a more serious danger. . . .

TO A CRITICAL BUT CHARITABLE READER.

(Undated)

Yes. I'm not surprised that a man who agreed with me in *Screwtape* (ethics served with an imaginative seasoning) might disagree with me when I wrote about religion. We can hardly discuss the whole matter by post, can we? I'll only make one shot. When people object, as you do, that if Jesus was God as well as

Man, then He had an unfair advantage which deprives Him for them of all value, it seems to me as if a man struggling in the water shd. refuse a rope thrown to him by another who had one foot on the bank, saying 'Oh but you have an unfair advantage'. It is because of that advantage that He can help. But all good wishes; we must just differ; in charity I hope. You must not be *angry* with me for believing, you know; I'm not angry with you.

I feel sure you will not be offended if I tell you that I have—with great reluctance—sent your gift straight on to someone else, whose need is much greater than mine . . . an elderly lady who has always had a struggle to make both ends meet and who . . . is now on the verge of actual want. . . . Amongst the elderly, living on dwindling investment income in a world of rising prices, there is already discomfort, hardship, and I fear in many cases, real suffering. . . .

TO THE PRIME MINISTER'S SECRETARY, *in reply to the offer of a C.B.E.*

3 December 1951

I feel greatly obliged to the Prime Minister, and so far as my personal feelings are concerned this honour would be highly agreeable. There are always however knaves who say, and fools who believe, that my religious writings are all covert anti-Leftist propaganda, and my appearance in the Honours List wd. of course strengthen their hands. It is therefore better that I shd. not appear there. I am sure the Prime Minister will understand my reason, and that my gratitude is and will be none the less cordial.

TO A LADY.

26 December 1951

I am v. glad you have discovered François de Sales. I would regard his prose and Geo. Herbert's verse as the *sweetest* of religious writings. And how remarkable it is that such a man's mere statement that anxiety is a great evil at once helps you to escape from that evil. That indeed seems to be one of the magical Laws of this very creation in which we live; that the thing we know already, the thing we have said to ourselves a hundred times, when said by *someone else* becomes suddenly operative. It is part of C. Williams' doctrine, isn't it?—that no one can paddle his own canoe but everyone can paddle someone else's. . .

TO MRS. L. (*See pp.* 218–221 *and* 227.)

8 January 1952

'Whether it is any good praying for actual things'—the first question is what one means by 'any good'. Is it a good thing to do? Yes: however we explain it, we are *told* to ask for particular things such as our daily bread. Does it 'work'? Certainly not like a mechanical operation or a magical spell. It is a *request* which of course the Other Party may or may not, for His own good reasons, grant. But how can it change God's will? Well—but how v. odd it would be if God in His actions towards me were bound to ignore what I did (including my prayers). Surely He hasn't to forgive me for sins I didn't commit or to cure me of errors into which I have never fallen? In other words His will (however changeless in some ultimate metaphysical sense) must be related to what I am and do? And once grant that, and why should my asking or not asking not be *one* of the things He takes into account? At any rate He *said* He would—and he ought to know. (We often talk as if He were not very good at Theology!)

I certainly believe (now *really*, long since with a merely intellectual assent) that a sin once repented and forgiven, is gone, annihilated, burnt up in the fire of Divine Love, white as snow. There is no harm in continuing to 'bewail' it, i.e. to express one's sorrow, but not to ask for pardon, for that you have already—one's sorrow for being that sort of person. Your conscience need not be 'burdened' with it in the sense of feeling that you have an unsettled account, but you can still in a sense be *patiently* and (in a sense) *contentedly* humbled by it. . . .

TO SISTER PENELOPE C.S.M.V.

10 January 1952

I have, if not thought, yet imagined a good deal about the other kinds of men. My own idea was based on the old problem, 'Who was Cain's wife?' If we follow scripture it would seem that she must have been no daughter of Adam's. I pictured the true men descending from Seth, then meeting Cain's not perfectly human descendants (in Genesis VI. 1–4, where I agree with you) interbreeding and thus producing the wicked Antediluvians. Oddly enough I, like you, had pictured Adam as being physically the son of the anthropoids on whom God worked after birth the miracle which made him Man; said in fact, 'Come out. Forget thine own people and thy father's house'. The call of Abraham would be a far smaller instance of the same sort of thing, and regeneration in each one of us wd. be an instance too tho' not a smaller one. That all seems to fit in historically and spiritually. I don't quite feel we shd. gain anything by the doctrine that Adam was a hermaphrodite. As for the rudimentary presence in each sex of organs proper to the other, does not that occur in other mammals as well as humans? Surely pseudo-organs of lactation are externally visible in the male dog? If so there wd. be no *more* ground for making men, I mean humans, hermaphrodite than any other mammal.... No doubt these rudimentary organs have a spiritual significance; there ought spiritually to be a man in every woman and a woman in every man. And how horrid the ones who haven't got it are; I can't bear 'a man's man' or a 'woman's woman'....

TO A LADY.

31 January 1952

That suffering is not *always* sent as a punishment is clearly established for believers by the book of Job and by John IX. 1–4. That it *sometimes* is, is suggested by parts of the Old Testament and Revelation. It wd. certainly be most dangerous to assume that any given pain was penal. I believe that all pain is contrary to

God's will, absolutely but not relatively. When I am taking a thorn out of my own finger (or a child's finger) the pain is 'absolutely' contrary to my will; i.e. if I could have chosen a situation without pain I would have done so. But I *do* will what caused the pain, relatively to the given situation; i.e. granted the thorn I prefer the pain to leaving the thorn where it is. A mother spanking a child would be in the same position; she would rather cause it this pain than let it go on pulling the cat's tail, but she would like it better if no situation which demands a smack had arisen.

On the heathen, see Tim. IV. 10. Also in Matt. XXV. 31–46 the people don't sound as if they were believers. Also the doctrine of Christ's descending into Hell (i.e. Hades, the land of the dead; not Gehenna the land of the lost) and preaching to the dead; and that would be outside time and would include those who died long after Him as well as those who died before He was born as Man. I don't think we know the details; we must just stick to the view that (a) all justice and mercy will be done, (b) but nevertheless it is our duty to do all we can to convert unbelievers.

TO A LADY.

29 February 1952

I learn from Mrs. Arnold that you are taking the plunge. As you have been now for so long in my prayers, I hope it will not seem intrusive to send you my congratulations. Or I might say condolences and congratulations. For whatever people who have never undergone an adult conversion may say, it is a process not without its distresses. Indeed they are the very sign that it is a true initiation. Like learning to swim or to skate, or getting married, or taking up a profession. There are cold shudderings about all these processes. When one finds oneself learning to fly *without* trouble one soon discovers (usually—there *are* blessed exceptions where we are allowed to take a real step without that difficulty) by waking up, that it was only a dream. All blessings and good wishes.

TO THE SAME.

18 March 1952

Don't bother at all about that question of a person being 'made a Christian' by baptism. It is only the usual trouble about words being used in more than one sense. Thus we might say a man 'became a soldier' the moment that he joined the army. But his instructors might say six months later 'I think we have made a soldier of him'. Both usages are quite definable, only one wants to know which is being used in a given sentence. The Bible itself gives us one short prayer which is suitable for all who are struggling with the beliefs and doctrines. It is: Lord I believe, help Thou my unbelief.

Would something of this sort be any good?: 'Almighty God, who art the father of lights and who hast promised by thy dear Son that all who do thy will shall know thy doctrine: give me grace so to live that by daily obedience I daily increase in faith and in the understanding of thy Holy Word, through Jesus Christ our Lord. Amen.'

TO A LADY.

1 April 1952

The advantage of a fixed form of service is that we know what is coming. *Ex tempore* public prayer has this difficulty; we don't know whether we can mentally join in it until we've heard it—it might be phoney or heretical. We are therefore called upon to carry on a *critical* and a *devotional* activity at the same moment: two things hardly compatible. In a fixed form we ought to have 'gone through the motions' before in our private prayers; the rigid form really sets our devotions *free*. I also find the more rigid it is, the easier it is to keep one's thoughts from straying. Also it prevents getting too completely eaten up by whatever happens to be the preoccupation of the moment (i.e. war, an election, or what not). The *permanent* shape of Christianity shows through. I don't see how the *ex tempore* method can help becoming provincial, and I think it has a great tendency to direct attention to the minister rather than to God. Quakers—well I've been unlucky in mine. The ones I know are atrocious bigots whose religion seems to consist almost entirely in attacking other people's religions. But I'm sure there are as good ones as ever.

TO MRS. L. (*See pp.* 218–221, 227, *and* 236.)

13 May 1952

In Bp. Gore's *Sermon on the mount*. . . . I find the view that Christ forbade 'divorce in such a sense as allowed re-marriage'. The question is whether He made an exception by allowing divorce in such sense as allowed re-marriage when the divorce was for adultery. In the Eastern Church re-marriage of the innocent party is allowed; not in the Roman. The Anglican Bps. at Lambeth in 1888 denied re-marriage to the guilty party, and added that 'there has always been a difference of opinion in the Ch. as to whether Our Lord meant to forbid re-marriage of the innocent party in a divorce'.

It would seem then that the only question is whether you can divorce your husband in such a sense as wd. make you free to re-marry. I imagine that nothing is further from your thoughts. I believe that you are free as a Christian woman to divorce him especially since the refusal to do so does some harm to the innocent children of his mistress; but that you must (or should) regard yourself as no more free to marry another man than if you had not divorced him. But remember I'm no authority on such matters, and I hope you will ask the advice of one or two sensible clergymen of our own Church. Our own Vicar whom I have just rung up, says that there *are* Anglican theologians who say that you must not divorce him. His own view was that in doubtful cases the Law of Charity shd. always be the over-riding consideration, and in a case such as yours charity directs you to divorce him. . . .

TO A LADY.

15 May 1952

Thanks for your letter of the 9th. All our prayers are being answered, and I thank God for it. The only (possibly, not necessarily) unfavourable symptom is that you are just a trifle too excited. It is quite right that you should feel that 'something terrific' has happened to you.... Accept these sensations with thankfulness as birthday cards from God, but remember that they are only greetings, not the real gift. I mean that it is not the sensations that are the real thing. The real thing is the gift of the Holy Spirit which can't usually be—perhaps not ever—experienced as a sensation or emotion. The sensations are merely the response of your nervous system. Don't depend on them. Otherwise when they go and you are once more emotionally flat (as you certainly will be quite soon), you might think that the real thing had gone too. But it won't. It will be there when you can't feel it. May even be most operative when you can feel it least.

Don't imagine it is all 'going to be an exciting adventure from now on'. It won't. Excitement, of whatever sort, never lasts. This is the push to start you off on your first bicycle: you'll be left to lots of dogged pedalling later on. And no need to feel depressed about it either. It will be good for your spiritual leg muscles. So enjoy the push while it lasts, but enjoy it as a treat, not as something normal.

Of course none of us have 'any right' at the altar. You might as well talk of a non-existent person 'having a right' to be created. It is not *our* right but God's free bounty. An English peer said, 'I like the order of the Garter because it has no dam' nonsense about merit'. Nor has Grace. And we must keep on remembering that as a cure for Pride. Yes, pride is a perpetual nagging temptation. Keep on knocking it on the head, but don't be too worried about it. As long as one knows one is proud one is safe from the worst form of pride. If S—— answers your letter, then let the correspondence drop. He is not a great philosopher (and none of my scientific colleagues think much of him as a scientist) but he is strong enough to do some harm. You're not David and no one has told you to fight Goliath. You've only just enlisted. Don't go off challenging enemy champions. Learn your drill. I hope this doesn't sound all like cold water. I can't tell you how pleased I was with your letter. God bless you.

TO DOM BEDE GRIFFITHS, O.S.B.

28 May 1952

It isn't chiefly *men* I am kept in touch with by my huge mail: it is *women*. The female, happy or unhappy, agreeing or disagreeing, is by nature a much more *epistolatary* animal than the male.

Yes, Pascal does contradict several passages in Scripture and must be wrong. What I ought to have said was that the Cosmological argument is, for some people at some times, ineffective. It always has been for me. (By the way, do read K. Z. Lorenz's *King Solomon's Ring* on animal—especially bird—behaviour. There are instincts I had never dreamed of: big with the promise of real morality. The wolf is a v. different creature from what we imagine.)

The stories you tell about the two perverts belong to a terribly familiar pattern: the man of good will, saddled with an abnormal desire wh. he never chose, fighting hard and time after time defeated. But I question whether in such a life the successful operation of Grace is so tiny as we think. Is not this continued avoidance either of presumption or despair, this ever renewed struggle itself a great triumph of Grace? Perhaps more so than the (to human eyes) equable virtue of some who are psychologically sound. I am glad you think J. Austen a sound moralist. I agree. And not platitudinous, but subtle as well as firm.

TO A LADY

20 June 1952

I would prefer to combat the 'I'm special' feeling not by the thought 'I'm no more special than anyone else', but by the feeling 'Everyone is as special as me'. In one way there is no difference, I grant, for both remove the speciality. But there is a difference in another way. The first might lead you to think, 'I'm only one of the crowd like everyone else'. But the second leads to the truth that there isn't any crowd. No one is like anyone else. All are 'members' (organs) in the Body of Christ. All different and all necessary to the whole and to one another; each loved by God individually, as if it were the only creature in existence. Otherwise you might get the idea that God is like the government which can only deal with the people in the mass.

About confession, I take it that the view of our Church is that everyone may use it but none is obliged to. I don't doubt that the Holy Spirit guides your decisions from within when you make them with the intention of pleasing God. The error wd. be to think that He speaks *only* within, whereas in reality He speaks also through Scripture, the Church, Christian friends, books etc. . . .

TO A LADY.

(Undated)

Incense and Hail Marys are in quite different categories. The one is merely a question of ritual; some find it helpful and others don't, and each must put up with its absence or presence in the church they are attending with cheerful and charitable humility. But Hail Marys raise a doctrinal question; whether it is lawful to address devotions to any *creature*, however holy. My own view would be that a *salute* to any saint (or angel) cannot in itself be wrong any more than taking off one's hat to a friend; but that there is always some danger lest such practices start one on the road to a state (sometimes found in R.C.s) where the B.V.M. is treated really as a divinity and even becomes the centre of the religion. I therefore think such salutes are better avoided. And if the Blessed Virgin is as good as the best mothers I have known, she does not *want* any of the attention which might have gone to her Son diverted to herself. . . .

TO CHARLES MOORMAN, *who had made enquiries concerning Charles Williams and also* That Hideous Strength.

2 October 1952

I am sure you are on a false scent. Certainly most, perhaps all the poems in [Charles Williams'] *Taliessin* volume were written before the last novel, *All Hallows Eve*, was even conceived, and there had been Arthurian poems (not of much value) in his earlier manner long before. I can't tell you when he first became interested in the Arthurian story, but the overwhelming probability is that, like so many English boys, he got via Tennyson into Malory in his 'teens. The whole way in which he talked of it implied a life-long familiarity. Much later (but even so, before I met him) came the link-up between his long-standing interest in *Arthuriana* and a new interest in Byzantium. Everything he ever said implied that his prose fiction, his 'pot boilers', and his poetry all went on concurrently; there was no 'turning from' one to the other. He never said anything to suggest that he felt his themes 'would not fit with ease into tales of modern life'. What would have expressed the real chronological relation between the novels would have been the words (tho' I don't think he ever actually said them) 'I haven't got much further with my Arthurian poems this week because I've been temporarily occupied with the idea for a new story'. The question when did he first come across the doctrine of 'Caritas' puzzled me. What doctrine do you mean? If you mean the ordinary Christian doctrine that there are three theological virtues and 'the greatest of these is charity' of course he would never remember a time when he had not known it. If you mean the doctrine of Coinherence and Substitution, then I don't know when he first met these. Nor do I know when he began the *Figure of A*. His knowledge of the earlier Arthurian documents was not that of a real scholar; he knew none of the relevant languages except (a little) Latin.

The VII Bears and the Atlantean Circle are pure inventions of my own, filling the same purpose in the narrative that 'noises off' wd. in a stage play. Numinor is a mis-spelling of Numenor which, like the 'true West', is a fragment from a vast private mythology invented by Professor J. R. R. Tolkien. At the time we all hoped that a good deal of that mythology would soon become public through a romance which the Professor was then contemplating. Since then the hope has receded. . . .

TO A LADY.

20 October 1952

I think you are perfectly right to change your manner of prayer from time to time and I should suppose that all who pray seriously do thus change it. One's needs and capacities change and also, for creatures like us, excellent prayers may 'go dead' if we use them too long. Whether one shd. use written prayers composed by other people, or one's own words, or wordless prayers, or in what proportion one should mix all three, seems entirely a question for each individual to answer from his own experience. I myself find prayers without words the best *when* I can manage it, but can do so only when least distracted and in the best spiritual and bodily health (or what I think best). But another person might find it quite otherwise.

Your question about old friendship where there is no longer spiritual communion is a hard one. Obviously it depends very much on what the other party wants. The great thing in friendship (as in all other forms of love) is, as you know to turn from the demand to *be* loved (or helped or amused) to the wish to love (or help or amuse). Perhaps in so far as one does this one also discovers how much time one shd. spend on the sort of friends you mention. I don't think a decay in one's desire for mere 'society' or 'acquaintance' or 'the crowd' is a bad sign. (We mustn't take it as a sign of our increasing spirituality of course; isn't it merely a natural neutral development as one grows older?)

All that Calvinist question—Free-will and Predestination—is to my mind indiscussible, insoluble. Of course (we say) if a man repents God will accept that. Ah yes (say they), but the fact of his repenting shows that God has already moved him to do so. This at any rate leaves us with the fact that in *any concrete case* the question never arises as a practical one. But I suspect it is really a meaningless question. The difference between Freedom and

Necessity is fairly clear on the bodily level; we know the difference between making our teeth chatter and just finding them chattering with the cold. It begins to be less clear when we talk about human love (leaving out the *erotic* kind). 'Do I like him because I choose or because I must?' There are cases where this has an answer, but others where it seems to me to mean nothing. When we carry it up to relations between God and Man, has the distinction become perhaps nonsensical? After all, when we are most free, it is only with freedom God has given us; and when our will is most influenced by Grace, it is still *our will*. And if what *our will* does is not voluntary, and if 'voluntary' does not mean 'free', what are we talking about? I'd leave it alone.

TO ROGER LANCELYN GREEN.

21 October 1952

I have just finished Vol. I of Henry James' letters. An interesting man, tho' a dreadful prig; but he did appreciate Stevenson. A *phantasmal* man, who had never known God, or earth, or war, never done a day's compelled work, never had to earn a living, had no home and no duties. . . .

TO A LADY.

8 November 1952

I am returning your letter with the questions in it numbered so that you'll know wh. I am answering.

(1) Some call me Mr. and some Dr. And I not only don't care but usually don't notice which.

(2) Distinguish (A) A second chance in the strict sense, i.e., a new earthly life in which you cd. attempt afresh all the problems you failed at in the present one (as in religions of Reincarnation. (B) Purgatory; a process by which the work of re-

demption continues, and first perhaps begins to be noticeable after death. I think Charles Williams depicts (B) and not (A).

(3) We are never given any knowledge of 'What would have happened if . . .'

(4) I think that every prayer which is sincerely made even to a false god or to a very imperfectly conceived true God, is accepted by the true God and that Christ saves many who do not think they know Him. For he is (dimly) present in the *good* side of the inferior teachers they follow. In the parable of the Sheep and the Goats (Matt. XXV. 31 and following) those who are saved do not seem to know that they have served Christ. But of course our anxiety about unbelievers is most usefully employed when it leads us, not to speculation but to earnest prayer for them and the attempt to be in our own lives such good advertisements for Christianity as will make it attractive.

(5) It is Christ Himself, not the Bible, who is the true word of God. The Bible, read in the right spirit and with the guidance of good teachers, will bring us to Him. When it becomes really necessary (i.e. for our spiritual life, not for controversy or curiosity) to know whether a particular passage is rightly translated or is myth (but of course myth specially chosen by God from among countless myths to carry a spiritual truth) or history, we shall no doubt be guided to the right answer. But we must not use the Bible (our fathers too often did) as a sort of Encyclopedia out of which texts (isolated from their context and not read with attention to the whole nature and purport of the books in which they occur) can be taken for use as weapons.

(6) *Kill* means *murder*. I don't know Hebrew; but when Our Lord quotes this commandment he uses the Greek φονεύειν . . . .

(7) The question of what you wd. 'want' is off the point. Capital punishment might be wrong tho' the relations of the murdered man wanted him killed; it might be right tho' they did not want this. The question is whether a Xtian nation ought or ought not to put murderers to death; not what passions interested individuals may feel.

(8) There is no doubt at all that the natural impulse to 'hit back' must be fought against by the Xtian whenever it arises. If one I love is tortured or murdered my desire to avenge him must be given no quarter. So far as nothing but this question of

retaliation comes in 'turn the other cheek' *is* the Christian law. It is however quite another matter when the neutral public authority (*not* the aggrieved person) may order killing of either private murderers or of public enemies in mass. It is quite clear that St. Paul . . . approved of capital punishment—he says 'the magistrate bears the sword and should bear the sword'. It is recorded that the soldiers who came to St. John Baptist asking, 'What shall we do?' were *not* told to leave the army. When Our Lord Himself praised the Centurion He never hinted that the military profession was in itself sinful. This has been the general view of Christendom. Pacifism is a v. recent and local variation. We must of course respect and tolerate Pacifists, but I think their view erroneous.

(9) The symbols under which Heaven is presented to us are (a) a dinner party, (b) a wedding, (c) a city, and (d) a concert. It would be grotesque to suppose that the guests or citizens or members of the choir didn't know one another. And how can love of one another be commanded in this life if it is to be cut short at death?

(10) When I have learnt to love God better than my earthly dearest, I shall love my earthly dearest better than I do now. In so far as I learn to love my earthly dearest at the expense of God and *instead* of God, I shall be moving towards the state in which I shall not love my earthly dearest at all. When first things are put first, second things are not suppressed but increased. If you and I ever come to love God perfectly, the answer to this tormenting question will then become clear and will be far more beautiful than we cd. ever imagine. We can't have it now.

TO MRS. EDWARD A. ALLEN.

19 January 1953

I don't wonder that you got fogged in *Pilgrim's Regress*. It was my first religious book and I didn't then know how to make things easy. I was not even trying to very much, because in those days I never dreamed I would become a 'popular' author and hoped for no readers outside a small 'highbrow' circle. Don't waste your time over it any more. The *poetry* is my own. . . .

TO A LADY.

6–7 April 1953

I don't think gratitude is a relevant motive for joining an Order. Gratitude might create a state of mind in which one became aware of a vocation; but the vocation would be the proper reason for joining. They themselves would surely not wish you to join *without* it? You can show your gratitude in lots of other ways. Is there in this Order, even for lay members such as you would be, not something like a noviciate or experimental period? If so, that would be the thing, wouldn't it? If not, I think I can only repeat my previous suggestion of undergoing a sort of unofficial noviciate by living according to the Rule for 6 months or so and seeing how it works. Most of the things you probably do anyway and are things we ought to do. (The only one I'm doubtful about is the 'special intention' clause. I'm not quite sure what the theological implications are). . . . Is the vow irrevocable or can you contract out again?

About putting one's Christian point of view to doctors and other unpromising subjects I'm in great doubt myself. All I'm clear about is that one sins if one's real reason for silence is simply the fear of looking a fool. I suppose one is right if one's reason is that the other party will be repelled still further and only confirmed in his belief that Christians are troublesome and embarrassing people, to be avoided whenever possible. But I find it a dreadfully worrying problem. (I am quite sure that an importunate bit of evangelisation from a comparative stranger would *not* have done me any good when I was an unbeliever.)

I think our official view of Confession can be seen in the form for the Visitation of the Sick, where it says, 'Then shall the sick person be moved (i.e. advised, prompted) to make a . . . Confession . . . if he feel his conscience troubled with any weighty matters'. That is, where Rome makes Confession compulsory for all, we make it permissible for any; not 'generally necessary' but profitable. We do not doubt that there can be forgiveness without it. But, as your own experience shows, many people do not *feel* forgiveness, i.e. do not effectively believe in 'the forgiveness of sins', without it. The quite enormous advantage of coming *really* to believe in forgiveness is well worth the horrors (I agree that they *are* horrors) of a first Confession. Also, there is the gain in self-knowledge; most of us have never really faced the facts about ourselves until we uttered them aloud in plain words, calling a spade a spade. I certainly feel that I have profited enormously by the practice. At the same time I think we are quite right not to make it generally obligatory, which might force it on some who are not ready for it and might do harm. . . .

TO A LADY.

17 July 1953

I'm v. glad you've seen that Christianity is as hard as nails; i.e. hard *and* tender at the same time. It's the *blend* that does it; neither quality would be any good without the other. You needn't worry about not feeling brave. Our Lord didn't—see the scene in Gethsemane. How thankful I am that when God became man He did not choose to become a man of iron nerves; that would not have helped weaklings like you and me nearly so much. Especially don't *worry* (you may of course pray) about being brave over merely possible evils in the future. In the old battles it was usually the reserve, who had to *watch* the carnage, not the troops who were in it, whose nerve broke first. Similarly I think you in America feel much more anxiety about atomic bombs than we do; because you are further from the danger. If and when a horror turns up you will then be given Grace to help you. I don't think one is usually given it in advance. 'Give us our daily bread' (not an annuity for life) applies to spiritual gifts too; the little *daily* support for the *daily* trial. Life has to be taken day by day and hour by hour.

The writer you quote *was* very good at the stage at wh.

you met him; now, as is plain, you've got beyond him. Poor boob—he thought his mind was his own. Never his own until he makes it Christ's; up till then, merely a result of heredity, environment, and the state of his digestion. I became my own only when I gave myself to Another. 'Does God seem real to me?' It varies; just as lots of other things I firmly believe in (my own death, the solar system) *feel* more or less real at different times. I have dreamed dreams but not seen visions; but don't think all that matters a hoot. And the saints say that visions are unimportant. If Our Lord *did* seem to appear to you at your prayers (bodily) what after all could you do but go on with your prayers? How cd. you know that it was not an hallucination? . . .

No, no, I'm not committed to a real belief in Aslan, all that comes in a *story*. I haven't the faintest idea whether there was a real Grail or not. Of course I believe that people are still healed by faith; whether that has happened in any particular case one can't of course say without getting a real doctor who is also a real Christian to go through the whole case-history. . . .

TO MRS. EMILY MCLAY.

3 August 1953

I take it as a first principle that we must not interpret any one part of Scripture so that it contradicts other parts, and specially we must not use an apostle's teaching to contradict that of Our Lord. Whatever St. Paul may have meant, we must not reject the parable of the sheep and the goats (Matt. xxv. 30–46). There, you see there is nothing about Predestination or even about Faith—all depends on works. But how this is to be reconciled with St. Paul's teaching, or with other sayings of Our Lord, I frankly confess I don't know. Even St. Peter you know admits that he was stumped by the Pauline Epistles (II Peter. iii. 16–17).

What I think is this. Everyone looking back on *his own* conversion must feel—and I am sure the feeling is in some sense true—'It is not I who have done this. I did not choose Christ; He chose me. It is all free Grace which I have done nothing to earn'. That is the Pauline account; and I am sure it is the only true account of every conversion *from the inside*. Very well. It then seems to us logical and natural to turn this personal experience into a general rule, 'All conversions depend on God's choice'. But this I believe is exactly what we must not do; for generalizations are legitimate only when we are dealing with matters to which our faculties are adequate. Here, we are not. How our individual experiences are in reality consistent with (a) our idea of Divine justice, (b) the parable I've just quoted, and lots of other passages, we don't and can't know. What is clear is that we can't find a consistent formula.

I think we must take a leaf out of the scientists' book. They are quite familiar with the fact that for example, Light has to be regarded *both* as a wave in the ether and as a stream of particles. No-one can make these two views consistent. Of course reality must be self-consistent; but till (if ever) we can *see* the consistency it is better to hold two inconsistent views than to ignore one side of the evidence. The real inter-relation between God's omnipotence and Man's freedom is something we can't find out. Looking at the Sheep and the Goats, every man can be quite sure that every kind act he does will be accepted by Christ. Yet equally, we all do feel sure that all the good in us comes from Grace. We have to leave it at that. I find the best plan is to take the Calvinist view of my own virtues and other people's vices; and the other view of my own vices and other people's virtues. But tho' there is much to be puzzled about, there is nothing to be *worried* about. It is plain from Scripture that, in whatever sense the Pauline doctrine is true, it is not true in any sense which excludes its (apparent) opposite. You know what Luther said, 'Do you doubt if you are chosen? Then say your prayers and you may conclude that you are'.

TO MRS. EMILY MCLAY.

8 August 1953

Your experience in listening to those philosophers gives you the technique one needs for dealing with the dark places in the Bible. When one of the philosophers, one whom you knew on other grounds to be a sane and decent man, said something you didn't understand, you did not at once conclude that he had gone off his head. You assumed that you'd missed the point. Same here.

The two things one must *not* do are (a) to believe on the strength of Scripture or on any other evidence that God is in any way evil (In Him is no *darkness* at all) (b) to wipe off the slate any passage which seems to show that He is. Behind the shocking passage be sure there lurks some great truth which you don't understand. If one ever *does* come to understand it, one sees that it is good and just and gracious in ways we never dreamed of. Till then it must just be left on one side.

But why are baffling passages left in at all? Oh, because God speaks not only for us little ones but for the great sages and mystics who *experience* what we can only *read about*, and to whom all the words have therefore different (richer) contents. Would not a revelation which contained nothing that you and I did not understand, be for that very reason rather suspect? To a child it would seem a contradiction to say both that his parents made him and God made him, yet we see how both can be true.

TO MRS. EDWARD A. ALLEN.

9 January 1954

Thank you for your nice woody and earthy (almost like Thoreau or Dorothy Wordsworth) letter of the 6th. I think I go with you in preferring trees to flowers in the sense that if I had to live in a world without one or the other I'd choose to keep the trees. I certainly prefer tree-like people to flower-like people—the staunch and knotty and storm-enduring kind to the frilly and fragrant and easily withered. . . .

I think what makes even beautiful country (in the long run) so unsatisfactory when seen from a train or a car is that it whirls each tree, brook, or haystack close up into the foreground, *soliciting* individual attention but vanishing before you can give it. . . . Didn't someone give a similar explanation of the weariness we feel in a crowd where we can't help seeing individual faces but can do no more than see them so that (he said) 'it is like being forced to read the first page, but no more, of 100 books in succession'? . . .

TO DOM BEDE GRIFFITHS, O.S.B. *who was concerning himself with the problems of Christian missionary work in India.*

16 January 1954

I suspect that a great going-to-meet-them is needed, not only on the level of thought but in method. A man who had lived all his life in India said, 'That country might be Christian now if there had been *no* Missions in our sense but many single missionaries walking the roads with their begging bowls. For that is the sort of Holy Man India believes in, and she will never believe in any other'. Of course we must beware of thinking about 'the East' as if it were homogeneous. I suppose the Indian and the Chinese *ethos* are as alien to each other as either is to us.

The article on Tolerance in that same issue made my flesh creep. What do they mean by 'Error has no rights'? Of course Error has no rights because it is not a person: in the same sense Truth has no rights. But if they mean 'Erroneous persons have no rights', surely this is as contrary to the plain dictates of Natural Law as any proposition could be?

Quite a different question. Has anyone composed prayers for children, NOT in the sense of special prayers supposed suitable for their age (which easily leads to wish-wash) BUT simply in the sense of *translations* of ordinary prayers into the easiest language. And wd. it be worth doing?

TO DOM BEDE GRIFFITHS, O.S.B.

23 January 1954

I *have* a taste for Dickens but don't think it a low one. He is the great author on mere affection (*storge*); only he and Tolstoi (another great favourite of mine) really deal with it. Of course his error lies in thinking it will do instead of *agape*. Scott, as D. Cecil said, has not the critical *mind* but the civilized *heart*. Unforced nobility, generosity, liberality, flow from him. But Thackeray I positively dislike. He is the voice of 'the world' and his supposedly 'good' women are revolting: jealous *pharisiennes*. The publicans and sinners will go in before Mrs. Pendennis or Lady Castlewood.

TO DOM BEDE GRIFFITHS, O.S.B.

30 January 1954

Yes, I certainly rule out Little Emily and Little Nell and all the 'littles'. The Marchioness is the real thing. The trouble in Thackeray is that he can hardly envisage goodness except as a kind of εὐήθεια; all his 'good' people are not only simple but simpletons. That is a subtle poison which comes in with the Renaissance: the Machiavellian (intelligent) villain presently producing the idiot hero. The Middle Ages didn't make Herod clever, and knew the devil was an ass. There is really an un-faith about Thackeray's ethics; as if goodness were somehow charming and infantile. No conception that the purification of the will (*ceteris paribus*) leads to the enlightenment of the intelligence.

TO A LADY.

18 February 1954

Of course taking in the poor illegitimate child is 'charity'. *Charity* means love. It is called Agape in the New Testament to distinguish it from Eros (sexual love), Storge (family affection) and Philia (friendship). So there are 4 kinds of love, all good in their proper place, but Agape is the best because it is the kind God has for us and is good in all circumstances. There are people I mustn't feel Eros towards, and people I can't feel Storge or Philia for; but I can practise Agape to God, Angels, Man and

Beast, to the good and the bad, the old and the young, the far and the near. You see Agape is all giving, not getting. Read what St. Paul says about it in First Corinthians Chap. 13. Then look at a picture of Agape in action in St. Luke, Chap. 10, vv. 30–35. And then, better still, look at Matthew Ch. 25, vv. 31–46; from which you see that Christ counts all that you do for *this* baby exactly as if you had done it for Him when He was a baby in the manger at Bethlehem; you are in a sense sharing in the things His mother did for Him. Giving money is only *one* way of showing charity; to give time and toil is far better and (for most of us) harder.

And notice, tho' it is all giving,—you needn't expect any reward—how you *do* get rewarded almost at once. Yes. I know one doesn't even *want* to be cured of one's pride because it gives pleasure. But the pleasure of pride is like the pleasure of scratching. If there is an itch one does want to scratch; but it is much nicer to have *neither* the itch nor the scratch. As long as we have the itch of self-regard we shall want the pleasure of self-approval; but the happiest moments are those when we forget our precious selves and have neither but have everything else (God, our fellow humans, animals, the garden and the sky) instead. . . .

TO MRS. URSULA ROBERTS

31 July 1954

I am certainly unfit to advise anyone else on the devotional life. My own rules are (1). To make sure that, wherever else they may be placed, the main prayers should *not* be put 'last thing at night'. (2). To avoid introspection in prayers—I mean not to watch one's own mind to see if it is in the right frame, but always to turn the attention outwards to God. (3). Never, never to try to generate an emotion by will power. (4). To pray without words when I am able, but to fall back on words when tired or otherwise below par. With renewed thanks. Perhaps *you* will sometimes pray for *me*?

TO MRS. EDWARD A. ALLEN.

1 November 1954

I think it would be dangerous to suppose that Satan had created all the creatures that are disagreeable or dangerous to us for (a) those creatures, if they could think, wd. have just the same reason for thinking that *we* were created by Satan. (b). I don't think evil, in the strict sense, can *create*. It can spoil something that Another has created. Satan may have corrupted other creatures as well as us. Part of the corruption in us might be the unreasoning horror and disgust we feel at some creatures quite apart from any harm they can do us. (I can't abide a spider myself). We have scriptural authority for Satan originating diseases—see Luke XIII. 16.

Do you know, the suffering of the innocent is *less* of a problem to me v. often than that of the wicked. It sounds absurd; but I've met so many innocent sufferers who seem to be gladly offering their pain to God in Christ as part of the Atonement, so patient, so meek, even so at peace, and so unselfish that we can hardly doubt they are being, as St. Paul says, 'made perfect by suffering'. On the other hand I meet selfish egoists in whom suffering seems to produce only resentment, hate, blasphemy, and more egoism. They are the real problem.

Christian Scientists seem to me to be altogether too simple. Granted that all the evils are illusions, still, the existence of that illusion wd. be a real evil and presumably a real evil permitted by God. That brings us back to exactly the same point as we began from. We have gained nothing by the theory. We are still faced with the great mystery, not explained, but coloured, transmuted, all through the Cross. Faith, not wild over-simplifications, is what will help, don't you think? Is it so v. difficult to believe that the travail of all creation which God Himself descended to share, at its most intense, may be necessary in the process of turning finite creatures (with free wills) into—well, into Gods. . . .

TO DOM BEDE GRIFFITHS, O.S.B.

1 November 1954

Your book came at a moment of low spiritual temper, external worry, and (mild) physical pain. I had prayed v. hard a couple of nights before that my faith might be strengthened. The response was immediate and your book gave the finishing touch. It did me a great deal of good: apart, of course from its lower gains in the way of interest and enjoyment. This made an objective literary judgement v. difficult, but I think you have probably done it very well. It must have been a job to keep it so short without becoming perfunctory, and so subjective without being (and it is not in the least) mawkish or suffocating. Much that you said about the Sacraments was v. illuminating. One felt how Paganism does not merely survive but first becomes really itself in the v. heart of Christianity. By the way wd. you agree that the un-Christening of Europe (much of it) is an even bigger change than its Christening? So that the gap between Professor Ryle and, say Dante, is *wider* than that between Dante and Virgil?

TO MRS. VERA GEBBERT (NÉE MATHEWS).

17 December 1954

Would you believe it; an American school girl has been expelled from her school for having in her possession a copy of my *Screwtape*. I asked my informant whether it was a Communist school, or a Fundamentalist school, or an RC school, and got the shattering answer, 'No, it was a *select* school'. That puts a chap in his place, doesn't it? . . .

TO JOCELYN GIBB, *his publisher; who had sent him handsomely-bound copies of* Surprised by Joy *and* Mere Christianity.

22 December 1954

I never had a handsomer present (both in a bibliophile's and in Mr. Wodehouse's sense of the word *handsome*). Perhaps these two charming volumes will teach me at last to have for the bodies of my own books the same reverence I have for the bodies of all other books. For it is a curious fact that I never can regard them as being really *books*; the boards and print, in however mint a condition, remain a mere pretence behind which one sees the scratchy, inky old MS. You might do a little research to find out if it is so with all authors. Thank you so much. Who did them?

I am always glad to hear of anyone's taking up that Cinderella, *The Great Divorce*.

With renewed thanks and all good wishes for Christmas and the New Year.

TO I. O. EVANS.

22 December 1954

About the word 'hiking' my own objection wd. lie only against its abuse for something so simple as going for a walk, i.e. the passion for making specialised and self-conscious stunts out of activities which have hitherto been as ordinary as shaving or playing with the kitten. Kipling's 'Janeites' where he makes a sort of secret society ritual out of (of all things) reading Jane Austen is a specimen. Or professionals on the BBC playing to an audience the same games we used to play for ourselves as children. . . .

There is a grain of seriousness in my sally against the Civil Service. I don't think you have worse taste or worse hearts than other men. But I do think the State is increasingly tyrannical and you, inevitably, are among the instruments of that tyranny. . . . This doesn't matter for you who did most of your service when the subject was still a free man. For the rising generation it will become a real problem at what point the policies you are ordered to carry out have become so iniquitous that a decent man must seek some other profession. . . .

TO THE MILTON SOCIETY OF AMERICA, *which on 28 December 1954 held 'A Milton Evening in Honour of Douglas Bush and C. S. Lewis'.*

(Undated)

Mr. Hunter informs me that your Society has done me an honour above my deserts. I am deeply grateful to be chosen for it and also delighted by the very existence of such a Society as yours. May it have a long and distinguished history.

The list of my books which I send . . . will I fear strike you as a very mixed bag . . . (but) there is a guiding thread. The imaginative man in me is older, more continuously operative, and in that sense more basic than either the religious writer or the critic. It was he who made me first attempt (with little success) to be a poet. It was he who, in response to the poetry of others, made me a critic, and, in defence of that response, sometimes a critical controversialist. It was he who after my conversion led me to embody my religious belief in symbolical or mythopeic forms, ranging from *Screwtape* to a kind of theologised science-fiction. And it was of course he who has brought me, in the last few years, to write the series of Narnian stories for children; not asking what children want and then endeavouring to adapt myself (this was not needed) but because the fairy tale was the genre best fitted for what I wanted to say. . . .

TO A LADY.

2 February 1955

Thanks for your letter. The day before it I got a letter from someone else asking me if the *Silent Planet* was a true story. It's not the first I've had. So I'm beginning to think that some people (and if you don't look out I'll have to include you!) just don't understand what fiction is. When you say what is natural with the intention of making people believe it, that's lying. When you say it with no such intention, that's fiction. But it may be perfectly serious in the sense that people often express their deepest thoughts, speculations, desires etc. in a story. Of course it would have been wrong for R. to talk about the land of the Pf. when he hadn't really been there, as if he had; because *inside the book* R. is supposed (or pretended) to be telling his story as true. Surely we can have a character in a story telling a lie, and distinguish it from what he ought to have said, although the v. things he is lying about are themselves (from *our* point of view who live outside the story) imaginary? As for 'writing stories about God', it would be rather a tall order to have a story strictly about God (beginning 'One day God decided' . . .). But to imagine what God might be supposed to have done in other worlds does not seem to be wrong; and a story is only imagining out loud.

It is right and inevitable that we shd. be much concerned about the salvation of those we love. But we must be careful not to expect or demand that their salvation shd. conform to some ready-made pattern of our own. Some Protestant sects have gone very wrong about this. They have a whole programme of conversion etc. marked out, the same for everyone, and will not believe that anyone can be saved who doesn't go through it 'just so'. But (see the last chapter of my *Problem of Pain*) God has His own way with each soul. There is no evidence that St. John underwent the same kind of 'conversion' as St. Paul. It's not essential to believe in the Devil; and I'm sure a man can get to Heaven without being accurate about Methuselah's age. Also, as Macdonald says 'the time for *saying* comes seldom, the time for *being* is always here'. What we practise, not (save at rare intervals) what we preach, is usually our great contribution to the conversion of others. . . .

TO THE SAME.

16 March 1955

I am afraid I am not going to be much help about all the religious bodies mentioned in your letter of March 2nd. I have always in my books been concerned simply to put forward 'mere' Christianity, and am no guide on these (most regrettable) 'inter-denominational' questions. I do however strongly object to the tyrannic and unscriptural insolence of anything that calls itself a Church and makes teetotalism a condition of membership. Apart from the more serious objection (that Our Lord Himself turned water into wine and made wine the medium of the only rite He imposed on all His followers), it is so provincial (what I believe you people call 'small town'). Don't they realize that Christianity arose in the Mediterranean world where, then as now, wine was as much part of the normal diet as bread? It was the 17th Century Puritans who first made the universal into a rich man's luxury. . . .

I think I can understand that feeling about a housewife's work being like that of Sisyphus (who was the stone-rolling gentleman). But it is surely in reality the most important work in the world. What do ships, railways, mines, cars, government etc. exist for except that people may be fed, warmed, and safe in their own homes? As Dr. Johnson said, 'To be happy at home is the end of all human endeavour'. (1st to be happy to prepare for being happy in our own real home hereafter; 2nd in the meantime to be happy in our houses). We wage war in order to have peace, we work in order to have leisure, we produce food in order to eat it. So your job is the one for which all others exist. . . .

TO THE SAME.

14 May 1955

My own view about Elisha and the Bears (not that I haven't known small boys who'd be much improved by the same treatment!) and other such episodes is something like this. If you take the Bible as a whole, you see a process in which something which, in its eccentric levels (these aren't necessarily the ones that come first in the Book as now arranged) was hardly moral at all, and was in some ways not unlike the Pagan religions, is gradually purged and enlightened till it becomes the religion of the great prophets, and of Our Lord Himself. That whole process is the greatest revelation of God's true nature. At first hardly anything comes through except mere power. Then (v. imperfect) the truth that He is One and there is no other God. Then justice, then mercy, last wisdom.

Of course Our Lord never drank *spirits* (they had no distilled liquors) but of course the wine of the Bible was real fermented wine and alcoholic. The repeated references to the sin of drunkenness in the Bible, from Noah's first discovery of wine down to the warnings in St. Paul's epistles, make this perfectly plain. The other theory could be (honestly) held only by a v. ignorant person. One can understand the bitterness of some temperance fanatics if one has ever lived with a drunkard; what one finds it harder to excuse is any educated person telling such lies about history.

I think myself that the shocking reply to the Syrophenician woman (it came alright in the end) is to remind all us Gentile Christians—who forget it easily enough and even flirt with anti-Semitism—that the Hebrews are spiritually *senior* to us, that God *did* entrust the descendants of Abraham with the first revelation of Himself. . . .

TO MRS. VERA GEBBERT.

25 June 1955

My lecture has proved a best seller and I've no copies left. . . . You've got it nearly right; the only error being that instead of saying the Great Divide came between the Middle Ages and the Renaissance, I said at great length and emphatically that it *didn't*. But of course 'not' is a very small word and one can't get every fine shade just right!

TO FR. PETER MILWARD.

22 September 1955

What Malory meant I have no idea. I doubt if he had any clear intention. To use an image I have used before, I think his work is like one of our old English cathedrals to which many generations have contributed in many different styles, so that the total effect was foreseen by no one and must be regarded as something midway between a work of art and a work of nature. I therefore give up asking what M. meant; we can only ask what his book in fact *means*. And to me it means primarily neither the Grail story nor the Lancelot story but precisely the tension and interlocking between the two.

I know v. little about the Albigensians (except that Denis de Rougement talks manifest nonsense). If I undertook a study of the Grail, I shd. begin by making up (you perhaps know it already) the history—with v. exact chronology—of the doctrine of Transubstantiation and of contemporary controversies and reactions. I suspect the story is closely connected with these.

It is certainly a remarkable fact (I hadn't noticed it before) that the post-medieval interest in Arthur has been almost exclusively Protestant. But one must beware of seeking causes too deep. Might it not be simply that the only nation wh. cd. regard Arthur as a *national* hero was a Protestant nation....

TO A CHILD IN AMERICA.

16 October 1955

In this country we hardly ever have any snow worth talking about till January or later. Once we had it at Easter after all the spring leaves were out. So the snow could lie on the trees far heavier than if they had been bare, and there was great destruction in the way of broken branches. We had our first frost last night—this morning the lawns are all grey, with a pale bright sunlight on them: wonderfully beautiful. And somehow *exciting*. The first beginning of the winter always excites me; it makes me want adventures. I expect our autumn has gentler colours than your fall and it goes far slower. The trees, especially beeches, keep their leaves for weeks and weeks after they have begun to change colour, turning from yellow to gold and from gold to flame colour.

I never knew a guinea-pig that took any notice of humans (they take plenty of one another). Of those small animals I think Hamsters are the most amusing . . . and, to tell you the truth, I am fond of mice. But the guinea-pigs go well with learning German. If they talked I'm sure that is the language they would speak.

TO EDWARD A. ALLEN.

5 December 1955

Oddly enough the week-end journeys [to and from Cambridge] are no trouble at all. I find myself perfectly content in a slow train that crawls through green fields stopping at every station. Just because the service is so slow and therefore in most people's eyes *bad*, these trains are almost empty. . . . I get through a lot of reading and sometimes say my prayers. A solitary railway journey I find quite excellent for this purpose. . . .

TO FR. PETER MILWARD.

17 December 1955

Thank you for yr. letters of Nov. 17. The enclosed card was one of the v. few I have been pleased at getting. Christmas cards in general and the whole vast commercial drive called 'Xmas' are one of my pet abominations; I wish they could die away and leave the Christian feast unentangled. Not of course that even secular festivities are, on their own level, an evil; but the laboured and organized jollity of this—the spurious childlikeness—the half-hearted and sometimes rather profane attempts to keep up some superficial connection with the Nativity—are disgusting. But yr. card is most interesting as an application of Japanese style to a Christian subject; and *me judice* extremely successful.

Albigensianism and ancient Celtic paganism are both increasingly popular 'sources' for medieval story; but I fear they are an *asylum ignorantiae*, chosen because we know so v. little about either. The facts I'd try to hold onto are (1). The name Galahad (Gilead). (2). The resemblance of the Grail to *manna* (see I think 'Wisdom'; the reference is at Cambridge.) (3). The (I think proved) Cistercian *provenance*. *Enthusiasm* is Ronny Knox's worst book. And of course you won't be misled by de Rougemont's nonsense in 'L'Amour et l'Occident' (Not that the ethics of the last chapter—'l'amour cesse d'être un demon quand il cesse d'être un dieu'—aren't excellent; but the historical parts are mildly speculative).

One quite sees the *chivalric* idea in St. Ignatius, but of course the chivalry of *Amadis* (an excellent romance by the way) is pretty different from that of Arthuriana in general, let alone the Sangrealiana in particular. . . .

TO DOM BEDE GRIFFITHS, O.S.B.

8 February 1956

Yes, I do feel the old Magdalen years to have been a v. important period in both our lives. More generally, I feel the whole of one's youth to be immensely important and even of immense length. The gradual *reading* of one's own life, seeing a pattern emerge, is a great illumination at our age. And partly, I hope, getting freed from the past as past by apprehending it as structure. If I ever write a story about someone like She or the Wandering Jew who lived for millenia, I shd. make a great point of this; he wd., after 10,000 years, still feel his first 50 years to be the biggest part of his life. I am glad you found a Chestertonian quality in the book. Actually it seems to me that one can hardly say anything either bad enough or good enough about life. The one picture that is utterly false is the supposed realistic fiction of the XIX century where all the real horrors and heavens are excluded. The reality is a queer mixture of idyll, tragedy, farce, melodrama: and the characters (even the same character) far better *and* worse than are ever imagined.

I wd. have preferred your book on Mysticism to be a Penguin, for I think they reach a larger audience than anything else. I look forward to it v. much. I think it is just the thing for you to do. You are (as you well know) on dangerous ground about Hinduism, but someone must go to dangerous places. One often wonders how different the content of our faith will look when we see it in the total context. Might it be as if one were living in an infinite earth? Further knowledge wd. leave our map of the Atlantic say, quite *correct*, but if it turned out to be the estuary of a great river—and the continent through which that river flowed turned out to be itself an island—off the shores of a still greater continent—and so on. You see what I mean? Not one jot of Revelation will be proved false; but so many new truths might be added.

By the way, that business of having to look up the same word ten times in one evening is no proof of failing powers, you have simply forgotten that it was exactly like that when we began Latin or even French.

Your Hindus certainly sound delightful. But what do they *deny*? That has always been my trouble with Indians—to find any proposition they wd. pronounce false. But truth must surely involve exclusions? I am reading Runciman's *History of the Crusades*; a terrible revelation—the old civilization of the E. Mediterranean destroyed by Turkish barbarians from the East and Frankish barbarians from the West.

TO A LADY.

13 March 1956

You'll find my views about drinks in *Christian Behaviour*. . . . Smoking is much harder to justify. I'd like to give it up but I'd find this v. hard, i.e. I can abstain, but I can't concentrate on anything else while abstaining—not smoking is a whole time job.

Birth control I won't give a view on; I'm certainly not prepared to say that it is always wrong. The doctrines about the Blessed Virgin which you mention are R.C. doctrines, aren't they? And as I'm not an R.C. I don't think I need bother about them. But the habit (of various Protestant sects) of plastering the landscape with religious slogans about the Blood of the Lamb etc. is a different matter. There is no question here of doctrinal difference; we agree with the doctrines they are advertising. What we disagree with is their taste. Well, let's go on disagreeing but don't let us *judge*. What doesn't suit us may suit possible converts of a different type. My model here is the behaviour of the congregation at a 'Russian Orthodox' service, where some sit, some lie on their faces, some stand, some kneel, some walk about, and *no one takes the slightest notice of what anyone else is doing*. That is good sense, good manners, and good Christianity. 'Mind one's own business' is a good rule in religion as in other things. . . .

TO MRS. R. E. HALVORSON.

(Undated)

One must first distinguish the effect which music has on people like me who are musically illiterate and get only the emotional effect, and that which it has on real musical scholars who perceive the structure and get an intellectual satisfaction as well. Either of these effects is, I think, ambivalent from the religious point of view: i.e. *each* can be a preparation for or even a medium for meeting God, but can also be a distraction and impediment. In that respect music is not different from a good many other things, human relations, landscape, poetry, philosophy. The most relevant one is wine which can be used sacramentally or for getting drunk or neutrally.

I think every *natural* thing which is not in itself sinful can become the servant of the spiritual life, but none is automatically so. When it is not, it becomes either just trivial (as music is to millions of people) or a dangerous idol. The emotional effect of music may be not only a distraction (to some people at some times) but a delusion: i.e. feeling certain emotions in church they mistake them for religious emotions when they may be wholly natural. That means that even genuinely religious emotion is only a servant. No soul is saved by having it or damned by lacking it. The love we are commanding to have for God and our neighbour is a state of the *will*, not of the affections (though if they ever also play their part so much the better). So that the test of music or religion or even visions if one has them—is always the same—do they make one more obedient, more God-centred and neighbour-centred and *less self-centred*? 'Though I speak with the tongues of Bach and Palestrina and have not charity etc.!'

TO A LADY.

2 April 1956

I'm a little, but unamusedly, surprised that my *Surprised by Joy* causes you envy. I doubt if you really would have enjoyed my life much better than your own. And the whole modern world ludicrously over-values books and learning and what (I loathe the word) they call 'culture'. And of course culture itself is the greatest sufferer by this error; for second things are always corrupted when they are put first. . . .

TO FR. PETER MILWARD.

9 May 1956

You need not be afraid of telling me 'only what I know already' about the Grail legend, for I know v. little. If you think otherwise you are perhaps confusing my interest in C(harles) W(illiams) with C.W.'s interest in the legend. For my own part, I am v. puzzled as to what exactly we are doing when we study —not this or that work of art—but a myth in abstract. Supposing that what people mean when they say 'The Grail is the Caldron of the Dead' is true, *what* do they mean? More briefly what does 'is' mean in such a sentence? It is not the 'is' of equality (2×6 is 3×4) nor classification (a horse is a mammal) nor of allegory (this rock is Christ). How can an imagined object in one story 'be' an imagined object in another story?

About my Inaugural—aren't you rather forgetting that I was trying to fix merely the cultural change? From my angle, you remember, even the original conversion of Europe had to be ranked as a minor change. After that, you cd. hardly expect the Reformation to be v. prominent. To be sure, if my point of view had been different, it wd. have become fundamental and you and I would of course differ v. widely about its character.

TO A CHILD IN AMERICA.

26 June 1956

You describe your Wonderful Night v. well. That is, you describe the place and the people and the night and the feeling of it all very well—but not the *thing* itself—the setting but not the jewel. And no wonder. Wordsworth often does just the same. His *Prelude* (you're bound to read it about 10 years hence. Don't try it now or you'll spoil it for later reading), is full of moments in which everything except the thing itself is described. If you become a writer you'll be trying to describe the *thing* all your life; and lucky if out of dozens of books, one or two sentences, just for a moment, come near to getting it across.

About *amn't I*, *aren't I* and *am I not*, of course there are no right and wrong answers about language in the sense in which there are right and wrong answers in Arithmetic. 'Good English' is whatever educated people speak; so that what is good in one place or time wd. not be so in another. *Amn't I* was good 50 years ago in the North of Ireland where I was brought up, but bad in Southern England. *Aren't I* wd. have been hideously bad in Ireland but was good in England. And of course I just don't know which (if either) is good in modern Florida. Don't take any notice of teachers and text-books in such matters. Nor of logic. It is good to say 'More than one passenger was hurt', although 'more than 1' equals at least two and therefore logically the verb ought to be plural 'were' and not singular 'was'. What really matters is:—

(1) Always try to use the language so as to make quite clear what you mean, and make sure your sentence couldn't mean anything else.
(2) Always prefer the plain direct word to the long vague one. Don't 'implement' promises, but 'keep' them.
(3) Never use abstract nouns when concrete ones will do. If you mean 'more people died', don't say 'mortality rose'.
(4) In writing. Don't use adjectives which merely tell us how you want us to feel about the thing you are describing. I mean, instead of telling us a thing was 'terrible', describe it so that we'll be terrified. Don't say it was 'delightful', make *us* say 'delightful' when we've read the description. You see, all those words (horrifying, wonderful, hideous, exquisite) are only saying to your readers 'Please will you do my job for me'.
(5) Don't use words too big for the subject. Don't say 'infinitely' when you mean 'very'; otherwise you'll have no word left when you want to talk about something *really* infinite.

TO FR. PETER MILWARD.

22 September 1956

Tolkien's book [*The Fellowship of the Ring*] is not an allegory—a form he dislikes. You'll get nearest to his mind on such subjects by studying his essay on Fairy Tales in the *Essays presented to Charles Williams*. His root idea of narrative art is 'sub-creation'—the making of a secondary world. What you wd. call 'a pleasant story for the children' wd. be to him *more serious* than an allegory. But for *his* views read the essay, wh. is indispensible. *My* view wd. be that a good myth (i.e. a story out of which ever varying meanings will grow for different readers and in different ages) is a higher thing than an allegory (into which *one* meaning has been put). Into an allegory a man can put only what he already knows; in a myth he puts what he does not yet know and cd. not come by in any other way.

TO A LADY.

14 November 1956

I wish you would pray very hard for a lady called Joy Gresham and me. I am likely v. shortly to be both a bridegroom and a widower, for she has cancer. You need not mention this till the marriage (which will be at a hospital bedside if it occurs) is announced. I'll tell you the whole story some day. . . .

TO *one who had commented upon the apparent absence of humour from the New Testament.*

6 December 1956

(1) I think there may be *some* humour. Matt. IX. 12 (People who are well don't need doctors) could well be said in a way that wd. by v. funny to everyone present except the Pharisees. So might Matt. XVII. 25. And in Mark X. 30—quickly slipping in 'tribulations' among all the assets—that cd. be funny too. And of course the Parable of the Unjust Steward (its comic element is well brought out in Dorothy Sayers' excellent *Man born to be King*).

(2) If there were more humour, should we (modern Occidentals) *see* it? I've been much struck in conversation with a Jewess by the extent to which Jews see humour in the O.T. where we don't. Humour varies so much from culture to culture.

(3) How much wd. be recorded? We know (John XXI. 25) that we have only a tiny fraction of what Our Lord said. Wd. the Evangelists, anxious to get across what was vitally necessary, *include* it? They told us nothing about His appearance, clothes, physical habits—none of what a modern biographer would put in.

TO FR. PETER MILWARD.

10 December 1956

Thanks for your letter of Nov. 5th. One historical point first. There cd. not have been an allegory about the atomic bomb when Tolkien began his romance for he did so before it was invented. That however has little to do with the theoretical question; tho' it has much to do with the extreme danger, in individual cases, of applying allegorical interpretations. We should probably find that many particular allegories critics read into Langland and Spenser are impossible for just that sort of reason, if we knew all the facts. I am also convinced that the wit of man *cannot* devise a story in wh. the wit of some other man cannot find an allegory.

For the rest, I wd. agree that the word can be used in wider or narrower senses. Indeed, in so far as the things unseen are manifested by the things seen, one might from one point of view call the whole material universe an allegory. The truth is that it's one of those words which needs defining in each context where one uses it. It wd. be disastrous if anyone took your statement that the Nativity is the greatest of all allegories to mean that the physical event was merely *feigned*. . . .

TO PROFESSOR CLYDE S. KILBY.

10 February 1957

An author doesn't necessarily understand the meaning of his own story better than anyone else, so I give my account of *Till we have Faces* simply for what it is worth. The 'levels' I am conscious of are these.

(1) A work of (supposed) historical imagination. A guess of what it might have been like in a little barbarous state on the borders of the Hellenistic world of Greek culture, just beginning to affect it. Hence the change from the old priest (of a very normal fertility mother-goddess) to Arnom; Stoic allegorisations of the myths standing to the original cult rather as Modernism to Christianity (but this is a parallel, not an allegory). Much that you

take as allegory was intended solely as realistic detail. The wagon men are nomads from the steppes. The children made mud pies not for symbolic purposes but because children do. The Pillar Room is simply a room. The Fox is such an educated Greek slave as you might find at a barbarous court—and so on.

(2) Psyche is an instance of the *anima naturaliter Christiana* making the best of the Pagan religion she is brought up in and thus being guided (but always 'under the cloud', always in terms of her own imaginations or that of her people) towards the true God. She is in some ways like Christ because every good man or woman is like Christ. What else could they be like? But of course my interest is primarily in Orual.

(3) Orual is (not a symbol) but an instance, a 'case' of human affection in its natural condition, true, tender, suffering, but in the long run tyrannically possessive and ready to turn to hatred when the beloved ceases to be its possession. What such love particularly cannot stand is to see the beloved passing into a sphere where it cannot follow. All this I hoped would stand as a mere story in its own right. But—

(4) Of course I had always in mind its close parallel to what is probably happening at this moment in at least five families in your home town. Someone becomes a Christian, or in a family nominally Christian already, does something like becoming a missionary or entering a religious order. The others suffer a sense of outrage. What they love is being taken from them. The boy must be mad. And the conceit of him! Or: is there something in it after all? Let's hope it is only a phase! If only he had listened to his natural advisers. Oh come back, come back, be sensible, be the dear son we used to know! Now I, as a Christian, have a good deal of sympathy with those jealous, suffering, puzzled people (for they do suffer, and out of their suffering much of the bitterness against religion arises). I believe the thing is common. There is very nearly a touch of it in Luke II. 38, 'Son, *why hast thou* so dealt with us?' And is the reply easy for a loving heart to bear?

TO SISTER PENELOPE, C.S.M.V.

6 March 1957

Yes, it is true. I married (knowingly) a very sick, save by near-miracle, a dying woman. She is the Joy Davidman whose *Smoke on the Mountain* I think you read. She is in the Wingfield Morris Hospital at Headington. When I see her each week-end she is, to a layman's eyes (but not to a doctor's knowledge) in full convalescence, better every week. The disease is of course cancer; by which I lost my mother, my father, and my favourite aunt. She knows her own state of course; I would allow no lies to be told to a grown-up and a Christian. As you may imagine, new beauty and new tragedy have entered my life. You wd. be surprised (or perhaps you wd. not?) to know how much of a strange sort of happiness and even gaiety there is between us....

TO MRS. EDWARD A. ALLEN.

16 March 1957

I think I haven't yet told my news. I have lately married a lady who is very ill and probably dying; I shall be left with two stepsons. Thus, as you may guess, great beauty and great tragedy have come into my life. We need your prayers more than ever....

In my job one hardly works to a schedule of hours you know; nor, apart from lectures and committees, can one draw any hard and fast line between what is and what is not 'work'. I couldn't tell you which of the books I read are professional reading and which are for pleasure. In *writing* I do regard all non-academic works (all the ones you have read) as being leisure occupations. They have been done at odd moments; nothing unusual about that, for better authors would have said the same—Caesar, Chaucer, Sidney, Fielding, Lamb, Jane Austen and Trollope (the last incredibly copious; he wrote most of his novels on railway journeys).

TO SISTER MADELEVA, C.S.C.

8 May 1957

I was never less likely to come to America than now. I am newly married to a dying woman. Every moment is spent at her bedside. I am sure we may count on your prayers; add your prayer for help and guidance in the difficult responsibility of bringing up two orphan stepsons. I have only one qualification if it is one; these two boys are now facing the very same calamity that befell my brother and myself at about the same age.

TO SISTER PENELOPE, C.S.M.V.

12 May 1957

Joy is at home, completely bed-ridden. Though the doctors hold out no ultimate hope, the progress of the disease does seem to be temporarily arrested to a degree they never expected. There is little pain, often none, her strength increases and she eats and sleeps well. This has the paradoxical (but come to think of it, natural) result of giving her lower spirits and less peace. The more *general* health, of course the stronger the instinctive will to live. Forbidden and torturing hopes will intrude on us both. In short, a dungeon is never harder to bear than when the door is open and the sunshine and bird song float in. . . .

TO A CHILD IN AMERICA.

18 July 1957

They tell me that one shd. never try to learn Spanish and Italian at the same time. The fact that they are so alike of course helps one a bit over the meanings of words (but Latin wd. help almost equally well for both) but it makes a confusion in one's mind about grammar and idioms—in the end one makes a horrid soup out of both.

I don't know Spanish, but I know there are lovely things in Italian to read. You'll like Boiardo, Ariosto, and Tasso. By the way, good easy Latin reading to keep one's Latin up with is the New Testament in Latin. Any Roman Catholic bookshop will have one: say you want a copy of the Vulgate New Testament. *Acts* goes specially well in Latin.

I don't think being good *always* goes with having fun; a martyr being tortured by Nero, or a resistance man refusing to give away his friends when tortured by the Germans, were being good but not having fun. And even in ordinary life there are things which wd. be fun to me but I mustn't do them because they wd. spoil other people's fun. But *of course* you are quite right if you mean that giving up fun for no reason except that you think it's 'good' to give it up is all nonsense. Don't the ordinary old rules about telling the truth and doing as you'd be done by tell one pretty well which kinds of fun one may have and which not? But provided the thing is in itself right, the more one likes it and the less one has to 'try to be good' the better. A *perfect* man wd. never act from sense of duty; he'd always *want* the right thing more than the wrong one. Duty is only a substitute for love (of God and of other people) like a crutch which is a substitute for a leg. Most of us need the crutch at times; but of course it is idiotic to use the crutch when our own legs (our own loves, tastes, habits etc.) can do the journey on their own.

TO DOM BEDE GRIFFITHS, O.S.B.

24 August 1957

My wife's condition, contrary to the expectation of the doctors, has improved, if not miraculously (but who knows?) at any rate wonderfully. (How wd. one say that in Latin?) No one, least of all herself, encourages me to dream of a permanent recovery, but this is a wonderful reprieve. Tho' she is still a cripple her *general* health is better than I have ever seen it, and she says she has never been happier. It is nice to have arrived at all this by something which began in Agape, proceeded to Philia, then became pity, and only after that, Eros. As if the highest of these, Agape, had successively undergone the sweet humiliations of an incarnation.

My own troubles, after one terrible fortnight, have taken a turn for the better. No one suggests that the disease is *either* curable or *fatal*. It normally accompanies that fatal disease we call Senility, but no one knows why I have got it so (comparatively) early in life. . . .

TO MISS JANE GASKELL.

2 September 1957

My wife and I have just been reading your book and I want to tell you that I think it a quite amazing achievement—incomparably beyond anything I could have done at that age. The story runs, on the whole, very well and there is some real imagination in it. The idea of the gigantic spoiled brat (had you a horrid baby brother once?) is really excellent; perhaps even profound. Unlike most modern fantasies, your book also has a firm core of civilized ethics. On all these grounds, hearty congratulations.

On the other hand there is no reason at all why your next book should not be at least twice as good. I hope you will not think it impertinent if I mention (this is only one man's opinion of course) some mistakes you can avoid in future.

1. In all stories which take one to another world, the difficulty (as you and I know) is to make something happen when we've got there. In fact, one needs "filling". Yours is quite sufficient in *quantity* (almost too much) but not quite, I think, of the right sort. Aren't all these economic problems and religious differences too like the politics of our own world? Why go to faerie for what we already have? Surely the wars of faerie should be high, reckless, heroical, romantic wars—concerned with the possession of a beautiful queen or an enchanted treasure? Surely the diplomatic phase of them should be represented not by conferences (which, on your own showing, are as dull as ours) but by ringing words of gay taunt, stern defiance, or Quixotic generosity,

interchanged by great warriors with sword in hand before the battle joins?

2. This is closely connected with the preceding. In a fantasy every precaution must be taken never to break the spell, to do nothing which will wake the reader and bring him back with a bump to the common earth. But this is what you sometimes do. The moving bus on which they travel is a dull invention at best, because we can't help conceiving it as mechanical. But when you add upholstered seats, lavatories, and restaurants, I can't go on believing in faerie for a moment. It has all turned into commonplace technological luxury! Similarly even a half-fairy *must not* climb a fairyhill carrying a suitcase full of new nighties. All magic dies at this touch of the commonplace (Notice, too, the disenchanting implication that the faeries can't make for themselves *lingerie* as good as they can get—not even in Paris, which wd. be bad enough—but, of all places, in London).

3. Never use adjectives or adverbs which are mere appeals to the reader to feel as you want him to feel. He won't do it just because you ask him: you've got to *make* him. No good *telling* us a battle was "exciting". If *you* succeed in exciting us the adjective will be unnecessary; if you don't, it will be useless. Don't tell us the jewels had an "emotional" glitter; make us feel the emotion. I can hardly tell you how important this is.

4. You are too fond of long adverbs like "dignifiedly", which are not nice to pronounce. I hope, by the way, you always write by ear not by eye. Every sentence shd. be tested on the tongue, to make sure that the sound of it has the hardness or softness, the swiftness or languor, which the meaning of it calls for.

5. Far less about clothes, please! I mean, ordinary clothes. If you had given your fairies strange and beautiful clothes and described *them*, there might be something in it. But your heroine's tangerine skirt! For whom do you write? No *man* wants to hear how she was dressed, and the sort of woman who does seldom reads fantasy; if she reads anything it is more likely to be the women's magazines. By the way, these are a baneful influence on your mind and imagination. Beware! they may kill your talent. If you *can't* keep off them, at least, after each debauch, give your imagination a good mouth-wash by a reading (or wd. it be a re-reading) of the *Odyssey*, Tolkien's *Lord of the Rings*,

E. R. Eddison's *The Worm Ouroboros*, the romances of James Stephens, and all the early mythical plays of W. B. Yeats. Perhaps a touch of Lord Dunsany too.

6. Names not too good. They ought to be beautiful and suggestive as well as strange; not merely odd like *Enaj* (wh. sounds as if it came out of Butler's *Erewhon*).

I hope all this does not enrage you. You'll get so much bad advice that I felt I must give you some of what I think good.

TO SISTER PENELOPE, C.S.M.V.

6 November 1957

Whatever our state had been, a letter from you wd. always have cheered and comforted. In reality it is beyond all that we dared to hope. When they sent Joy here from hospital last April, they sent her home to die. The experienced nurses expected her life to be a matter of weeks. She could not be moved in bed without a lifting squad of three of us, and with all our care we nearly always hurt her. Then it began to appear that the cancer had been arrested; the diseased spots in the bone were no longer spreading or multiplying. Then the tide began to turn—they were disappearing. New bone was being made. And so little by little the woman who could hardly be moved in bed began to walk about the house and in the garden—limping, and with a stick, but walking. She even found herself getting up *unconsciously* to answer the telephone the other day. It is the unconsciousness that is the real triumph—the body that would not obey the most planned volition now begins to act on its own. General health and spirits excellent. *Of course* the sword of Damocles still hangs over us; or should I say, we are forced to be aware of the sword wh. really hangs over all mortals.

Did I tell you that I also have a bone disease? It is neither mortal nor curable; a prematurely senile loss of calcium. I was very crippled and had much pain all summer, but am in a good spell now. I was losing calcium just about as fast as Joy was gaining it, a bargain (if it was one) for wh. I am very thankful. . . .

TO JOCELYN GIBB, *his publisher; who had sent him some honey.*

25 December 1957

Your parcel, as it happened, was opened before your letter, so you had a good joke *in absentia*. We did wonder a little whether there were any core or whether we were peeling an onion. But the golden treasure surpassed the wrappings in value more than they surpassed it in bulk; I had a stanza of this edible poem for breakfast to-day with much enjoyment. Thank you very much.

Marry gup! The hymn which you miscall a psalm, truly hath in that place "to pay the price of sinne", which paying the price of sinne I do suppose to be all one with redeeming. Go to. You lie at the catch, neighbour. Nor is it unfit that I admonish printers concerning printing and publishers concerning publishing, the which if I now were to handle I might chance to recall that old sawe *ex sutore medicus* and scribble the ultracrepidations of cobblers. With what stomach, think you, would Tullie have born the Salii going about to mend his periods?

Mid-day dinner with a generous burgundy is perhaps a mistake.... *Vinum locutum est.* I wish you a merry Christmas retrospectively.

TO MRS. EDWARD A. ALLEN.

1 February 1958

I quite agree with the Archbishop that no *sin*, simply as such, should be made a *crime*. Who the deuce are our rulers to enforce their opinions about sin on us?—a lot of professional politicians, often venal time-servers, whose opinion on a moral problem in one's own life we shd. attach very little value to. Of course many acts which are sins against God are also injuries to our fellow-citizens, and must on that account, but only on that account, be made crimes. But of all the sins in the world I shd. have thought homosexuality was the one that least concerns the State. We hear too much of the State. Government is at its best a necessary evil. Let's keep it in its place.

TO MISS MURIEL BRADBROOK.

18 April 1958

I am glad you raised this question. I was maintaining yesterday that when a bifurcation of meaning is sufficiently old and wide, the resulting senses often enter the linguistic consciousness of each new generation as mere homophones, and their reunion has the explosion of a pun. But on the other hand, when the bifurcation is less wide there may be a period during which the speakers really do not know in which sense they are using the word. When *we* speak of a 'simple meal' do we always know whether we mean (*a*) not complicated, (*b*) modest, not 'posh', or (*c*) easy to prepare? (Of course they needn't coincide. A haunch of venison is more 'posh' than a shepherd's pie, but *less* complicated, and helpings of caviare out of a jar are easier to prepare than either). In the passage you quote, almost all of the senses of 'sad' (including that which would yield a tautology) seem to me possible, and I suggest that Webster may not have made up his mind between them. Cf. the passage in Boswell where Goldsmith lets Johnson tell him what he meant by 'slow' in the first line of the *Traveller*.

TO A LADY.

30 October 1958

I don't often see television, but my brother, who sometimes looks in on a friend's set, says. . . . that to him the most terrible part of the business is the implicit assumption that progress is an inevitable process like decay, and that the only important thing in life is to increase the comfort of homo sapiens at whatever cost to posterity and the other inhabitants of the planet. I can well imagine how a 'scientific' programme would jar after watching such a stately ceremony as the opening of Parliament. . . .

TO A LADY.

29 December 1958

By an allegory I mean a composition (whether pictorial or literary) in wh. immaterial realities are represented by feigned physical objects; e.g. a pictured Cupid allegorically represents erotic love (which in reality is an experience, not an object occupying a given area of space) or, in Bunyan, a giant represents Despair.

If Aslan represented the immaterial Deity in the same way in which Giant Despair represents Despair, he would be an allegorical figure. In reality however he is an invention giving an imaginary answer to the question, 'What might Christ become like, if there really were a world like Narnia and He chose to be incarnate and die and rise again in *that* world as He actually has done in ours?' This is not allegory at all. So in *Perelandra*. This also works out a *supposition*. ('Suppose, even now, in some other planet there were a first couple undergoing the same that Adam and Eve underwent here, but successfully').

Allegory and such supposals differ because they mix the real and the unreal in different ways. Bunyan's picture of Giant Despair does not start from supposal at all. It is not a supposition but a *fact* that despair can capture and imprison a human soul. What is unreal (fictional) is the giant, the castle, and the dungeon. The Incarnation of Christ in another world is mere supposal; but *granted* the supposition, He would really have been a physical object in that world as He was in Palestine and His death on the Stone Table would have been a physical event no less than his death on Calvary. Similarly, if the angels (who I believe to be real beings in the actual universe) have that relation to the Pagan gods which they are assumed to have in Perelandra, they might *really* manifest themselves in real form as they did to Ransom. Again, Ransom (to some extent) plays the role of Christ not because he allegorically represents Him (as Cupid represents falling in love) but because in reality every real Christian is really called upon in some measure to *enact* Christ. Of course Ransom does this rather more spectacularly than most. But that does not mean that he does it allegorically. It only means that fiction (at any rate my kind of fiction) chooses extreme cases.

There is no conscious connection between any of the phonetic elements in my 'Old Solar' words and those of any actual language. I am always playing with syllables and fitting them together (purely by ear) to see if I can hatch up new words that please me. I want them to have an emotional, not intellectual, suggestiveness; the heaviness of *glund* for as huge a planet as Jupiter, the vibrating, tintillating quality of *viritrilbia* for the subtlety of Mercury, the liquidity. . . . of Maleldil. The only exception I am aware of is *hnau* which *may* (but I don't know) have been influenced by Greek *nous*.

TO PROFESSOR CLYDE S. KILBY.

20 January 1959

As to Professor van Til's point it is certainly scriptural to say that 'to as many as believed He gave power to become the sons of God', and the statement 'God became Man that men might become gods' is Patristic. Of course van Til's wording 'that man must *seek* to *ascend* in the *scale* of life' with its suggestions (*a*) that we could do this by our own efforts, (*b*) that the difference between God and Man is a difference of position on a 'scale of life' like the difference between a (biologically) 'higher' and a (biologically) 'lower' creature, is wholly foreign to my thought.

I think an anthology of extracts from a living writer would make both him and the collector look rather ridiculous and I'm sure publishers would not agree to the plan. I am sorry to reply so ungraciously to a proposal which does me so much honour. But I'm convinced it would not do.

TO *the clergyman who had married Jack and Joy, and who now wrote asking for prayers.*

29 April 1959

Indeed, indeed, we both will. I don't see how any degree of faith can exclude the dismay, since Christ's faith did not save Him from dismay in Gethsemane. We are not necessarily doubting that God will do the best for us; we are wondering how painful the best will turn out to be. In a case like the one you refer to, where the growth is detected in its primary state and in the most operable part, there are of course solid grounds for an entirely optimistic view. But then *one* of your fears and hers, is of all the fears you *will* have to suffer before you are out of the wood. The monotony of anxiety—the circular movement of the mind—is horrible. As far as possible I think it is best to treat one's own anxiety as being also an illness. I wish I could help. Can I? You did so much for me.

As to the 'frightening monotony' I think this disease now ranks as a *plague* and we live in a plague-stricken population.

God bless you both. I shall have no need to 'remind' myself to remember you. Let us have news as soon as there is any.

If you find (some do) that mental anguish produces an inclination to eat more—paradoxical but it can—I should jolly well do so.

TO DOM BEDE GRIFFITHS, O.S.B.

30 April 1959

Thanks for *Christ and India*. It confirms what I had, less clearly, thought already—that the difficulty in preaching Christ in India is that there is no difficulty. One is up against true Paganism—the best sort of it as well as the worst—hospitable to all gods, naturally religious, ready to take any shape but able to retain none. . . .

About the Semitic genius, my wife, who is a Jewess by blood, holds two views wh. will interest you.

(1) That the only living Judaism is Christianity. Where her own people still have any religion it is archaic, pedantic, and so-to-speak, sectarian, so that being a devout Jew is rather like being a Plymouth Brother.

(2) That we Goyim misread much of the O.T. because we start with the assumption that its sacred character excludes *humour*. That no-one who knew the Jewish *ethos* from inside would fail to see the fully accepted comic element in Abraham's dialogue with God (Genesis XVIII) or in Jonah.

While we are on exegesis, am I right in thinking that the key to the Parable of the Unjust Steward is to grasp that the Master in it is the *world*? The dismissal is the notice—apparently now being served on you and long since served on me—that our present tabernacle will soon be taken down. The moral is 'cheat your master'. If he gives us wealth, talent, beauty, power etc. use them for your own (external) purposes—spoil the Egyptian. If you won't do that, even with *his* kind of property, who will trust you with the true kind? It wd. be very nice to meet when you are in Europe if that should be at all possible. . . .

TO PROFESSOR CLYDE S. KILBY.

7 May 1959

Whatever view we hold in the divine authority of scripture must make room for the following facts:

(1) The distinction which St Paul makes in I. Cor. VII between v. 10 and v. 12.
(2) The apparent inconsistencies between the genealogies in Matt. I and Luke III. Between the accounts of the death of Judas in Matt. XXVII 5 and Acts I. 18–19.
(3) St. Luke's own account of how he obtained his matter (I. 1–4).
(4) The universally admitted unhistoricity (I do not of course say falsity) of at least some narratives in scripture (the parables), which may well extend also to Jonah and Job.

(5) If every good and perfect gift comes from the Father of Light then all true and edifying writings, whether in scripture or not, must be *in some sense* inspired.

(6) John XI. 49–52. Inspiration may operate in a wicked man without his knowing it, and he can then utter the untruth he intends *as well as* the truth he does not intend.

It seems to me that 2 and 4 rule out the view that every statement in scripture must be *historical* truth. And 1, 3, 5 and 6 rule out the view that inspiration is a single thing in the same sense that, if present at all, it is always present in the same mode and the same degree. Therefore, I think, rules out the view that any one passage taken in isolation can be assumed to be inerrant in exactly the same sense as any other—e.g. that the numbers of O.T. armies (which in view of the size of the country, if true, involves continuous miracle) are statistically correct because the story of the resurrection is historically correct. That the over-all operation of Scripture is to convey God's word to the reader (he also needs His inspiration) who reads it in the right spirit, I fully believe. That it *also* gives true answers to all the questions (often religiously irrelevant) which he might ask, I don't. The very *kind* of truth we are often demanding was, in my opinion, never even envisaged by the ancients.

TO CHARLES MOORMAN, *who was proposing a literary enquiry into a group of writers.*

15 May 1959

I don't think your project at all 'presumptuous', but I do think you may be chasing after a fox that isn't there. Charles Williams certainly influenced me and I perhaps influenced him. But after that I think you would draw a blank. No one ever influenced Tolkien—you might as well try to influence a bandersnatch. We listened to his work, but could affect it only by encouragement. He has only two reactions to criticism; either he begins the whole work over again from the beginning or else takes no notice at all. Dorothy Sayers was not living in Oxford at the time and I don't think she ever in her life met Tolkien. She knew Charles Williams well, and me much later. I am sure she neither exerted nor underwent any literary influence at all. Of course it may be that, just because I was in it myself, I don't see (objectively) what was really going on. But I give my honest impression for what it is worth.

To be sure, we had a common point of view, but we had it before we met. It was the cause rather than the result of our friendship. . . .

TO KATHLEEN RAINE (MRS. MADGE).

19 June 1959

One must (and will) write poetry if one can. That one must therefore return to the place where the Muse once appeared, as if she were bound to appear there again, is quite a different proposition. The gods will not be met by appointment. They never give us their addresses. And tho' the Faculty has not been able to give you what you, reasonably, want, it does not follow that they don't want you. At any rate *postpone*. There will never be a time when you can't leave Cambridge; there could easily be one when you couldn't return.

TO A LADY.

8 September 1959

No one, I presume, can imagine life in the glorified body. On this, and on the distinction (in general) between belief and imagination, I have said all I can in *Miracles*. Lor' bless us, I can picture very few of the things I believe in. I can't picture will, thought, time, atoms, astronomical distance, New York, nor even (at this moment) my mother's face.

Your whole worry about the word *Christian* comes from ignoring the fact that words have different meanings in different contexts. The best parallel is the word *poet*. We can argue till the cows come home whether 'Pope is a poet'. On the other hand a librarian, putting 'poets' in one shelf and prose in another, after a single glance at one page of Pope, classifies him as a 'poet'. In other words, the word has a deep, ambiguous, disputable and (for many purposes) useless sense; also a shallower, clear, useful sense. In the second sense it seems to be more useful not to classify Quakers as Christians. But this is a linguisitic, not a religious question. . . .

TO DOM BEDE GRIFFITHS, O.S.B.

5 November 1959

The best Dickens always seems to me to be the one I have read last. But in a cool hour I put *Bleak House* top, for its sheer prodigality of invention. About death I go through different moods, but the times when I can *desire* it are never, I think, those when this world seems harshest. On the contrary, it is just when there seems to be most of Heaven already here that I come nearest to longing for a *patria*. It is the bright frontispiece which whets one to read the story itself. All joy (as distinct from mere pleasure, still more amusement) emphasises our pilgrim status; always reminds, beckons, awakens desire. Our best havings are wantings.

TO SIR HENRY WILLINK, *Master of Magdalene; who had just lost his wife.*

3 December 1959

I have learned now that while those who speak about one's miseries usually hurt one, those who keep silence hurt more. They help to increase the sense of *general* isolation which makes a sort of fringe to the sorrow itself. You know what cogent reason I have to feel *with* you; but I can feel *for* you too. I know that what you are facing must be worse than what I must shortly face myself, because your happiness has lasted so much longer and is therefore so much more intertwined with your whole life. As Scott said in like case "What am I to do with that daily portion of my thoughts which has for so many years been hers?" People talk as if grief were just a feeling—as if it weren't the continually renewed shock of setting out again and again on familiar roads and being brought up short by the grim frontier post that now blocks them. I, to be sure, believe there is something beyond it; but the moment one tries to use that as a consolation (that is not its function) the belief crumbles. It is quite useless knocking at the door of heaven for earthly comfort; it's not the sort of comfort they supply there.

You are probably very exhausted physically. Hug that and all the little indulgences to which it entitles you. I think it is tiny little things which (next to the very greatest things) help most at such a time.

I have myself twice known, after a loss, a strange excited (but utterly un-spooky) sense of the person's presence all about me. It may be a pure hallucination. But the fact that it always goes off after a few weeks proves nothing either way.

I wish I had known your wife better. But she has a bright place in my memory. It was so reassuring to the Oxford deserter to meet someone from L.M.H. and be able to talk about "the Hippo".[1] She will be very greatly missed—on their own account, quite apart from any sympathy with you—by every fellow of this College.

And poor Horace[2] too—"the single talent well employed."

I shall not be at the funeral. You can understand and forgive my desire, now, to spend every possible moment at home. Forgive me if I have said anything amiss in this letter. I am too much involved myself to practise any skill.

[1] Miss Lynda Greer.

[2] A kitchen porter in Magdalene.

TO DR. ALASTAIR FOWLER.

10 December 1959

I only once detected a pupil offering me some one else (Elton) as his own work. I told him I was not a detective nor even a schoolmaster, nor a nurse, and that I absolutely refused to take any precaution against this puerile trick; that I'd as soon think it my business to see that he washed behind his ears or wiped his bottom. . . . He went down of his own accord the next week and I never saw him again. I think you ought to make a general announcement of that sort. You must not waste your time constantly reading me and Dowden and Churton Collins as a sort of police measure. It is bad for them to think this is 'up to you'. Flay them alive if you *happen* to detect them; but don't let them feel that you are a safeguard against the effects of their own idleness. What staggers me is how any man can prefer the galley-slave labour of transcription to the freeman's work of attempting an essay on his own. . . .

TO A SCHOOLGIRL IN AMERICA, *who had written (at her teacher's suggestion) to request advice on writing.*

14 December 1959

It is very hard to give any general advice about writing. Here's my attempt.

(1) Turn off the Radio.
(2) Read all the good books you can, and avoid nearly all magazines.
(3) Always write (and read) with the ear, not the eye. You shd. hear every sentence you write as if it was being read aloud or spoken. If it does not sound nice, try again.
(4) Write about what really interests you, whether it is real things or imaginary things, and nothing else. (Notice this means that if you are interested *only* in writing you will never be a writer, because you will have nothing to write about. . . .)

(5) Take great pains to be *clear*. Remember that though you start by knowing what you mean, the reader doesn't, and a single ill-chosen word may lead him to a total misunderstanding. In a story it is terribly easy just to forget that you have not told the reader something that he wants to know—the whole picture is so clear in your own mind that you forget that it isn't the same in his.

(6) When you give up a bit of work don't (unless it is hopelessly bad) throw it away. Put it in a drawer. It may come in useful later. Much of my best work, or what I think my best, is the re-writing of things begun and abandoned years earlier.

(7) Don't use a typewriter. The noise will destroy your sense of rhythm, which still needs years of training.

(8) Be sure you know the meaning (or meanings) of every word you use.

TO DELMAR BANNER.

17 May 1960

I'm glad you liked the book [*The Four Loves*]. I quite agree with you about homosexuals; to make the thing criminal cures nothing and only creates a blackmailer's paradise. . . . But I couldn't well have a digression on that. One is fighting on two fronts, (*a*) for the persecuted homo against snoopers and busy-bodies, (*b*) for ordinary people *against* the widespread freemasonry of the highbrow homos who dominate so much of the world of criticism and won't be v. nice to you unless you are in their set. . . .

TO MRS. VERA GEBBERT.

15 June 1960

Alas, you will never send anything along 'for the three of us' again, for my dear Joy is dead. Until within ten days of the end we hoped, although noticing her increasing weakness, that she was going to hold her own, but it was not to be. Last week she had been complaining of muscular pains in her shoulders, but by Monday 11th seemed much better, and on Tuesday, though keeping her bed, said she felt a great improvement; on that day she was in good spirits, did her 'crossword puzzle' with me, and in the evening played a game of Scrabble. At quarter past six on Wednesday morning my brother, who slept over her, was wakened by her screaming and ran down to her. I got the doctor, who fortunately was at home, and he arrived before seven and gave her a heavy shot. At half past one I took her into hospital in an ambulance. She was conscious for the short remainder of her life, and in very little pain thanks to drugs; and died peacefully in my company about 10.15 the same night. . . . You will understand that I have no heart to write more, but I hope that when next I send a letter it will be a less depressing one.

TO SIR HENRY WILLINK, *Master of Magdalene.* (*The College was at this time about to reach a decision on the publication of Pepys's Diary in its unexpurgated entirety.*)

17 June 1960

Francis[1] flatters me with the idea that, if there is a division as to printing those "curious" passages in our new Pepys, my opinion might be asked for. Since I can't be sure of coming to the next meeting of the Governing Body, I have decided to let you have it in writing.

A prudential and a moral problem are both involved.

The prudential one is concerned (*a*) with the chances of a prosecution, and (*b*) with the chances of disrepute and ridicule.

[1]Mr. F. McD. C. Turner, a Fellow of Magdalene at the time.

On (*a*) it would be ridiculous for me to express an opinion in your presence and Mickey's.[1] As to (*b*), a spiteful or merely jocular journalist would certainly make us for a week or two malodorous in the public nostril. But a few weeks, or years, are nothing in the life of the College. I think it would be pusillanimous and unscholarly to delete a syllable on that score.

The moral problem comes down to the question "Is it probable that the inclusion of these passages will lead anyone to commit an immoral act which he would not have committed if we had suppressed them?" Now of course this question is strictly unanswerable. No one can foresee the odd results that any words may have on this or that individual. We ourselves, in youth, have been both corrupted and edified by books in which our elders could have foreseen neither edification nor corruption. But to suggest that in a society where the most potent aphrodisiacs are daily put forward by the advertisers, the newspapers, and the films, any perceptible increment of lechery will be caused by printing a few obscure and widely separated passages in a very long and expensive book, seems to me ridiculous, or even hypocritical.

A very severe moralist might argue that it is not enough to be unable to foresee harm; that we ought, before we act, to be able to foresee with certainty the absence of harm. But this, as you see, would prove too much. It is really an argument against doing, or not doing, any action whatever. For they all go on having consequences, mostly unforeseeable, to the world's end.

I am therefore in favour of printing the whole unexpurgated Pepys.

TO MRS. VERA GEBBERT.

5 August 1960

I believe in the resurrection. . . . but the state of the dead *till* the resurrection is unimaginable. Are they in the same *time* that we live in at all? And if not, is there any sense in asking what they

[1] R. W. M. Dias, Fellow of Magdalene and University Lecturer in Law.

are 'now'?. . . . Perhaps being maddeningly busy is the best thing for me. Anyway I am. This is one of those things which makes the tragedies of real life so *very* unlike those of the stage.

TO A GERMAN ENQUIRER.

(Undated: August 1960)

My *Out of the Silent Planet* has no factual basis and is a critique of our own age only as any Christian work is implicitly a critique of any age. I was trying to redeem for genuinely imaginative purposes the form popularly known in this country as 'science-fiction'—I think you call it 'futur-romanz'; just as (*si parva licet componere magnis*) *Hamlet* redeemed the popular revenge play.

TO FR. PETER MILWARD.

26 September 1960

First, about the Grail. I think it important to keep on remembering that a question can be v. interesting without being answerable and one of my main efforts as a teacher has been to train people to say those (apparently difficult) words "We don't know". We haven't even got anything that can be quite accurately called "*the* Grail legend". We have a number of romances which introduce the Grail and are not consistent with one another. No theory as to the ultimate origin is more than speculative. The desire to make that origin either Pagan or (less commonly) heretical is clearly widespread, but I think it springs from psychological causes, not from any evidence.

I do not myself doubt that it represents in a general way an imaginative and literary response to the doctrine of Transsubstantiation and the visible act of the elevation. But we must be on our guard against abstraction. A story does *not* grow like a tree nor breed other stories as a mouse begets other mice. Each story is told by an individual, voluntarily, with an unique artistic purpose. Hence the real germination goes on where historical, theological, or anthropological studies can never reach it—in the mind of some man of genius, like Chrétien or Wolfram. Those who have written stories themselves will come nearer to understanding it than those who have "studied the Grail legend" all their lives.

The whole (unconscious) effort of the orthodox scholars is to remove the individual author and individual romance and substitute the picture of something diffusing itself like an infectious disease or a fashion in clothes. Hence the (really senseless) question "What is the Grail?" The Grail is in each romance just what that romance exhibits it to be. There is no "Grail" over and above these "Grails". Hence, again, the assumption that the mystery in each romance could be cleared up if we knew more about the Celtic Caldron of Plenty or the Cathari or what you will. It never occurs to the scholars that this mysteriousness may be a calculated and wholly effective literary technique.

I am entirely on the side of your society for shutting de Chardin up. The enormous boosts he is getting from scientists who are very hostile to you seem to me v. like the immense popularity of Pasternak among anti-Communists. I can't for the life of me see his merit. The cause of Man against men never needed championing *less* than now. There seems to me a dangerous (but also commonplace) tendency to Monism or even Pantheism in this thought. And what in Heaven's name is the sense of saying that before there was life there was "pre-life"? If you choose to say that before you switched on the light in the cellar there was "pre-light", of course you may. But the ordinary English word for "pre-light" is darkness. What do you gain by such nicknames?

TO MRS. VERA GEBBERT.

16 October 1960

I wasn't at all questioning the life after death you know; only saying that its character is for us unimaginable. The things you tell me about it are all outside my powers of conception. To say, 'They are now as they were then' and add next moment, 'unhampered of course by the body' is to me like saying, 'They are exactly the same but of course unimaginably different'. But don't let us trouble one another about it. We shall know when we are dead ourselves. The Bible seems scrupulously to avoid any *description* of the other world, or worlds, except in terms of parable or allegory....

TO A LADY.

(Undated: February 1961)

There are, as you know, two schools of Existentialism, one anti-religious and one religious. I know the anti-religious school only through one work—Sartre's *L'Existentialisme est un Humanisme*. I learned from it one important thing—that Sartre is an artist in French prose, has a sort of wintry grandeur which partly explains his immense influence. I couldn't see that he was a real philosopher; but he is a great rhetorician. The religious school I know only from having heard a lecture by Gabriel Marcel and reading (in English) Martin Buber's *I and Thou*. They both say almost exactly the same thing, though I believe they reached their common position quite independently. (As a man Marcel was a perfect old dear.) And what they are saying is impressive—as a mood, an *aperçue*, a subject for a poem. But I didn't feel that it really worked out as a philosophy. I had been classifying Tillich more as an interpreter of the Bible than as a philosopher. I dare say you are right in thinking that for some people at some moments what I call semi-Christianity may be useful. After all, the road into the city and the road out of it are usually the same road; it depends on which direction one travels in.

At the back of religious Existentialism lies Kierkegaard. They all revere him as their pioneer. Have you read him? I haven't or hardly at all.

TO DR. ALASTAIR FOWLER.

4 May 1961

You talk of Evolution as if it were a substance (like individual organisms) and even a rational substance or person. I had thought it was an abstract noun. So far as I know it is not impossible that in addition to God and the individual organisms there might be a sort of *daemon*, a created spirit, in the evolutionary process. But that view must surely be argued on its own merits? I mean we mustn't unconsciously and without evidence, slip into the habit of hypostatising a noun. . . .

TO MRS. MARGARET GRAY.

9 May 1961

How right you are when you say "Christianity is a terrible thing for a lifelong atheist to have to face"! In people like us—adult converts in the 20th century—I take this feeling to be a good symptom. By the way, you have had in most respects a tougher life than I, but there's one thing I envy you. I lost my wife last summer after a very late, very short, and intensely happy married life, but I have not been vouchsafed (and why the deuce should I be?) a visit like yours—or certainly not except for one split second. Now about reading.

For a good ("popular") defence of our position against modern woffle, to fall back on, I know nothing better than G. K. Chesterton's *The Everlasting Man*. Harder reading, but very protective, is Edwyn Bevan's *Symbolism and Belief*. Charles Williams' *He Came Down from Heaven* doesn't suit everyone, but try it.

For meditative and devotional reading (a little bit at a time, more like sucking a lozenge than eating a slice of bread) I suggest *The Imitation of Christ* (astringent) and Traherne's *Centuries of Meditation* (joyous). Also my selection from Macdonald, *George Macdonald: an Anthology*. I can't read Kierkegaard myself, but some people find him helpful.

For Christian morals I suggest my wife's (Joy Davidman) *Smoke on the Mountain*; Gore's *The Sermon on the Mount* and (perhaps) his *Philosophy of the Good Life*. And possibly (but with a grain of salt, for he is too puritanical) William Law's *Serious Call to a Devout and Holy Life*. I know the very title makes one shudder, but we have both got a lot of shuddering to get through before we're done!

You'll want a mouth-wash for the *imagination*. I'm told that Mauriac's novels (all excellently translated, if your French is rusty) are good, though very severe. Dorothy Sayers' *Man Born to be King* (those broadcast plays) certainly is. So, to me, but not to everyone, are Charles Williams' fantastic novels. *Pilgrim's Progress*, if you ignore some straw-splitting dialogues on Calvinist theology and concentrate on the story, is first-class.

St Augustine's *Confessions* will give you the record of an earlier adult convert, with many very great devotional passages intermixed.

Do you read poetry? George Herbert at his best is extremely nutritious.

I don't mention the Bible because I take that for granted. A modern translation is for most purposes far more useful than the Authorised Version.

As regards my own books, you might (or might not) care for *Transposition*, *The Great Divorce*, or *The Four Loves*.

Yes—"being done good to"—gru! I never asked even to *be*.

TO A LADY

28 October 1961

I'm not well enough to answer your letter properly. . . . The nearest I can put up as a Scriptural warrant for prayers for the dead is the place in one of the Epistles about people being 'baptized for the dead'. If we can be baptized for them, then surely we can pray for them? I'd like to give you the reference, but my Concordance is upstairs and—my heart being one of the things that is wrong with me—I'm not allowed to go upstairs.

TO DOM BEDE GRIFFITHS, O.S.B.

3 December 1961

Thank you for your letter of 27 Nov. Your hand, though not yet nearly as bad as mine, deteriorates. But the bits I could read were all very interesting. The difficulty about Hinduism, and indeed about all the higher Paganisms, seems to me to be our double task of reconciling and converting. The activities are almost opposites, yet must go hand in hand. We have to hurl down false gods and also elicit the peculiar truth preserved in the worship of each. . . .

Try to time your next letter so that it does not arrive near Christmas. Every year the merciless spate of correspondence makes this season more pestilential and less festal for me.

I forget whether you know that my wife died in July. Pray for us both. I am learning a great deal. Grief is not, as I thought, a state but a process; like a walk in a winding valley which gives you a new landscape every few miles. All blessings. I am tired and slightly ill at the moment, otherwise I wd. answer your letter more as it deserves.

TO DOM BEDE GRIFFITHS, O.S.B.

20 December 1961

To lose one's wife after a very short married life may, I suspect, be less miserable than after a long one. You see, I had not grown *accustomed* to happiness. It was all a 'treat', I was like a child at a party. But perhaps earthly happiness, even of the most innocent sort, is I suspect, addictive. The whole being gets geared to it. The withdrawal must be more like lacking bread than lacking cake. . . .

About Nature—you are apparently meeting, at an unusually late hour, the difficulty which I met in adolescence and which was for years my stock argument against Theism. Romantic Pantheism has in this matter led us all up the garden path. It has taught us to regard Nature as divine. But she is a creature, and surely a creature lower than ourselves. And a fallen creature—not an evil creature but a good creature corrupted, retaining many beauties but all tainted. . . . The Devil cd. *make* nothing but has *infected* everything. I have always gone as near Dualism as Christianity allows—and the N.T. allows one to go v. near. The Devil is the (usurping) lord of this age. It was he, not God, who 'bound this daughter of Abraham'.

Even more disturbing, as you say, is the ghastly record of Christian persecution. It had begun in Our Lord's time—'Ye know not what spirit ye are of' (John of all people!). I think we must fully face the fact that when Christianity does not make a man v. much better, it makes him v. much worse. It is, paradoxically, dangerous to draw nearer to God. Doesn't one find in one's own experience, that every advance (if one ever has advanced) in the spiritual life opens to one the possibility of blacker sins as well as brighter virtues? Conversion may make of one who was, if no better, no worse than an animal, something like a devil. Satan was an *angel*. I wonder have any of us taken seriously enough the prohibition of casting pearls before swine? This is the point of Our Lord's remarks after the parable of the Unjust Steward. We are denied many graces that we ask for because they would be our ruin. If we can't be trusted even with the perishable wealth of this world, who will trust us with the real wealth? (The 'Lord' in this parable is of course not God but the world). . . .

I am rather seriously ill. Prostate trouble, by the time it was diagnosed, had already damaged my kidneys, blood, and heart, so that I'm now in a vicious circle. They can't operate until my biochemistry gets right and it looks as if that can't get right until they operate. I am in some danger—not sentenced but on trial for my life. I know I shall have your prayers. My temptation is not to impatience. Rather, I am far too inclined to snuggle down in the enforced idleness and other privileges of an invalid.

Have you read anything by an American Trappist called Thomas Merton? I'm at present on his *No Man Is an Island*. It is the best new spiritual reading I've met for a long time.

TO A LADY, *further to the letter of 28 October.*

28 December 1961

I've found the passage—I Cor. XV. 20. Also I Pet. III 19–20 bears indirectly on the subject. It implies that something can be done for the dead. If so, why should we not pray for them?

Beware of the argument, 'the Church gave the Bible and therefore the Bible can never give us grounds for criticising the Church'. It is perfectly possible to accept B on the authority of A and yet regard B as a higher authority than A. It happens when I recommend a book to a pupil. I first send him to the book, but having gone to it he knows (for *I've* told him) that the author knows more about the subject than I.

TO DR. AUSTIN FARRER.

29 December 1961

I've read your book [*Love Almighty and Ills Unlimited*] with great enjoyment. You once said that you wrote with difficulty, but no one would guess it; this is full of felicities that sound as unsought as wildflowers. . . .

Of course admiration is not always agreement. I stick at the diagnosis, 'Emotional reaction rather than rational conviction'. . . . How do people decide what is an emotion and what is a value judgement? Not presumably just by introspection wh. will certainly be hard put to it to find a value judgement chemically pure from emotion. . . . I find however that the problem of animal pain is just as tough when I concentrate on creatures I dislike as on ones I cd. make pets of. Conversely, if I removed all emotion from, say my view of Hitler's treatment of Jews, I don't know how much value judgement would remain. I loathe hens. But my conscience would say the same things if I forgot to feed them as if I forgot to feed the cat. . . .

TO WAYNE SHUMAKER.

21 March 1962

Thanks for the article on *Paradise Lost.* I think I agree with all you say, especially your distinction between what is common to all the myths and what is peculiar to *Paradise Lost.* Possibly that kind of distinction should be pressed even further. Thus the child is not like the savage *simpliciter* but like a savage in close contact with and subject to civilization; controlled, protected, corrupted and elevated by it at every turn. Again, does not a myth built into a systematic and *fully* believed theology differ, by that very fact, from a myth told by primitive man (usually in explanation of a ritual)? For I doubt whether primitives stand to their myths in a relation of full credal affirmation such as one finds in Christianity and Islam. All this had happened to the Fall story long before Milton. Indeed M's great success lies in practising the credal affirmation without losing the *quality* of myth. M *does* lose this (for me) in Books XI and XII, I'm afraid.

TO T. S. ELIOT.

25 May 1962

You need not sympathize too much; if my condition keeps me from doing some things I like, it also excuses me from doing a good many things I don't. There are two sides to everything!

We must have a talk—I wish you'd write an essay on it—about Punishment. The modern view, by excluding the retributive element and concentrating solely on deterrence and cure, is hideously immoral. It is vile tyranny to submit a man to compulsory 'cure' or sacrifice him to the deterrence of others, unless he *deserves* it. On the other view what is there to prevent any of us being handed over to Butler's 'Straighteners' at any moment?

I'd have to know more about the Greek of that period to make a real criticism of the N(ew) E(nglish) B(ible) (N.T. which is the only part I've seen). Odd, the way the less the Bible is read the more it is translated.

TO AN ENQUIRER.

31 July 1962

I shall be glad to help if I can. It is however rather a big IF, for my knowledge of children's literature is really very limited. The real expert is Roger L. Green, Poulton-Lancelyn, Bebington, Wirral, Cheshire. My own range is about exhausted by MacDonald, Tolkien, E. Nesbit, and Kenneth Graham. The *Alice* books are, aren't they, in a totally different category, the effect being exclusively comic-nonsensical: not, in my experience, fully appreciated by children. Oh by the way, don't miss the utterly unexpected influence of Rabelais on Kingsley's *Water Babies.*

TO CHRISTOPHER DERRICK.

10 August 1962

Yes, I jolly well have read Gombrich and give him alpha with as many plusses as you please. The writers on art have hopelessly outstripped the writers on literature in our period. Seznoc, Wind, and Gombrich are a very big three indeed. I am much better: still dieted and—well, plumbered, but otherwise almost normal.

TO DOM BEDE GRIFFITHS, O.S.B.

(Undated: August 1962)

By being an invalid I meant that even if the operation comes off and delivers me from . . . the low-protein diet, I shall have to be careful about my heart—no more bathing or real walks, and as few stairs as possible. A very mild fate: especially since nature seems to remove the desire for exercise when the power declines.

Syriac too! I envy you the wide linguistic conquests you have made, though I hardly share one of the purposes for which you use it. I cannot take an interest in liturgiology. I see very well that some ought to feel it. If religion includes cult and if cult requires order it is somebody's business to be concerned with it. But not, I feel, mine. Indeed, for the laity I sometimes wonder if an interest in liturgiology is not rather a snare. Some people talk as if it were itself the Christian faith.

I am deeply interested by what emerged from that Hindu-Christian debate, but not surprised. I always thought the real difference was the rival conceptions of God. A ticklish question. For I suppose that we, by affirming three Persons implicitly say that God is not *a* person. Wd. it be fair to say that He is revealed to us as *super*-personal, which is very different from being *im*-personal?

I am delighted to hear that there is some chance of seeing you in England again.

:O HENRY NOEL, *with reference to a theme central to* The Great Divorce.

14 November 1962

About all I know of the 'Refrigerium' is derived from Jeremy Taylor's sermon on 'Christ's advent to judgement' and the quotations there given from a Roman missal printed at Paris in 1626, and from Prudentius. See Taylor's *Whole Works*, edit. R. Heber, London 1822, Vol. V, p. 45.

The Prudentius says, 'Often below the Styx holidays from their punishments are kept, even by the guilty spirits. . . . Hell grows feeble with mitigated torments and the shadowy nation, free from fires, exults in the leisure of its prison; the rivers cease to burn with their usual sulphur'.

TO A LADY.

21 November 1962

I think I share to excess your feelings about a move. By nature I demand from the arrangements of this world just that permanence which God has expressly refused to give them. It is not merely that nuisance and expense of any big change in one's way of life that I dread, it is also the psychological uprooting and the feeling—to me or to you intensely unwelcome—of having ended a chapter. One more portion of oneself slipping away into the past. I would like everything to be immemorial—to have the same old horizons, the same garden, the same smells and sounds, always there, changeless. The old wine is to me always better. That is, I desire the 'abiding city' where I well know it is not and ought not to be found. I suppose all these changes should prepare us for the greater change which has drawn nearer even since I began this letter. We must 'sit light' not only to life itself but to all its phases. The useless word is 'encore'.

TO AN ENQUIRER.

2 December 1962

. . . .

(5) I turned to fairy tales because that seemed the form which certain ideas and images in my mind seemed to demand; as a man might turn to fugues because the musical phrases in his head seemed to him to be 'good fugal subjects'.

(6) When I wrote the *Lion* I had no notion of writing the others.

(7) Writing 'juveniles' certainly modified my habits of composition. Thus (*a*) it imposed a strict limit on vocabulary. (*b*) excluded erotic love, (*c*) cut down reflective and analytical passages, (*d*) led me to produce chapters of nearly equal length for convenience in reading aloud.

All these restrictions did me great good—like writing in a strict metre.

TO SISTER PENELOPE, C.S.M.V.

17 September 1963

What a pleasant change to get a letter which does *not* say the conventional things! I was unexpectedly revived from a long coma, and perhaps the almost continuous prayers of my friends did it—but it wd. have been a luxuriously easy passage, and one almost regrets having the door shut in one's face. Ought one to honour Lazarus rather than Stephen as the protomartyr? To be brought back and have all one's dying to do again was rather hard.

When you die, and if 'prison visiting' is allowed, come down and look me up in Purgatory.

It *is* all rather fun—solemn fun—isn't it?

TO SIR HENRY WILLINK: *on the writer, having resigned his fellowship, being made an Honorary Fellow of the College.*

25 October 1963

The ghosts of the wicked old women in Pope "haunt the places where their honour died". I am more fortunate, for I shall haunt the place whence the most valued of my honours came.

I am constantly with you in imagination. If in some twilit hour anyone sees a bald and bulky spectre in the Combination Room or the garden, don't get Simon to exorcise it, for it is a harmless wraith and means nothing but good.

If I loved you all less I should think much of being thus placed ("so were I equall'd with them in renown") beside Kipling and Eliot. But the closer and more domestic bond with Magdalene makes that side of it seem unimportant.

TO MISS JANE DOUGLASS.

27 October 1963

Thanks for your note. Yes, autumn is really the best of the seasons; and I'm not sure that old age isn't the best part of life. But of course, like autumn, it doesn't *last*.

(My brother's autumn lasted, like the year's, a few weeks longer; and on that note very characteristic of his last days—peaceful acceptance, combined with enduring grief for 'mutabilitie'—I end my selection from his correspondence. W. H. L.)